CRITICAL ESSAYS
ON ISRAELI SOCIETY, RELIGION,
AND GOVERNMENT

DISCARDED
From Nashville Public Library

A PUBLICATION FROM *THE ASSOCIATION FOR ISRAEL STUDIES*

SUNY Series in Israeli Studies
Russell Stone, editor

Critical Essays
on Israeli Society, Religion,
and Government

Books on Israel, Volume IV

Kevin Avruch and Walter P. Zenner, Editors

State University of New York Press

Published by
State University of New York Press, Albany

For information, address State University of New York Press,
State University Plaza, Albany, N.Y., 12246

Production by E. Moore
Marketing by Bernadette LaManna

Library of Congress Cataloging-in-Publication Data

Critical essays on Israeli society, religion, and government / Kevin
  Avruch and Walter P. Zenner, editors.
      p.   cm. — (Books on Israel ; v. 4) (SUNY series in Israeli
  studies)
      "A publication from the Association for Israel Studies."
      Includes bibliographical references and index.
      ISBN 0-7914-3253-X (HC : alk. paper). — ISBN 0-7914-3254-8
  (PB : alk. paper)
      1. Israel—Book reviews. 2. Judaism—Israel—Book reviews.
  3. Popular culture,—Israel—Book reviews.   I. Avruch, Kevin.
  II. Zenner, Walter P.   III. Series.   IV. Series: SUNY series in
  Israeli studies.
  DS102.95.B66   1988 vol. 4
  956.94—dc20
                                                        96-17788
                                                          CIP

                10   9   8   7   6   5   4   3   2   1

CONTENTS

INTRODUCTION

Walter P. Zenner and Kevin Avruch

This is the fourth volume to be published under the aegis of the Association for Israel Studies which brings together scholars from a variety of disciplines and perspectives in reviewing recent work on modern Israel. The previous volumes in this series, all published by the State University of New York Press, are: *Books on Israel*, vol. 1 (I. Lustick, ed.), 1988; *Critical Essays on Israeli Society, Politics, and Culture* (Books, vol. 2) (I. Lustick and B. Rubin, eds.), 1991; and *Critical Essays on Israeli Social Issues and Scholarship* (Books, vol. 3) (R. Stone and W. Zenner, eds.), 1994. Although no volume by itself pretends to offer a comprehensive coverage of this broad topic, as a series, *Books on Israel* offers interested students of contemporary Israel a "state-of the art" view of current literature in selected fields—perhaps most usefully literature outside the field of the reader's own specialization—and of the important questions being asked in each. Each chapter is especially written for this volume, and, while the authors have structured their contributions as "review essays," this format is intended to serve as a platform for a critical reflection on the work or works reviewed, and on their importance for an understanding of Israeli society and culture.

When the third volume of this series, *Critical Essays on Israeli Social Issues and Scholarship* went to press in 1994, the peace process among Israel, the Palestinians, and the Arab states seemed to be dead in the water. How differently the situation looks today. While the peace process between the Israelis and Palestinians is still unstable, it has resulted in the establishment of a PLO-led authority in Gaza and Jericho, the virtual withdrawal of the Israel Defense Forces (IDF) from some West Bank towns, open diplomatic contacts between Israel and several Arab states, and a treaty between Israel and Jordan. However, it has led also to a new round of violence, including the assassination of Prime Minister Yitzhak Rabin in November 1995 by a disgruntled Jewish law student with extreme religious-nationalist leanings (and, perhaps most disturbingly, with the apparent blessing of some Israeli and other rabbis).

Nevertheless, the issues on which diplomats, politicians, scholars, and the general public have been fixated for forty-odd years have been transformed. Instead of concern with how obdurate each side is on these issues, they can now turn to the solution of specific problems, one of the most crucial of which will be water resource management, the subject of Ofira Seliktar's chapter in this volume. Meanwhile, Mohammed Abu-Nimer focuses on the human dimensions of the Israeli-Palestinian peace process by examining the dilemmas which face peace activists on both sides. His chapter continues an exploration of themes taken up by Ilan Peleg's essay in the third volume of this series to which we have previously referred—"The Arab-Israeli Conflict and the Victory of Otherness"—and, in the same volume, by Efraim Inbar in "The Intercommunal Dimension in the Arab-Israeli Conflict: The Intifada." Abu-Nimer shows in particular how difficult Jews in the peace camp have found the bridging of the "Great Rift Valley" that separates Jews and Arabs in Israel. In this vein, readers should also consult the essay by Myron Aronoff in "The Ambiguities of a 'Binational' Israel" found in the second volume of the series.

Turning to issues of government and society, the chapters in this volume by Efraim Ben-Zadok and Samuel Krislov direct our attention to institutions that have been neglected previously by students of Israeli government. In contrast to the more usual concern with Israel's national government and politics, Ben-Zadok concentrates on local governance. He reviews some of the current literature on local government and protest movements, showing the new dynamism in local governance in Israel, and how closely government on the local level reflects ethnic and other rifts within the body social. Krislov focuses on the courts, and places issues surrounding the court system and Israeli legal culture in general within the larger context of Israel's multicultural—and particularly its Judaic—background.

Jeff Halper's contribution, reviewing studies of Jerusalem, is a departure for this series in that it concentrates on one locality. Jerusalem is, of course, unique among Israeli cities, but review articles could be written about other localities as well. While never losing sight of the particular policy and planning problems that the city faces and creates, Halper brings out many aspects of this city's character, both sacred and secular, and Jewish and Arab. Each of these chapters in some way, engages questions of ethnicity in Israel, which are also considered in previous volumes, such as by Walter Zenner in volume 1 in "Ethnic Factors in Israeli Life," and Walter Weiker in volume 3 in "Studies on Ethnicity."

Three chapters in this volume deal with Judaism and Israeli society, particularly relating to ethnic and gender issues. Zvi Zohar considers the relationship between Orthodox Judaism and secular Jews, crosscut by the division between European and Middle Eastern Jews. He analyzes the views and philosophy of a respected Sephardic Orthodox rabbi, especially as they touch on politics. His sophisticated analysis leads us away from thinking of all Orthodox Jews as either zealous anti-Zionists or as irredentist religious nationalists. (For a view of the latter, see, Kevin Avruch's piece on "Jewish Fundamentalism in Israel" in the series' second volume.) As is Zohar, Walter Zenner is concerned with the plurality of views within Sephardi Orthodox Jewry. He deals with this in relationship to issues of ethnic identity among Jews in Israel. (See also the essays on ethnicity already mentioned above on this introduction as well as in earlier volumes of this series.) Zenner's essay, as does Zohar's (and Nancy Berg's, to be discussed later), points to the need to deal with Sephardim as authors—indeed, as *agents*—rather than merely as objects of research by Ashkenazim. Taking up the theme of "locality" emphasized in different ways by Ben-Zadok and Halper, Kevin Avruch argues for the need to pay attention to localized forms of Judaic expression. As was Zenner, Avruch is concerned with Orthodoxy, but Orthodoxy now refracted through the lens of gender. He reviews two books by anthropologists on Orthodox women, one of Middle Eastern origin, and the other Ashkenazi *haredot*. Both ethnographies give voice to the subjects of study, rather than viewing them simply as victims of male domination. (See also Madeleine Tress's essay— "Does Gender Matter?"—in the third volume of this series.)

The three essays in the last part of this volume take multifaceted approaches to large issues in Israeli literature, cinema, and culture. Ostensibly reviewing three examples from the genre of autobiography and memoir—all written by former generals in the IDF—Pnina Lahav ranges far (and critically) to explore decision-making processes of more than twenty years ago, at the time of the Yom Kippur War. Reflecting on the uses and abuses of memory and memoir, Lahav offers a cultural critique of top military leaders during that period. She analyzes them, and the period, in psychocultural terms.

Nancy Berg's chapter on *ma'abara*—or immigrants' transition camp—literature points to the division between European and Middle Eastern Jews in Israel, which is considered by Zohar and Zenner in religious terms. In showing how the Middle Eastern immigrants were introduced to a heavily Europeanized Israeli society, Berg also argues for the new "voice" which the Middle Easterners have now found, partly through literature, to recover aspects of their own past. This reiterates points made by Walter Zenner and Abraham Marthan in their essays on Amnon Shamosh in volume 3 of this series.

Nurith Gertz deals with Israeli literature and cinema of the 1980s and 1990s, but she also takes up some problems broached by Abu-Nimer in his discussion of the dilemmas of the peace process. Gertz, that is, focuses on some prominent films made by members of Israel's "peace camp." As was Lahav, Gertz is sympathetic to a fairly radical critique of Zionism from within this intellectual segment of Jewish Israeli society—a critique, incidentally, covered in previous volumes of this series in articles that dealt with the beginning of revisionist historical treatments of the founding of Israel. See, for example, Steven Heydemann's "Revisionism and the Reconstruction of Israeli History," in the second volume of this series. In addition to Heydemann's essay, works by Donna R. Divine in volume 1 ("Political Discourse in Israeli Literature"), and Aviad Raz in the third volume ("Rewriting the Holocaust: An Israeli Case Study in the Sociology of the Novel"), also exemplify the series' ongoing attention to culture and the arts, particularly in literature, in contemporary Israel.

In sum, we are pleased to present these eleven critical essays on diverse aspects of Israeli society, religion, and government as the fourth in a continuing series sponsored by the Association for Israel Studies.

Part I

The Arab-Israeli Conflict

Both scholars and practitioners of the art-and-science of conflict resolution have come to realize that conflicts often come in two parts. One part involves a disagreement by the parties over so-called "hard" resources or things that are typically scarce or not easily divisible, and subject to zero-sum calculations and materialist or realist theorizing. Let's call them "interests." The other part involves the realm of communications and miscommunication, or mutual perceptions and misperceptions, or social constructions of reality, including histories and futures. Here, we leave rational and perhaps zero-sum calculi, and narrowly materialist thinking, to enter the domains of language, metaphor, and affect. Let's call these things "interpretations."

The chapters by Ofira Seliktar and Mohammed Abu-Nimer neatly exemplify both of these faces of the Arab-Israeli conflict—respectively, the interest-based and interpretation-based aspects of the conflict. Seliktar reviews six books dealing with aspects of that most-scarce of Middle Eastern resources—water—and focuses appropriately on the solutions, usually technological, proposed by technocrats and specialists. Abu-Nimer, on the other hand, talks about problems of perception and role-enactment that he sums up by way of a master metaphor—"crossing the red line" between Israeli and Palestinian peace activists, and their larger respective societies. Arab-Israeli negotiations about water issues did not significantly occur until progress was made on the peace process, Seliktar notes. However, Abu-Nimer reminds us that, in deeply rooted conflicts, the parties will never be able to get to the point of negotiating interests until prior problems of perception and affect and trust—those of interpretation—are addressed as well. The assassination of Prime Minister Rabin also reminds us that the costs borne by those who cross red lines in these deeply rooted conflicts can be very great indeed.

1. Water in the Arab-Israeli Struggle: Conflict or Cooperation?

Ofira Seliktar

Natasha Beschorner, *Water and Instability in the Middle East* (London: The International Institute for Strategic Studies, 1992).

John Bulloch and Adel Darwish, *Water Wars. Coming Conflicts in the Middle East* (London: Victor Gollancz, 1993).

Elisha Kally with Gideon Fishelson, *Water and Peace. Water Resources and the Arab-Israeli Peace Process* (Westport, Conn: Praeger, 1993).

Nurit Kliot, *Water Resources and Conflict in the Middle East* (London: Routledge, 1994).

Miriam R. Lowi, *Water and Power. The Politics of a Scarce Resource in the Jordan River Basin* (Cambridge: Cambridge University Press, 1993).

Arnon Soffer, *Rivers of Fire. The Conflict of Water in the Middle East* (Tel-Aviv: Am Oved, 1992) (Hebrew).

Although the struggle over water resources has been a feature of the Arab-Israeli conflict since its beginning, the phenomenon has only recently received serious academic attention. Whether the potential for conflict has actually increased or not, water scarcity has come to be perceived as a real issue, with some observers presenting it as a possible *casus belli* in the future.

The six books considered in this essay offer a wide-ranging overview of the issues involved in the water struggles of the Middle East, including the Tigris-Euphrates, Jordan-Yarmuk, and the Nile basins. Rather than attempt to cover the entire subject, this review will focus on the contested waters between Israel and her Arab coriparians. Whenever relevant, references will be made to other watersheds in the region, especially to demonstrate how problems there impact the Arab-Israeli water conflict.

I

Well before the emergence of independent states in the Middle East, it was recognized that its river systems form unitary basins—the area of land drained by a river and its tributaries. All six books share the premise that arbitrary political divisions are detrimental to a rational utilization of these water basins. They also agree that nowhere has this been more evident than in the Jordan-Yarmuk basin. Kliot described it as representing "an extreme case of an international river with a very small amount of water bitterly fought over by Israel and its Arab neighbours" (p.272). Indeed, Kally and Fishelson argue that all the development plans in Mandatory Palestine were based on the assumption that the waters of the region would be cooperatively developed (pp. 5–20). Estimation of the availability of water was part of the broader calculations of the "economic absorptive capacity" which the British Mandatory authority undertook after promulgating its first immigration ordinance in 1920. Given the anticipated influx of Jewish immigrants, the White Paper of 1922 presented a scientific formula for estimating the numbers of Jews and Arabs that Palestine could support.[1]

While the formula became subsequently politicized—with Arabs and Jews claiming different numbers of potential settlers—all the various plans to develop the Jordan-Yarmuk river system remained cooperative. In 1938, Dr. Walter

Lowdermilk, an American land-conservation expert, proposed the ambitious Jordan Valley Authority project. Conceived in the spirit of the American Tennessee Valley Authority, the venture would have utilized the waters of the Jordan-Yarmuk, Yarkon, and possibly the Litani. Lowdermilk also envisioned a Med-Dead Sea Canal to generate electricity. In 1939, M. G. Ionides, an advisor to the Transjordanian government, published a plan that would have used the water of the Jordan River for irrigation of large areas of land. Among other cooperative measures, Ionides designated the Sea of Galilee as a storage facility for the excess of winter floods.

During the same period, the World Zionist Organization appointed the American engineer, J. B. Hays, to prepare a comprehensive plan entitled "Water Resources in the Land of Israel." Hays included Syria, Lebanon, and Transjordan in his scheme for pooling water resources in the basin. The plan called for a regional storage facility in Beith Netofa Valley, a large water carrier and a possible Med-Dead Sea Canal. Hays's projection was, by far, the most optimistic in terms of the level of cooperation. He estimated that, in addition to irrigation, the pooled water and electricity generated would provide a base for a population of four million in Palestine. In 1947, the special United Nations Commission on Palestine, UNSCOP, reexamined Hays's projections and found them to be exaggerated. The British Mandatory authority suggested a more limited alternative which included the waters of the Litani, a multiyear storage facility and electric plant in the Sea of Galilee, and an annual reservoir in Beith Netofa.

II

Attempts at cooperative utilization of the Jordan-Yarmuk system were terminated after the riparians received independence. The intense state of hostility between Israel and her Arab neighbors precluded any joint efforts. What was worse, optimal water-resource development of surface flows, although technically feasible, gave way to unilateral abstraction by

Israel, Jordan, and Syria. In 1951, Israel unveiled its "All-Israel Plan" which included drainage of the Hula swamps, diversion of the northern Jordan River and construction of the National Water Carrier to service the coastal plain and the Negev. At the same time, Jordan started implementing a modified version of the Bunger Plan, named for the American engineer, M. E. Bunger. The Great Yarmuk Project included two dams on the Yarmuk (Mukheiba and Maqarin) and the West Ghor Canal, with a siphon across the Jordan River connecting it to the East Ghor Canal. After failing to negotiate an agreement with Israel and Syria, Jordan built the East Ghor Canal which transfers water from the Yarmuk River and its southern tributaries to the Jordan Valley. In 1953, Syria signed an agreement with Jordan to utilize the Yarmuk River, but international opposition forced a change. Since then, Syria has been constructing a series of smaller dams to collect the water of the small tributaries of the Yarmuk, thus depleting its yield. Finally, in 1954, Lebanon embarked upon an ambitious project to develop the Litani River. The Litani River Authority eventually came to include a major storage dam near Qirawn, two hydroelectric systems, and an irrigation project in the Bakka Valley.

While all of the authors bemoan the unilateral exploitation of the Jordan-Yarmuk basin, only Lowi provides a systematic answer to the question of why riparians prefer such suboptimals pattern of development. Placing her analysis within the framework of international relations theory, Lowi points out that there are two approaches to viewing conflict and cooperation among states. The political realists and their descendants, the neorealists, argue that, under conditions of political-structural anarchy prevalent in international relations, states are motivated by fear and distrust which lead to competition and conflict. In the absence of an enforceable world order, states become preoccupied with autonomy, security, and power. As a result, they tend to shun cooperative outcomes—a posture that the neo-realists also explain as stemming from the fear that cooperation might give a prospective partner the benefit of a larger relative gain (p. 4).

The liberals and their philosophical soul mates—the functionalists and liberal-institutionalists—claim that cooperation is more the norm in international relations. In order to achieve optimal solutions in an increasingly interdependent world, states consider and join partnerships and cooperative endeavors. To facilitate cooperative outcomes, the liberal school in general, and the liberal-institutionalist in particular, favor an activist role for metanational institutions. International agencies, transgovernmental bodies, and multinational corporations can all play important parts in bringing national actors into the cooperative fold. The functionalists postulate that small, but cumulative, "confidence-building measures" will increase the overall propensity to cooperate (p. 5).

However, as Lowi conclusively shows, the actions of Israel and her coriparians have been motivated by realist concerns. To illustrate, she notes that, in the 1950s, the Eisenhower Administration, in a bid to defuse tensions over the various unilateral diversion efforts, followed the functionalist formula. The Johnston Unified Plan—named for the American negotiator, Eric Johnston—was conceived as a comprehensive scheme for sharing, distributing, and allocating water from the Jordan-Yarmuk system to Israel, Jordan, Syria, and Lebanon. Under the terms of the 1956 agreement, Israel was allocated a total of 400 million cubic meters (MCM) of water (31 percent); Jordan, 720 MCM (56 percent); Syria, 132 MCM (10.3 percent); and Lebanon, 35 MCM (2.7 percent). There were also plans for cooperative projects, such as transboundary storage facilities. The hidden agenda was, however, to use limited technical cooperation to induce a measure of conciliation into the larger conflict. However, general Middle East tension overshadowed the negotiations, leading Lowi to conclude that "when the context is acute hostility, states will not elect to cooperate on most issues, if they get away with it" (p. 197).

The limited technical cooperation which has occurred—including the de facto acceptance of the Johnston Plan by Israel and Jordan—is attributed by Lowi to the resource needs and dependency of the riparians (p. 202). Israel was interested in legitimizing its National Water Carrier, and, thus, considered the plan binding. Jordan, a lower riparian with a overburdened demand schedule, was highly dependent on whatever water it could get, and was, therefore, in no position to reject the agreement. On the other hand, Syria, which had alternative water sources, was in a good position to play the "spoiler." Lebanon, with an abundance of water resources and a marginal stake in the system, could do likewise.[2]

The other authors agree on the dominance of the larger Arab-Israeli conflict over water matters. Beschorner openly doubts whether water-resource management could be used to improve international relations in the Middle East. Her emphatic assertion that "water-related disputes are a consequence of, rather than a catalyst for, deteriorating relations between states" is a real challenge to liberals, be they functionalists or institutionalists (p. 70). Kliot, in a meticulous comparative study, finds that the "conflict has determined the behavior of the riparians for almost forty years" (p. 173). The Arab effort to divert the headwaters of the Jordan River is a case in point. Conceived by the Arab League as a response to Israel's NWC, the 1964 plan called for the diversion of the Hasbani and Banias away from the Jordan River. The water was to be allocated to Lebanon, Syria, and Jordan through a series of technologically daunting construction projects. Kliot quotes a number of experts in support of her contention that the plan, carrying extremely high technical and economic costs, was only marginally feasible (p. 206). Likewise, Kally and Fishelson find the diversion project to be "a clear demonstration of the triumph of irrational ideology over rational considerations in international relations" (p. 32).

The larger Middle East conflict has also influenced the policy of "food security," which Kliot describes as an "elusive ideological concept" guiding governments' efforts to achieve self-sufficiency in food production (p. 78). Food security leads to "inefficient and unreasonable" policies of subsidizing the agricultural sector. Heavily subsidized water—a major component in food security programs, has lead to waste and inefficiency in water management in Israel, Jordan, and Syria, as well as Egypt.

III

Given the fact that all of the authors agree that the Arab-Israeli conflict has dominated the water issue, the obvious question is whether the contemporary peace process will alleviate tension over water, and even foster a spirit of cooperation. Although most of these books were published before current developments, a careful analysis of their thematic hypotheses allows a certain temporal extension of the conclusions. It should be emphasized that there is an overwhelming consensus that water shortages in the Middle East have reached a critical dimension. Bulloch and Darwish capture the spirit of this crisis well when they warn that "water in the Middle East has became a commodity as important as oil" (p. 198). Of course, this is not a new theme, and it has been debated before. A project commissioned by the Center for Strategic and International Studies warned that "by the year 2000, water—not oil—will be the dominant resource issue of the Middle East."[3] According to this widely shared view, the situation in the Jordan-Yarmuk basin is especially grim. By the end of the century, projected water requirements for Israel will be 2,500 MCM, or 130 percent of current renewable supplies. For Jordan, it will be 1,000 MCM (120 percent). Exact Syrian data are not available, but some estimates put its water deficit in the year 2000 at 1,000 MCM.[4] Projections for the West Bank and Gaza speak of an average deficit of 75 to 80 MCM, and 100 MCM respectively for nondrought and drought conditions.

There is less agreement among the authors, however, as to whether the projected shortages will lead to conflict or stimulate cooperation. Because the main sources of the projected shortages—rapid population growth; changing lifestyles mandating a higher water consumption per capita; expansion of agriculture and industry; and inefficient maintenance and operation of water facilities—are difficult to address, some experts believe that quiescent rivalries could be rekindled sometime in the future. Bulloch and Darwish write that water might change the power equation in the Middle East. Those who possess the precious resource could use it "as a means of leverage and a way of projecting power" . . . over those who lack adequate supplies, and "a prime concern of national security must be to increase what is available" (p. 198).

Although these two researchers confine their prediction to low-intensity conflicts or LICs—such as Syrian-sponsored Kurdish guerrilla attacks against Turkish water projects on the Tigris and Euphrates, or possible tension in the Nile basin—other experts do not hesitate to postulate a full-fledged conflict. This view is particularly popular with observers who espouse the "hydrological imperative" theory. First used to claim that Israel invaded Lebanon in order to divert the Litani, it has been more recently upgraded to fit a variant of the dependency paradigm in international relations.[5] Observers who subscribe to this paradigm claim that countries suffering from resource scarcity tend to compensate by reaching beyond their borders. According to one dependency-oriented scholar, Israel's continued occupation of southern Lebanon supports the Litani diversion theory.[6]

To a lesser extent, the conflict approach has also been applied to the West Bank. Arab sources have pointed out that Israel has drawn a disproportionate amount of water from the Mountain aquifer which is estimated to hold some 450 MCM of renewable fresh water, and an additional 180 MCM of brackish water.[7] As Palestinians are restricted to about 20 percent of the renewable yield, many see Israel's continued hold on the territory as a prime example of the hydrological imperative. Palestinian and other observers seem to believe that, unwilling or unable to forego their groundwater, Israel will be reluctant to give up complete control of the territories. Ironically, right-wing Israeli spokesmen have also embraced the hydrological imperative. One representative work in this category describes the water of the mountain aquifer as "an inevitable source of conflict." Because Israel is the downstream riparian of the aquifer, she would be in no position to stop an independent Palestinian state from overpumping or polluting the shared groundwater.[8]

On the other side of the predictive divide are scholars such as Beschorner and Soffer, who do not see any imminent danger of a conflict. Beschorner, in particular, is scornful of the "proliferation of alarmist prediction," which gives "water a degree of strategic prominence which it does not necessarily merit" (p. 3). Her main assertion is that water scarcity, far from leading to an inevitable struggle, can also produce cooperation. This argument is not new, and it can be traced to a well-known thesis of Frederick Frey and Thomas Naff who postulated that, unlike other resources, some characteristics of water can induce cooperation "precisely because it is essential to life and so highly charged, water can—perhaps even tends—produce cooperation even in the absence of trust between concerned actors."[9]

Although Beschorner does not explicate the theoretical underpinning of her assertion, she attributes to water disputes many of the characteristics found in stochastic models of change. In a nutshell, stochastic processes are embedded in situations for which fortuitous occurrences dominate decision making. Individual idiosyncracies, capricious or violent environmental changes, and natural or man-made disasters can stir the political course away from the direction predicted by an aggregation of factors derived from past observations. Stochastic models have been increasingly used in international relations theory, showing, as one scholar put it, that the "exact logic that leads from war in one instance may lead toward it in another."[10] The three sets of factors that Beschorner attributes to water crises—a meager water environment, economies of scarcity, and volatile politics—are all prone to unpredictable turns of events (p. 3). One of the major environmental concerns in this respect is the possible impact of the greenhouse effect on the region.

Yet, paradoxically, cooperative solutions to water scarcity in such a harsh environment are quite likely to develop because of the high opportunity cost of pursuing conflict.

Indeed, Soffer cogently argues that conflictual solutions carry a much higher price tag than do cooperative ones. Adopting what is known in resource literature as the "water-market approach," Soffer calculates the price of conflict as invariably higher than in-basin and out-of-basin water transfer. He concludes that, given the huge direct and indirect costs of war, the eventual cost of a cubic meter of water to any riparian will be prohibitive. This rationale also applies to LICs, such as the security zone in Lebanon from which, according to hydraulic imperative theorists, Israel is trucking water from the Litani to across the border. Soffer argues that the cost of a cubic meter of trucked water will vary between $3.50 to $5.00—almost four times the cost of desalinated water (p. 202). Not incidently, other experts who have used the "water-market approach" have reached the same conclusion about other water disputes in the Middle East. For instance, Kliot estimates that it would be less costly for Egypt to invest in new water technology than to contemplate aggressive steps with regard to Ethiopia or the Sudan (p. 95).

However, even if overt conflicts over water can be ruled out, there is no guarantee of automatic cooperation. Beschorner and Soffer argue that cooperation, although superior from the point of view of optimal utilization of the Jordan-Yarmuk basin, could be psychologically difficult for Israel and her Arab neighbors to achieve. Beschorner seeks to explain the psychological impediments by noting the historical sense of vulnerability of Middle East riparians and their mistrust of resource dependency. She points out that optimal or cooperative water utilization is incompatible with notions of food security, and she quotes a former Israeli Water Commissioner as stating that "Israel does not want to become dependent for water on any neighboring country, even in peacetime" (pp. 32, 65). Soffer—whose book is based on a 1988 report to the Israel Ministry of Foreign Affairs—apparently reflects official wariness of relying on large-scale transboundary out-of-basin water transfers. He argues that the Arab countries have no culture of cooperation among themselves nor with their non-Arab neighbors in the region. The Arabs, as does Israel, share a deep reluctance to become dependent on others for a strategic resource (p. 230–231). What is worse, Soffer notes that the relentless unilateral utilization in the Jordan-Yarmuk basin is irreversible. As more unilateral plans come on stream, opportunities for co-operative ventures are correspondingly reduced (p. 232).

Unlike Lowi, the other authors do not attempt to systematically analyze underpinnings of the choices which the riparians might make. Yet, international relations theory can provide a more structured insight into what types of behaviors riparians will engage in when contemplating solutions to their water problems. Game theory is particularly useful in this respect because it can incorporate both economic and psychological aspects into one decision-making model. For example, Wolf and Dinar argue that so-called "water games" in the Middle East can be conceived in three different ways.

Where there are strong political actors with clearly demarcated water rights, a game known as "Stag Hunt" will obtain, and mutual cooperation is the rational strategy of choice. When actors are either somewhat hostile or competitive—and water rights are disputed—a "Prisoners' Dilemma" will prevail. In the absence of compelling interests to cooperate, each player's rational interest will be to defect—that is, to engage in a noncooperative, but not necessarily hostile, posture. When hostilities are very high, the game of "Chicken" will be pursued, with each riparian trying to preempt his opponent by diverting the maximum amount of water.[11]

Finally, a theoretical model is also useful in explaining the prescriptions for solving the water conflict that the six books offer. As noted, whether each is aware of it, the authors' prescriptive formulas are grounded in theories of international relations.

IV

By far, the most cooperative solution is offered by Kally and Fishelson. Published in conjunction with the Armand Hammer

Fund for Economic Cooperation in the Middle East at Tel-Aviv University, this book envisions a large-scale conveyance project from the Nile to the Gaza Strip, Israel, and possibly the West Bank and Jordan. Water rents involved make the transfer economically attractive for both Egypt and Israel. As the energy requirements of conveying water from the Nile to the Negev is 0.5 kilowatt-hours per cubic meter, compared to 2 to 3 kilowatt-hours from the Sea of Galilee, the water carried in the project would be less expensive than the NWC. Based on these calculations, the authors suggest a larger exchange scheme. Water from the Nile would be conveyed to Negev, and water from the Sea of Galilee would be transferred to the West Bank, and possibly to Jordan. The proposed project would be based on an expansion of the El Salaam Canal and the Egyptian Sinal Canal—an initial annual capacity of 100 MCM would be required to feed water into the Gaza Strip, and 500 MCM per year to supply the other consumers (p. 67–69). Although the authors acknowledge that ideological factors defeated the original proposal of Anwar Sadat to sell water to Israel, they seem to be more sanguine about the project's present chances.

However, Bulloch and Darwish make an equally compelling case against optimistic expectations for regional water transfers. Even though the proposed scheme is designed to use only one percent of the water of the Nile, it has provoked considerable internal opposition in Egypt. A 1992 report prepared for the Egyptian parliament by Dr. Hamdi el-Taheri, a well-known water expert, warns against future water shortages in Egypt. In both his report, and a book on the subject of water in the Arab world, el-Taheri argues that Israel's one-percent demand on the Nile water is part of the larger Zionist "hydrologic slogan." He—and many influential Egyptian politicians—apparently believe that Israel is trying to exert indirect pressure on Egypt by becoming involved in water diversion projects in the Sudan and Ethiopia. Of special concern to Egyptian authorities are the alleged plans of Ethiopia to dam the Blue Nile (p. 92).

Bulloch and Darwish see similar problems with another highly publicized cooperative plan—the Turkish Peace Pipeline. Proposed in 1987 by Turgut Ozal, the former Turkish Prime Minister, the project proposed to transfer water from the Seyhan and Ceyhan Rivers in Anatolia through two pipelines. The Western 2,655-kilometer pipeline is to carry water to Syria, Jordan, and Saudi Arabia, at an estimated cost of eighty-four cents per cubic meter. The Gulf pipeline will serve the Gulf states as well as the eastern part of Saudi Arabia at an approximate cost of $1.07 per cubic meter. However, the Turkish proposal has been greeted with suspicion or hostility, especially from Syria and Iraq whose water supply has been affected by the Turkish GAP (like the American Tennessee Valley Authority) project. Other Arab states expressed reservations because they fear that Turkey will use water dependency to reestablish the Ottoman Empire.

Regional projects could generate other complications. As already pointed out, Bulloch and Darwish argue that large-scale water ventures are susceptible to political agitation, and, ultimately, might become a source of LICs. For instance, the Turkish Ministry of Foreign Affairs mentioned the sale of water to Israel only once, as an apparent indication of political sensitivity. Although alternative plans suggested transferring water from Turkey to Israel in special "meduza bag" containers, or large plastic bags, Soffer believes that the proposals are less than sound. Heavy financial investment in building port facilities in the two countries would make the cost of water prohibitive, and dependency on a monopolistic provider will present a considerable political danger to Israel (p.222–223).

Other authors support less ambitious transboundary in-basin cooperative ideas. The most helpful project for addressing Jordan's water deficit is the Maqarin Dam. This dam was part of the original Great Yarmuk Project, but it ran into problems in the 1960s, and work on a smaller model was abandoned after the 1967 Six Day War, when Israel occupied the northern bank of the river. Moves to revive the plan started in 1974, but disagreements among Israel, Jordan, and Syria—plus the high cost of the venture—prevented the completion of a scaled-back version. According to Kliot, the new project—renamed *el-Wahda* or Unity—would involve a 100-meter dam with a total storage capacity of 250 MCM. It would provide Jordan with 100 MCM of water a year, and generate some 45 million kilowatt-hours of electricity (p. 203). Syria will receive 75 percent of the electric output and a small amount of water, with the rest scheduled to ease chronic water shortages in Amman and other Jordanian cities (p. 203). However, as Soffer warns, even fruitful in-basin cooperation can only postpone the crisis. With an estimated 3 percent annual population growth in the Arab countries and mass immigration to Israel, additional steps are needed[12] (p. 232).

Given the added uncertainty of dependence, Soffer joins Kliot and Beschorner in urging unilateral efforts in water management. There are two dimensions, demand and supply management, involved in any such endeavor.

The first and most urgent is demand management. Both Israel and the Arab riparians have allowed the demand for water to grow over the years, with little regard to the developing deficit. In Israel, an ideological commitment to agriculture and a political structure that places the power to price water in the hands of the agricultural lobby has made subsidized water available for water-intensive and economically nonviable crops. Kliot quotes the scathing 1990 report of the Comptroller General to support her contention that this disastrous pricing policy has created an artificial demand for water and led to a severe overpumping of ground water, contributing significantly to the current water deficit. She also points out that a politicized decision-making system, and the multiplicity of water authorities, are highly detrimental to rational demand management. In addition, Israel also needs to upgrade its water-delivery system which, according to estimates, loses between 20 to 40 percent in some areas (p. 240–243).

Demand management in the West Bank and Gaza is plagued by a combination of Israeli administration policies, a rapidly growing population, and inefficient irrigation practices. As in other Arab countries, the product value of water—that is, its contribution to agricultural production—is much lower than the twenty cents per cubic meter in Israel. For Jordan, Kliot recommends improved irrigation efficiency. By converting open canals to pipelines, efficiency levels can be raised from the current 46 percent to about 70 percent. In addition, Jordan needs to upgrade its pipeline network, most notably in urban areas, in order to save the approximately 44 to 50 percent of the flow that is currently lost (p. 227).

Even if substantive reforms in demand management can be effected—a herculean task at best—the power of these measures should not be overstated. Soffer believes that the only effective long-term solution is for the Jordan-Yarmuk riparians—and, indeed, for all of the countries in the Middle East—to switch from agriculture to industry and services. Using a sophisticated convertability formula, Soffer shows that Israel, as an already advanced society, is well-positioned for such a move. However, Jordan, Syria, and Egypt would encounter considerable problems. Not the least of these problems is the long tradition of an agricultural livelihood in the Arab countries (p. 234–235), and the adherence to the strategic concept of food security (Beschorner, 65).

The parameters of the second dimension—supply management—are limited by the meager water sources of the basin. As no new natural water resources are expected to be discovered in the region, additional storage facilities can capture only small amounts of winter water flows which can be used outright and/or as a recharge tool. Israel is already using this method to recharge its Coastal Plain aquifer, and Kliot reports on the planned Gaza Storm Water Project which can replenish the devastated Gaza Strip aquifer with some 2 MCM annually (p. 245). Technical means to bolster supplies include waste water reclamation for agricultural use and desalination. Only Israel has made considerable progress in recycling effluence. From some 500 MCM of wastewater available annually, 160 MCM are fully treated, and 60 MCM are partially reclaimed.[13] Jordan is well behind in the reclamation effort. According to one estimate, only some 45 MCM of reclaimed effluence will be available for agricultural use in 1995.

Desalination is an alternative means of increasing water supplies. However, at present, the technology is too expensive for irrigation. At a cost of seventy cents to one dollar per cubic meter—as compared with fifteen to twenty-five cents for a cubic meter for agriculture—desalination is used mostly for producing potable water. However, Soffer echoes Israeli water policy makers in his belief that desalination—which might become less expensive as the technology improves—is a reasonable answer to the water deficit of Israel, Jordan, and the Palestinians. Although desalination is, in principle, a unilateral measure, it could be used for negotiations between Israel and Jordan and Israel and the Palestinians, with Israel offering desalinated water to offset shortages in Jordan and in the territories (p. 222).

V

The authors of the six books have persuasively argued that the water conflict between Israel and the Arabs can be solved peacefully, either through cooperative or unilateral measures. However, they are also mindful of the potential for a hostile competition. To avert such an outcome, they offer a number of suggestions for settling extant disputes. Unfortunately, as Kliot points out, the legal guidelines for water-conflict management in international rivers, as embodied in the Helsinki Rules of 1966 and other legal collections, are not entirely clear. The two most extreme water doctrines are based on the principles of *absolute territorial sovereignty* (Harmon Doctrine) and *absolute territorial integrity*. The former holds that a state has the right to use the waters which pass through its territory, regardless of the interests of other riparians. The latter proclaims that no state may utilize that water in a way that will be detrimental to any of the coriparians. Sovereignty is favored by upstream riparians who are reluctant to abide by the interests of lower riparians. Conversely, integrity is preferred by lower riparians, especially as it is tied to the prior or historical use of water. An intermediate principle—called "equitable utilization"—has been gaining acceptance in the international legal community, and has been defined in terms of some ten criteria ranging from geography and climate to economic and demographic needs of the coriparians and prior-use considerations.

Rules governing shared aquifers are even less clear. The Seoul Rules of the International Law Commission, a United Nations-sponsored body, call for the integrated management of aquifers, exchange of information, and prevention of pollution (p. 4–12). The Doctrine of Correlative Rights, adopted by certain United States jurisdictions, might also be applied to international law. Accordingly, a landowner's use of ground water should be limited to the amount which he can use beneficially, and subject to the corresponding rights of others who share the aquifer.[14]

The three major areas of conflict among the Middle-Eastern riparians pertain to elements of the Jordan-Yarmuk system, groundwater in the West Bank, and surface and groundwater in the Gaza Strip. Jordan has accused Israel of withdrawing 100 MCM of water from the Yarmuk, exceeding the Johnston quota of 25 MCM. Israel has denied the charge by arguing that, under the Johnston Plan, it is entitled to 40 MCM, including winter flows. Jordan has also accused Syria, the upper riparian on the Yarmuk, of taking 200 MCM from the river, well above the 90 MCM allotted to her in the Johnston plan. Palestinians now demand from Jordan the 100 MCM allocated to West Bank by Johnston. Jordanians contend that, as Syria has diverted a major portion of the Yarmuk River, they are unable to deliver the water. They also point out that the Kingdom is burdened by several hundred thousand Palestinian refugees who were absorbed after the various wars with Israel.

West-Bank groundwater presents a highly complex issue because the Mountain and Schem-Gilboa aquifers are shared by Israel and the Palestinians. Although only 5 percent of the combined recharge area of the two aquifers is located within the Green Line, they drain naturally into Israeli territory. Some 40 percent of Israel's groundwater comes from the West Bank, and has been utilized by Jewish farmers even prior to the establishment of Israel. Palestinians complain that Israel has restricted their use and created a highly inequitable distribution system whereby, in 1990, some 900,000 Palestinians received between 120 to 160 MCM of water, and the 100,000 Jewish settlers were allotted 160 MCM. They also point out that Israel has overpumped the aquifers, creating a 100-to-200 MCM deficit that has dried indigenous wells. The Israelis invoke the so-called "prior-use principle," claiming that, in 1967, the state was already abstracting 480 to 550 MCM while the Arabs used only 40 MCM. They deny increasing the level of abstraction beyond the 1967 level.

Gaza's groundwater and surface water is not trans-boundary in the larger legal sense, but it is very limited. The annual safe yield or replenishment amounts to 60 MCM, falling well below the annual demand of 100 to 120 MCM. Both Palestinian and Israeli experts agree that the overdraft has caused an average of 12-to-15 centimeters drop in the water table, and severe salinity in some of the wells. The Palestinians charge that Israeli settlements in Gush Katif have contributed to the problem by abstracting 5 MCM from the already overtaxed aquifer. In addition, they argue that Israel has increased salinity by drilling wells east of Gaza, and within the Green Line, as well as by building dams on Wadi Gaza/Absor River.

None of the disputes are easy to settle, but most of the authors remain optimistic that a combination of political flexibility and technological solutions can avert an all-out competitive utilization of resources. Indeed, the recent peace agreement between Israel and Jordan, and the interim agreement between Israel and the Palestinian National Authority, have alleviated much of the tensions over water usage. The Israeli-Jordanian accord provides for a more equitable allocation from the Jordan and the Yarmuk Rivers, and establishes a framework for future cooperative utilization of water. For instance, the two countries plan to build a diversion/storage dam on the Yarmuk River as well as a storage facility on the Jordan River. A Joint Water Commission will oversee all issues relevant to water management.

The agreement with the Palestinians is less satisfactory in the sense that the final allocation of water from the West Bank aquifers was deferred to the permanent status negotiations. In the interim period, the West Bank will receive an additional 28.6 MCM from a variety of wells. The Gaza Strip will receive 5 MCM from the Israeli system. The Joint Water Commission will provide a measure of coordination in managing the common water resources and dealing with water-related disputes.

These cooperative steps will help Israel, Jordan, and the Palestinian Authority to manage their water resources. In particular, storage and planned desalination should increase the pool of available water at a fraction of the cost of a war. The larger cooperative projects—such the Nile conveyance or the Turkish Peace Pipeline—would be even more efficient. However, those projects will probably have to await a fully peaceful environment in the Middle East.

Notes

1. Ilan Troen, "Calculating the 'Economic Absorptive Capacity' of Palestine: A Study of the Political Uses of Scientific Research." *Contemporary Jewry*. 10:2 (1989) 19–38.

2. For a detailed discussion, see Sara Reguer, "Controversial Waters: Exploitation of the Jordan River, 1950–1980," *Middle East Studies*, 29:1 (January 1993) 53–90; and David M. Wishart, "The Breakdown of the Johnston Negotiations over the Jordan Waters." *Middle East Studies*, 26 (October 1990) 536–546.

3. Joyce R. Starr and Daniel C. Stoll, "Water for the Year 2000." In Joyce R. Starr and Daniel C. Stoll, eds., *The Politics of Scarcity. Water in the Middle East* (Boulder, Colo.: Westview Press, 1988).

4. Aaron Wolf and John Ross, "The Impact of Scarce Water Resources on the Arab-Israeli Conflict." *Natural Resources Journal.* 32:4 (1992) 919–959.

5. Proponents of this theory, which describes the quest for water resources as the motivator for Israeli military conquests— both in Lebanon in 1979 and 1982, and earlier on the Golan Heights and West Bank in 1967—usually point out that early Zionist planners advocated the inclusion of the Litani River in Israeli borders. During the war in Lebanon, several analysts developed a number of assumptions which ranged from attributing to Israel the intention of diverting a modest 100 MCM annually from the lower Litani to an elaborate scheme of a permanent occupation of entire Bekaa Valley, along with destruction of the Qirawn Dam and Marhaba diversion tunnel, which would allow diversion of the entire 700 MCM annual flow of the river to Israel. For instance, see John K. Cooley, "The War Over Water." *Foreign Policy*. 54 (Spring 1984) 3–26; Uri Davis, Antonia Maks, and John Richardson, "Israel's Water Policies." *Journal of Palestinian Studies*. 9 (1980) 3–12; Leslie Schmida, *Keys to Control: Israel's Pursuit of Arab Water Resources*, American Education Trust, 1983.

6. Hussein A. Amery, "The Litani River of Lebanon." *The Geographical Review*. 83:3 (July 1993) 229–237.

7. This estimate is included in Karen Assaf, Nader al Khatib, Elisha Kally, Hillel Shuval, *A Proposal for the Development of a Regional Water Master Plan* (Jerusalem: Israel/Palestine Center for Research and Information, 1993) 30. There is considerable variation in the estimates. For instance, the Comptroller's Report estimates the potential at 330 MCM. *Report on the Management of the Water System in Israel* (Jerusalem: Office of Comptroller, 1990).

8. Martin Sherman, "Water as an Impassible Impasse in the Israeli-Arab Conflict." *Nativ*. 4, (1993) 3–11.

9. Frederick Frey and Thomas Naff, "Water: An Emerging Issue in the Middle East?" *The Annals of the American Academy of Political and Social Science*. 65:482 (1985) 65–84.

10. Michael D. Ward, "Things Fall Apart: A Logical Analysis of Crisis Resolution Dynamics." *International Interactions*. 15:1 (1988) 65–79.

11. Aaron T. Wolf and Ariel Dinar, "Middle East Hydropolitics and Equity Measures for Water-Sharing Agreements." *Journal of Social and Economic Studies*. 19:1 (Spring 1994) 69–93.

12. According to Assaf, et al., in the year 2000, the population of Israel will reach 6.6 to 8 million and the Palestinians in the West Bank and Gaza will stand at 2.9 to 3.7 million. The United Nations World Population Prospects projects the population of Jordan at 4.4 million and that of Syria at 17.6 million.

13. These figures are included in Kliot (p. 239). A 1993 report of the Water Commission estimates the wastewater potential at 360 MCM for 1990, of which 265 MCM are reclaimed and 195 MCM are used for irrigation.

14. Deborah Housen-Curiel, *Aspects of the Law of International Water Resources* (Tel-Aviv: The Armand Hammer Fund for Economic Cooperation in the Middle East, 1992) 5–6.

2. Dialogue and National Consensus in the Pre-Madrid Period: Dilemmas of Israeli and Palestinian Peace Activists

Mohammed Abu-Nimer[1]

Haim Gordon and Rivca Gordon, eds. *Israel/Palestine : The Quest for Dialogue* (New York: Orbis Books, 1991).

David Hall-Cathala. *The Peace Movement in Israel, 1967–1987* (New York: St. Martin's Press, 1990).

Deena Hurwitz, ed. *Walking the Red Line: Israelis in Search of Justice for Palestine* (Philadelphia: New Society Publishers, 1992).

I

*T*hese three books focus on the dilemma that Israeli and Palestinian activists have faced in their efforts to create and maintain a dialogue for peace between their communities. Most of the authors' interviews were conducted between 1988 and 1991, shortly after the Palestinian Intifada erupted and before the beginning of the current peace process.

The three books show how a comprehensive consideration of historical and socioeconomic contexts, coupled with the background of the largest group in the peace camp (Peace Now), can be an effective tool for understanding the perplexity, moral dilemma, and agony of an Israeli peace activist—an activist who is morally aware of the wrongdoing, but is unable, practically speaking, to "cross the red line," which occurs when peace activists are willing to adopt political attitudes and actions that will exclude them from the Israeli national consensus, as defined by the mainstream and right-wing Zionist parties. That consensus has included the legal ban on dialogue or public contact with the PLO; unquestioned participation, and acceptance of, compulsory military service, even in the occupied territories; and the avoidance of confrontation with the Israeli Defense Forces in the territories. Until September 1993, the signing of the Declaration Of Principles agreement between Yassir Arafat and Itzak Rabin, acting against any of the consensual principles would have meant "crossing the red lines" of the national consensus. Nevertheless, activists and members of the peace camp on both sides—Palestinians and Israelis—broke, and continue to break, their communities' defined consensual boundaries.

The three books considered in this chapter provide a valuable context in which to examine the attempts of peace activists to redefine the relationship between moral imperatives and political expediency.

For example, Hall-Cathala shows that the very emergence of Peace Now in Israel was, in itself, an attempt at redefinition. When a group of high-ranking army generals (Ashkenazi and middle class) took the initiative and wrote a letter to Prime Minster Begin in 1977, urging him to negotiate with Sadat, this shocked the entire country. However, it also served as a mobilizing force, a force that was translated into consolidation and expansion within the Israeli peace movement. At the same time, as Hall-Cathala indicates, it was the very connection with military men that limited the Peace Now movement from reaching out further to the Palestinian community. Therefore, since its inception in the late 1970s, it has remained within the consensus. In fact, Peace Now never really left the national Zionist camp. This connection provided Peace Now members with partial credibility within their society, and restricted their ability to engage in a dialogue with the Palestinian community or representatives based on symmetrical principles of justice and freedom.

Hall-Cathala argues persuasively that Israeli peace organizations have the basic infrastructure of a social movement. He mainly discusses the question of whether this movement—particularly in the case of Peace Now, the largest organization—functions as a restorative movement, restoring the balance between universalist and particularist values.

Hall-Cathala's book addresses the peace organizations in Israel and its relationships to the Palestinian issue. However, it has different objectives than do the other books. This book is directed to different audiences of academicians and researchers. In his description and analysis of the Israeli peace movement's development, and the historical and sociopolitical conditions that surrounded its emergence, Hall-Cathala is among the very few scholars—if not the only one—who conducted comprehensive research on the various political and educational activities that relate to the Israeli peace movement.

Using the framework of social movements theory, the book points to contradictions within the peace camp, as well as between the right wing and the peace camp. Hall-Cathala argues that, among the important reasons for the emergence of the peace camp, there was the need to defend a universalist set of ideas and values (p. 15). Those values had been threatened by particularist—or national and territorial—trends in Israel since the rise of the Gush Emunim and the Likud. To reveal further this contradiction between universalist and particularist approaches to peace and dialogue, Hall-Cathala identifies some basic important questions about the nature of the Israeli Peace Movement— particularly Peace Now.

1. Why did it emerge among the Ashkenazim?
2. Why did it emerge suddenly in the late 1970s as a mass movement?
3. Why did it emerge through thirty organizations rather than as one unified organization?

One impressive achievement of Hall-Cathala was his description of the Israeli peace movement in typologies that accurately reflect the scope and nature of the movement's complexity. In particular, he elucidates the relationships between the different peace groups, and left-wing political parties, and between peace groups and extraparliamentary factions.

Editor Deena Hurwitz presents her analysis and critique of Palestinian-Israeli relations in general, and of the Israeli peace camp in particular, in a long introduction to *Walking the Red Line*. Unlike Hall Cathala, Hurwitz has no intention of producing an academic or intellectual analysis of the peace movement or peace activism in Israel. Her objectives are twofold. First, she presents the perspectives of more radical activists—sixteen Jews and two Arabs—through their personal stories and involvement. These activists are ones that were marginalized—and even excluded—by the media, academics, mainstream Israeli public opinion, and even Peace Now. A second purpose of the book is to show—particularly to American Jews—that debates about Israel or Zionism are not inherently anti-Semitic. She also addresses the role of the United States in maintaining the conflict by selling arms to all the parties.

To accomplish her objectives, Hurwitz includes activists Roni Ben-Effrat and Mikado—both of whom were accused and indicted for contact with the Democratic Front for Liberation of Palestine—and Marcello—an activist who analyzes the Palestinian-Israeli conflict from a class perspective. She also includes the Sephardi community as a legitimate party in this class conflict. These activists crossed the red line, as defined by both the mainstream peace camp—as represented by Peace Now—and Israeli public opinion. Their analysis and activities are perceived as being more radical than that of Yosi Sarid and Shulamit Aloni—both currently parliament members of the left-wing party, Meretz—or other associates of the Peace Now movement.

The contributors in Gordon and Gordon's book are divided into categories: religion, law, education, and Palestinian women. Two additional sections—on dialogue and vision, and dialogue and integrity—include writings by prominent Palestinian and Israeli figures, such as Shulamit Aloni, Faisal Hussieni, and Abdu El-Shafi.[2] Some contributors—such as Zahiera Kamal, Zvi Gilat, and Abdu El-Shafi—use their life stories and their suffering to illuminate their commitment to peace and negotiation. Even so, the focus of the book is not on peace activists' personal testimonies, but on what each contributor thinks of the concept of dialogue.

Zahiera Kamal, for example, is a Palestinian political activist who was arrested by the Israeli military on several occasions. She presents the concept of justice as a condition for true dialogue, and as an alternative to be adopted by dialoguers. Zvi Gilat, an Israeli journalist who covered the Intifada, describes the impact of, one day realizing, the importance of empowerment and symmetry in conducting dialogue. He describes an encounter with Palestinians who had been sitting in the square of the civil administration building for days, waiting for identity cards to be released. Gilat writes on one encounter in particular:

> He invited me—an invitation that was more of a demand—to sit down beside him on the dirty pavement. And only when I was seated did he continue speaking. He was right. Dialogue is possible only when the partners are on the same level, when their eyes are leveled . . . (Gordon and Gordon, 167).

Among all the Palestinian contributors to both edited books, Hanan Ashrawi's article is the most analytical and articulate with respect to the developments and obstacles to dialogue. She analyzes—and, as it turned out, predicts—three "basic channels of dialogue which ultimately will convert into a holistic peace drive."

1. Grassroots popular dialogue;
2. International conferences with Palestinians and Israelis; and

3. Secret and indirect Israeli-Palestinian voluntary dialogue, which can be transformed into an official negotiation. (Ashrawi, 1991:109).

These predictions of how the three paths to dialogue would merge into one peace process proved to be correct when the Palestinians and Israelis agreed to join the initiative led by the United States after the Gulf War, and after the secret talks in Oslo were revealed in 1993.

Hurwitz's and the Gordons' books differ in their objectives, audiences, and the messages which each editor attempts to send. Gordon and Gordon are much more critical than is Hurwitz in their evaluation and analyses of their contributors' articles. They even express disappointment that many contributors "didn't get it," referring to the idea that contributors found it difficult to engage in the true dialogue mode, and to confront the evil in their communities (p. 13). Such a critique raises the question of what "true dialogue" really is, and who decides that? Is true dialogue what Martin Buber described based on his Jewish philosophical orientation.[3] Or is it according to Gandhi's teachings?

Gordon and Gordon don't adequately differentiate the power context which determines to what extent activists on either side can fight the evil in their respective societies or national groups. Do Palestinians have the same means or an equal or even similar opportunity to confront their evil forces? When they confront the evil in their own society, or when they engage in true dialogue, do the Palestinians—as individuals and as a group—pay a similar price as do the Israelis?

II

In all three books, most of the critique of the Israeli peace camp focuses on Peace Now activities, and several contributors—particularly Israeli Jews—emphasize the particularist character of this group. Mainly, they charge, Peace Now failed to provide an alternative view of Zionism in contrast to Gush Emunim's ideology. It functioned as an alternative that so-called "peaceniks" could live with, without having to pay a higher price—by the crossing of a red line.

Support for such a contention is found in Hurwitz's book, which questions the red line for Israeli peace activists. Is the line to be drawn at loyalty to the nation state, or at loyalty to universalistic values? It is in this context that a prominent member of the peace movement, such as Yael Dayan, could state, in describing her reactions to the Gulf War: "Sometimes there are wars that are necessary to attain peace. . . . Peace Now in Israel means war now." (Hurwitz, 7).

Another endorsement for such a view is provided by several Israelis, who openly discuss their inability to cross the different red lines or to break away from the Israeli national consensus. Dafna Golan, for example, notes that activists were morally aware of the occupation's consequences and their responsibility as members of the occupying force, but still, they could not do more because of the threat of alienation.

> I know we need radical measures to take us out of our paralyzed situation, or our feeling of hopelessness and failure. Yet, steps that we middle class, parents, people who still live too comfortably, will be able to adopt. Because you see, you are right, a total refusal is the only morally and politically sound form of participation in Israeli society during the occupation. This is something we can write about or say. It is not something we can do, or ready right now to do. . . . Not to risk too much of the comfort we have. (Hurwitz, 104)

Hurwitz also argues that the risk of being put outside of the consensus can seem enormous. Nevertheless, how can activists effect social change without leading their people outside the prison of the status quo and national consensus? It is this mode of thought that has brought the Israeli Peace activist to sing *Yorim Ve Bochim* ("Shooting and Crying").

The accuracy of Hall-Cathala's analysis is reflected in the concerns and ideas presented by the thirty-six contributors in the other two books. An example is the peace camp's division according to the activists' attitudes toward Zionism, a classification that Hall-Cathala utilizes on several occasions, as does Hurwitz in her introduction.[4] Significantly, every Jewish contributor classifies herself or himself as either Zionist or anti-Zionist, and most of the contributors express their personal commitment to some sort of Zionism. In fact, in his preface to Hurwitz's book, Rabbi Marshall T. Meyer reassured his American and Israeli Jewish readers by indicating "I am a Zionist"—three times in one page!

The Zionist identity allowed these activists to control the price they paid for their views. In this context, the options are to be universalist but marginalized, or particularist, and thus accepted in the family. A majority of the peace activists chose the second option, and remained members of the family—although perhaps as its black sheep. An example is Roni Ben-Effrat, an Israeli peace activist who was incarcerated for illegal contact with the PLO. In her article, "Being a Jewish Opposition During Intifada," she wrote:

> Although we were frequently subjected to harassment, such as being blacklisted and denied jobs, or unpleasant delays at the airport, in general the authorities always treated us as "part of the family," albeit black sheep. (Hurwitz, 146)

Obviously, placing oneself outside of the family is more costly, and—some peace activists argue—also politically ineffective. Ben-Effrat, for example, was fired from her job as a teacher in a Jewish school, because she refused to wear a pin that proclaimed, "I am a Zionist." A positive identification with Zionism is defined as a "red line" by both the mainstream peace camp and the government.

These red lines—set up by the mainstream and right-wing political parties and accepted by the peace movement—represent limits on efforts to bring about change. In some cases those who dared to cross the red lines lost their lives or were physically harmed. However, they still sent a powerful message to their people as they broke the consensus.[5] These are the activists that the society will remember when people witness their political leaders redefining the red lines—

and setting new restrictions on whom to talk with, or exclude and hate.[6]

Another self-imposed limit of the mainstream peace camp groups has been the strategy of separating the status and problems of Arabs in Israel from the conflict with Palestinians in the West Bank and Gaza. The peace organizations' leaders have avoided discussing Palestinian human rights inside Israel for the last two decades. Such avoidance was clear during every commemoration since 1976 of Land Day and Peace Day—memorial days created by the Higher Committee of local Arab municipalities to commemorate the killing of seven Arabs by the Israeli police, and to emphasize the Arabs' commitment to peace and equality in Israel.

III

The three books which we are discussing were written prior to the beginning of the current peace process in the region. They help to capture the mood among Israeli and Palestinian peace activists during and after the Gulf War—which was also the most desperate and helpless period that the Israeli peace camp had faced since 1967. In "Resuming the Struggle," Stanley Cohen, a peace activist and professor of social work at the Hebrew University, expresses that desperation by quoting from Beckett's *Waiting for Godot*. Cohen declares that, if peace activists look at the balance of forces within the society, there is no prospect in sight that the occupation will end or that a Palestinian state will be established. "The despair that I want to convey in these few pages is not yet Estragon's 'Nothing to be done,' but it is getting close to this." (Hurwitz, 184)

This feeling of despair was felt by most of the Israeli peace activists in the pre-Madrid period. Several of the activists who contributed to Gordon and Gordon's book describe their society as apathetic, passive, and indifferent. Gordon and Gordon assert, "We accept the deeds of the evil." The whole society became brutalized, and Israeli racism toward Arabs became more pronounced, particularly during and after the Gulf War.

Gela Sversky articulates the confusion among activists who were unable to escalate their resistance and avoided paying a higher price socially and politically. "My mind tries to grasp the horror of what is going on here. It doesn't bear thinking about. I would rather listen to some good music as I apply insulating tape around the window." (Hurwitz, 169)

In fact, Gordon and Gordon, and Hurwitz both indicate that their feelings of political impotency were among the main motivations for publishing their books. The withdrawal and unwillingness to pay a higher price is denounced by several contributors—such as Cohen, Mikado, and Marcello in Hurwitz's book—while others explain and, to some extent, justify it.

The peak of the frustration was felt during the Gulf War when some Palestinians danced on their roofs while Scud missiles landed on Israel. During that time, Yosi Sarid—currently Israeli Knesset member and a founding member of Peace Now—and others announced their support for the war and expressed their sense of betrayal. Peace activists wondered about the Palestinians' attitudes by asking, "How could they do that?" The peace camp accused Palestinians of betraying Israeli interests!

Such a reaction in the Israeli peace camp, particularly among Peace Now activists, can be explained by considering the different and asymmetrical motivation for dialogue in the first place. Israelis were motivated by the politics of bad conscience and enlightened self-interest, while Palestinians were motivated by the necessity of coming to terms with the oppressors. These were the bases for dialogue. Following Gordon and Gordon's assumption about the nature of dialogue, two real questions must be posed in reading the three texts, even though many contributors recognize the power imbalance.

First, were these activists engaged in a true and honest dialogue based on the belief of protecting basic human rights, equality, and freedom, defined as a universalist set of values? Or was their dialogue based on the values of pragmatic

and self-interested activities in a particularist and national-
istic set of values? Second, if the Israeli peace camp was
motivated by a particularist set of principles, then why was it
inappropriate for the Palestinians to act similarly from a
particularist set of principles—namely, their own.

IV

The asymmetrical balance of power regularly leads to reluctance on the part of parties engaged in conflict—and particularly those interested in political action and structural
changes—to become involved in a dialogue for peace with the
other side.[7] Most of the Palestinians who contributed to the
two books reflect this in their skepticism. They raise doubts
about the effects of dialogue's results, timing, and the way in
which it was conducted. They express suspicion and fear
that dialogue is politically manipulated, and it perpetuates
the status quo.

This fear is not without basis. The efforts of Peace Now
and the peace camp in Israel can be viewed as reformist, in
some cases, and, in other cases, a tool of political control for
maintaining the status quo, particularly when activists march
for keeping the territories under a limited Israeli control and
avoiding talks with PLO members. Dialogue has been seen
by some as an end in itself, rather than as a step toward
creating a formal negotiation process.

The Palestinian contributors—such as, Ashrawi, Atteek,
and Abdu El-Shafi—relate that one of the many pitfalls and
obstacles in dialogue is the asymmetric basis and conditions
of the dialogue process.[8] They emphasize "the failure of
dialoguers to recognize asymmetry and differences between
the two sides." They add that dialogue is manipulated politically, avoiding the present reality and projecting only on the
future relations. Dialogue pursues the objective of dialogue as
the end in itself, rather than becoming a step toward formal
negotiation. Perceiving dialogue as a cure to the problem of
occupation was identified by several Palestinian contributors
as a serious limitation for a genuine and fruitful negotiation.

Having such a high degree of skepticism brought one contributor, Ashrawi, to raise some fundamental questions. Is dialogue necessary? What are its pitfalls, its objectives, and its accomplishments?

In response to these questions, Palestinian contributors, utilizing the Intifada, present the dialogue as a national interest. They agree upon three national interests that could result from desired dialogue:

1. A popular empowerment of the Palestinian community;
2. Help in monitoring human rights; and
3. Bringing the occupation to Israeli homes.

Thus, a focal critique of the Israeli peace camp, particularly Peace Now, is the failure of its members to establish or recognize the differences in power and context of their Palestinian interlocutors. A clear example of such inadequacy is presented in the Gordon and Gordon's introduction of the conflict and requirement for dialogue as symmetrical and equal. They equalize the feelings of guilt and victimization on both sides, without any further comments on the differences in power and reality of living or context.

V

In addition to its neglect of the Palestinian minority in Israel, another shortcoming of Gordon and Gordon's work is its marginalization of Sephardim. Gordon and Gordon and their contributors do not mention the Sephardim at all. Nor do they consider the diversity of the peace groups in the Jewish society in Israel. In contrast, Hall-Cathala devotes two chapters to the involvement and contribution of the Sephardim to the peace movement, and their larger role in the Israeli historical and socioeconomic contexts—something rarely done by analysts or even peace activists.

Several of Hurwitz's contributors addressed the relationship between Israeli Sephardim and Ashkenazim Jews not only in the society, but within the peace groups, too. For example, Marcello depicts the class-based oppression, and exclusion of Sephardim from the Zionist ideology, which resulted in their cultural isolation. He challenges the inability of the peace movement to address the connection between Sephardim and the Palestinian question.

Further, Meir Amor suggests, in "The Fact of War," the desirability of a class-based alliance between Sephardim and Palestinians. In support of the thesis that Sephardim are subject to economic exploitation, he writes:

> Sephardim and Palestinians shared in the past, and share today a marginal position in Israeli society. . . . Israel-Palestine conflict *is really between two main camps, Ashkenazi and Palestinians.* [Emphasis added] (Hurwitz, 79)

It is not clear, however, how accurately this statement implicitly describes or reflects the national identity and political attitudes of the Sephardim, particularly those who serve in Israeli army units and in the Border Police, or those who live in the poorest neighborhoods of Jerusalem or Tel-Aviv, and have continued, since 1977, to vote for the radical right wing or Likud.

In regard to the role of Arabs in Israel, both Hall-Cathala and Hurwitz critique Israeli policies, pointing out that the definition of the Jewish state as democratic seems to ignore a discriminatory policy toward Arabs in Israel. Gordon and Gordon, in their critique of the Israeli government policy and democratic system, do not seem to be aware of such issues. They focus only on the lack of a constitution, and the continuation of the occupation. When the authors review the dialogue and peace and education, they rely only on materials that deal with Arab-Jewish relations in Israel, mainly because there are very few school-based dialogue projects or educational dialogue programs between Palestinians and Israelis.

When considering the point of view of Arabs in Israel, Hurwitz interviews a Christian cleric and a Druze poet, among the few Arabs included in the text. To some extent, both represent the interests and concerns of the Palestinian community. However, why not include a Moslem leader who could also talk about the peace movement in Israel? If we were to use the same criteria as the editor, how many Moslem Arabs have crossed the red lines of *their* state and nation?

Anticipating similar criticism, Gordon and Gordon offer a disingenuous disclaimer:

> We spent much effort in enlisting workers for dialogue from each faith who would show how their own request for dialogue concurs with their religious beliefs. Despite our ongoing efforts, we failed in our attempts to find such a Moslem writer. (Gordon and Gordon, 41)

This apparently means that Islam has no interest in dialogue or peaceful approaches to conflict. How can one establish a dialogue—particularly one based on Gordon and Gordon's philosophy and assumption that faith is a corner-stone of any true dialogue—when Islam is not included? As for finding a Moslem writer on the specific subject of dialogue and Islam, the editors could have interviewed any of the religious leaders from Israel, the West Bank, or Gaza who have supported negotiation and dialogue.[9]

Despite the discrimination toward Arabs in Israel, Hall-Cathala finds many Arab-Jewish educational organizations in Israel which promote coexistence and democracy in the Arab schools and community. Therefore, he views the Palestinians in Israel as contributors to the peace movement through their parliamentary representatives and extraparliamentary organizations.

VI

Israeli and Palestinian women have been a major force in leading and organizing the various peace groups and encounters for dialogue and solidarity. The role of Palestinian women became particularly distinct during the Palestinian Uprising in the West Bank and Gaza between 1987 and 1992.[10]

All three books seem to agree that women's groups have played a crucial role in injecting life and energy into different phases of the Palestinian-Israeli dialogue process, and in developing a peace movement. Hurwitz asserts that women's groups in both camps were the most successful of all groups within the peace movement. They succeeded in relating to each other as women, first, and then as Israelis or Palestinians. Such a connection assisted in creating a bridge between the two camps, and even in creating coalitions.

Gordon and Gordon select two Palestinian women (but no Israeli Jewish women) to reflect on the issue of dialogue and women—with no explanation for selecting them, except that both Mar'i and Kamal are Palestinian women who not only have suffered from the occupation and discrimination of Israeli policies, but also have fought for their freedom in chauvinistic societies. Considering the relative strength of feminist women in the Israeli peace movement—particularly Women in Black—the editors should have included at least one Jewish feminist, perhaps an activist who could deal with Israeli male chauvinism in a more direct and intensive way than do Mar'i and Kamal.

In general, the selected Israeli women peace activists are closer to the particularist, rather than universalist, end of the values continuum. For example, Shulamit Aloni, (in Gordon and Gordon) who criticizes the tribal nationalist mode and calls for a universal human rights approach, still espouses a practical strategy that continues to be very much within the mainstream Zionist and pragmatic peace camp.

Yvonne Deutsch, in "Israeli Women: From Protest to a Culture of Peace," uncommonly suggests that, before the creation of such a culture, there is a need to confront basic issues related to the Jewishness of the state. She emphasizes the need for Israeli activists to be integrated into the Middle East, rather than importing models of Western feminism.[11]

In a similar vein, Zahiera Kamal, in "Accounting for Fears and Aspiration: A View on the Palestinian-Israeli Dialogue," (in Gordon and Gordon) strongly criticizes dialogue. She identifies the asymmetric burden of occupation on Palestinian activists in comparison to Jewish peace activists.

She challenges the dialogue's lack of effect on the reality of occupation, even though it brings mutual understanding of fears. She writes, "Even if we shed the fears, that doesn't relate to reality." (p. 135)

VII

All three books focus on Judaism and dialogue when addressing the relationships among religion, peace, and dialogue—especially in the Gordon and Gordons and Hurwitz texts, which include religious Jews who derive their strength and philosophy of peace from Judaism.

Using Hall-Cathala and Hurwitz's topology of the peace activists' political and ideological orientations, the contributors are divided into Zionist and non-Zionist, on the one hand, and humanistic-universalist and particularist, on the other. However, these categories fall short of reflecting the ideas and attitudes presented by most of the religious contributors or activists. They all declared themselves to be Zionists, and most of them used both particularist and universalist terminology. However, they differ in the intensity, emphasis, and interpretations of their Judaic beliefs. It seems that a triple continuum might be more accurate in reflecting the contributors' and other activists' ideological orientations and positions in regard to certain political strategies, such as meeting and negotiating with the PLO, the state's Jewish identity, and other elements.

Particularist	Universalist
Zionist	Anti-Zionist
National consensus	"Crossed the red line"

Some activists expressed a clear universalist attitude in regard to equal civil rights. However, on other issues, such as religion and land, they were closer to the particularist end of the spectrum. For instance, consider Yehezkil Landau in "Blessing both Palestinians and Jews: A Zionist religious view," (in Hurwitz). Landau, a member of "Oz Veshalom" (Strength and Peace), affirms his loyalty to the national consensus and the particularist camp—at least partially. In order to remain within the family, he states:

> We in Oz Veshalom are not pacifist. We serve proudly in the Israel Defence Forces—as do those soldiers who choose, out of conscience, to sit in military prison rather than serve in the West Bank and Gaza Strip today. (Hurwitz, 121)

On the other hand, Landau derives from Talmudic interpretations the love between Ismael and Esau, an idea that is not widely accepted as a serious basis for cooperation by either most Israelis or Palestinians. Contrary to the universalist perspective—and as with any other Israeli Jewish particularist—Landau asserts the right of Jews to return, and does not propose or assume a similar right for the Palestinians.

In contrast, Rabbi Jeremy Milgrom is a religious Zionist who introduces more universalist values, He challenges the myth of equality in Israeli society, and then addresses the need to withdraw from the occupied territories.

> It took me almost ten years to wake up to the fact that Israel, too, neglected its "minorities," and another decade passed until I realized that this suffering was structural and not incidental—inflicted by the very elements of collective. . . . The Release of the Palestinian people is essential to the resurrection of Judaism, the very goal that Zionism set to accomplish. (Hurwitz, 31)

Rabbi Milgrom further reflects on the existing asymmetrical conditions of dialogue by comparing the military obstacles and restrictions that faced those Palestinians who came to meet him with obstacles that confront the Israeli peace activists. Milgrom joins the group of activists who make the connection between Israel, as a Jewish democratic state, and the discriminatory status of Arabs in Israel. In reflecting on the Palestinians in Israel—how they lost their birthright and blessing—he suggests communal reparation of refugees, rebuilding of three hundred to four hundred villages, and restoration of confiscated land. Few Jews—or even Arabs—

have voiced such a request. It would be perceived as being too radical and even anti-Zionist.

Understanding the motivation and significance of the Israeli religious peace activism requires the examination of its development following the emergence of the Gush Emunim movement. Hall-Cathala argues that the fanatic interpretations of the Torah, and its manipulation by right-wing religious settlers, were among the main reasons for the reactive emergence of Israeli religious peace activism. Such analysis provides an explanation for those religious peace activists who strictly adhere to Zionist ideology, as well as their hesitation to break the national consensus as often as do some secular activists. Theirs is an ongoing struggle with right-wing religious groups who compete in being the truest of Israeli Zionists, nationalists, and protectors of the Torah. One can, therefore, question to what extent these Zionist religious activists can ever conduct a dialogue with the Palestinians based on values of justice and symmetry, imprisoned as they are by a set of loyalty criteria defined by nationalist, right-wing religious ideology?

VIII

Ironically, the recent success in the peace movement has shifted the activists' attention from feelings of desperation and helplessness that characterized pre-Madrid conference period, to, since the signing of the Declaration of Principles in September 1993. a struggle to comprehend the political changes and redefinitions of their national consensus.

In the new reality, members of the peace camp—mainly Peace Now—had found themselves part of the last Israeli Government, and even held cabinet positions. They were expected to negotiate face-to-face with members of the PLO—the same individuals who were portrayed as terrorists only two years before even by Peace Now activists. In fact, some peace actvists were protecting PLO activists from Israeli settlers in the West Bank and Gaza. Members of the peace camp are accused of encouraging police brutality against

settler protests. In addition, fostering Israeli-Palestinian dialogue becomes not only legitimate, but also well-funded.[12]

The most stunning change on this level is the fact that
the Jewish settlers are being accused—by the peace camp
activists, media and others—of undermining the national consensus for peace and negotiation with the Palestinians, especially when they call for civil disobedience and when some
militant leaders of the settlers' movement encourage Israeli
soldiers to refuse military orders to evacuate them.[13] This is
the same cry which many peace activists struggled with in
the pre-Madrid conference, and which, in the past, was a red
line that the Israeli peace camp couldn't cross.

In Israeli elections in 1992, Meretz—the political party
which represented the Israeli left wing and many of the peace
camp groups—joined, for the first time since 1967, the labor
government coalition. Thus, the protest and dialogue movements found themselves in a new situation. Instead of operating from the periphery, they now became part of the central
political institution. This change influenced the level and
intensity of protest activities. As in the case of any other
social movement, when its members think that their objective has been achieved, then the movement must redefine its
existence and find new ways to sustain itself. Otherwise, it
would experience a phase of disintegration.[14]

Although it is clear that the Israeli peace camp has been
going through these stages since 1992, it is still too soon to
determine whether the Israeli peace camp—particularly Peace
Now—will disintegrate, or will redefine its objectives and manage to engage its followers again. Regardless of the future
development in the life of the peace camp groups, they are in
a stronger and more influential cycle than the phase of helplessness, impotency, and despair which the peace activists
experienced in the period of 1988 to 1992.

In conclusion, all three books, regardless of their specific strengths and weaknesses, represent the type of research that should be encouraged on both sides—Palestinian
and Israeli. It is only through our self-critique and evaluation

that we will be able to walk with our people on the lengthy and rambling road of peace.

On a personal note—and as a veteran and experienced member of Israeli and Palestinian dialogue and activist groups—it is clear to me that we need continuously to examine our own red lines—particularly those lines which are, too often, drawn by leaders who fear change.

Notes

1. I would like to thank Professor Kevin Avruch for his assistance in reviewing drafts of this article and Professor David Parson for his editorial assistance.

2. El-Shafi was the head of the Palestinian delegation to the negotiation with the Israeli officials in Madrid, and also was the first to resign from the negotiation when Arafat expressed his willingness to sign an agreement with Israel as a result of the secret negotiation in Oslo.

3. Martin Buber, a Jewish philosopher and theologist, wrote extensively on dialogue. The Gordons rely on Buber's vision of dialogue "the ontic quest for dialogue" which characterizes human existence (Gordon and Gordon, 10).

4. Hurwitz classifies peace activists as belonging to two different peace camps, based on her perceptions of the motivation and concerns of activists.

1. A Zionist mainstream peace camp that calls for a democratic Jewish state, and
2. A Progressive peace camp which is concerned with human rights and does not indicate the nature of the state.

5. Some of these figures include Sa'id Hammami, a PLO representative in London, and Isam Sartawi, PLO representative in Italy, who were assassinated by groups that opposed their contact with Israelis. Emil Grunzweig was a Peace Now activist who was killed by a hand-grenade in an antiwar march in Jerusalem in 1982. Uri Avneri was physically injured on several occasions after meeting with PLO members.

6. The recognition and legitimizations of the PLO in Israel—exemplified by the Rabin-Arafat meeting—is a perfect example of political leaders redefining their national consensus boundaries.

7. Mohammed Abu-Nimer, "Conflict Resolution between Arabs and Jews in Israel: A Study of Six Intervention Models." Doctoral dissertation. George Mason University, Fairfax, Va., 1993.

8. Several Palestinian and Israeli scholars and activists discussed the pitfalls and limitations of dialogue before these edited books were published. In a series of articles, Jonathan Kuttab and Edy Kaufman conducted an ongoing conversation on the nature and conditions required for an effective process of Palestinian Israeli dialogue. See, *Journal of Palestine Studies*, 17:2. Winter 1988.

9. In Jerusalem, for example, there is a group called "Hope" which includes Moslems, Christians, and Jews, who have been meeting for the last few years discussing interfaith dialogue.

10. Simona Sharoni, *Gender and the Israeli-Palestinian Conflict* (Syracuse, N.Y.: Syracuse University Press, 1995).

11. A majority of the feminist activists in the Middle East in general—and Israel in particular—adopted an approach and ideology of feminism that is based on Western and capitalist culture and social structure. Some activists question the applicability of such ideas in traditional and less industrialized societies. See, Dina Rothbards Margolis, "Women's Movements Around the World." *Gender and Society* 7:3, 1993. 379–399.

12. Since 1993, United States government agencies distributed many grants and aid to encourage dialogue and cooperation between Palestinians and Israelis.

13. "This Is Our Land," a new organization of the settler movement, announced intentions to break the Israeli law. In a recent protest activity in Jerusalem, members of the same organization injured eleven police officers. See, Ha'aretz, 13 September 1995.

14. Charles Stewart, Craig Allen Smith, and Robert Denton. *Persuasion and Social Movements*. Prospect Heights, Ill.: Waveland Press, 1989.

Part II

Society and Government

For a long time, the academic study of Israeli government and politics focused exclusively on the national levels of Knesset, cabinet, and parties. Academics could argue that this was, after all, where the action was—certainly not on the local levels of city, neighborhood, or ward. Increasingly this self-imposed limitation to the study of politics has become indefensible, for reasons made clear in Efraim Ben-Zadok's chapter on the vicissitudes of Project Renewal. While Project Renewal, and the various protest movements which he covers in his essay, did not change the general political structure of the state—or the class-system on which it is based—they have helped spearhead trends for decentralization and local participation. They also have helped to legitimate the cultures of Middle Eastern Jews—a pattern touched on, as well, in chapters by Walter Zenner and Zvi Zohar elsewhere in this volume.

Samuel Krislov, on the other hand, returns us to the center of Israeli politics and governance, but, academically speaking, to a hitherto neglected part of it, namely, the Israeli judiciary. Focusing on a single book, Krislov, nevertheless, ranges widely in his discussion of judicial institutions and behavior. He especially notes the strong—if not always straight-forward—influence of Judaism, as well as the continuities between diaspora Jewish culture and Israel.

With Jeff Halper's review of studies of Jerusalem we return to a locality, but, perhaps simultaneously, also to the so-called "center." Jerusalem is, after all, a sort of *axis mundi* for the three great Middle Eastern religions. Halper stresses this special character of Jerusalem, as well as the way in which Jews, Muslims, and Christians interact within its precincts. Halper reminds us as well that, inevitably Jerusalem will figure prominently on the terminal agendas of future Israeli-Palestinian peace accords.

3. Neighborhood Renewal through the Establishment and through Protest

Efraim Ben-Zadok

Shlomo Hasson, *Urban Social Movements in Jerusalem: The Protest of the Second Generation* (Albany: State University of New York Press, 1993). (Originally published in Hebrew, Jerusalem Institute for Israel Studies, Research Series 26, 1987.)

Frederick A. Lazin, *Politics and Policy Implementation: Project Renewal in Israel* (Albany: State University of New York Press, 1994).

Decentralization and Local Autonomy

*T*he Israeli political system has been led since its inception by a powerful central government burdened with national tasks in defense, economy, and immigrant absorption. Hence, Israeli social scientists, preoccupied with the salient characteristics of their own political system, have studied extensively their central government and national politics. Since the early 1970s, the relationship between the central government and local governments have been gradually decentralized. The central government began to share

53

power with local governments, and the latter became more
autonomous in their negotiations with central bureaucratic
agencies. Israeli social scientists then began to pay more
attention to the study of center-local relations as well as
local community politics.

A growing number of studies on center-local relations
and local community politics in Israel appeared in the 1970s.[1]
Although these studies continued to describe the central government as dominant, they also documented the first signs
of decentralization in center-local relations, and local autonomy. That trend was clearly marked by Daniel Elazar's
argument that the Israeli society of the 1970s was transformed from national-central-based politics into territorial
based politics.[2] This distinction between national and local
politics was formalized in the 1975 local elections law passed
by the Knesset. Mayors used to be elected by the local council on the basis of its party list, thus frequently representing
the national-level party which dominated the council. After
1975, mayors were elected as individuals, separately from
the council, and directly representing the local voters.

The trend toward decentralization and local autonomy
was also characterized by an increasing number of citizen-
participation groups, such as local voluntary associations,
planning committees, and environmental councils. This trend
also included a rise in the number of local public protests,
such as strikes and demonstrations. A substantial number
of studies describing these citizen participation groups and
public protests appeared in the 1980s.[3] Citizen participation
in Project Renewal was most extensive, both as a subject of
research and in practice.[4] The public protest of the Black
Panthers, although less researched, has been perhaps the
most intriguing protest in practice.[5]

A number of books published in the early 1990s—such
as those by Efraim Ben-Zadok and Sam Lehman-Wilzig—
integrated the subjects of local politics, citizen participation,
and public protest in Israel.[6] The two volumes reviewed in
this chapter represent good examples of this genre.

The volume by Frederick Lazin is primarily about local politics and citizen participation in Project Renewal, with some discussion of public protest. The volume by Shlomo Hasson is primarily about the local politics and public protest of the Black Panthers and other urban social movements, with some discussion of citizen participation. The two volumes also cover center-local relations and report on the growing trend, since the early 1970s, toward decentralization and local autonomy in Israel.

How these two volumes converge—but also diverge—in their coverage of the same topics, is the main focus of this chapter. The first section of the chapter discusses how the two volumes converge in their coverage of the population of working-class Oriental neighborhoods in Israel since the early 1970s. It also discusses how Lazin focuses on the upper stratum of this population—residents of Israel's relatively small development towns. Meanwhile, Hasson focuses on the lowest stratum of this population—residents of a large urban center. The second section of the chapter elaborates on the theoretical approach proposed in the two volumes which is based on the same two elements—structures and processes. However, whereas Lazin emphasizes structures, Hasson emphasizes processes. The third section describes the beginning of Project Renewal, and the protest movement which emerged from demands for improvement in social service, housing, and urban infrastructure. Interestingly, whereas Lazin's analysis is limited to the political behavior of the actors during this formative stage in the context of their organizations, Hasson's analysis also includes the political behavior of the actors as independent of the organizations and based on their individual perceptions. The fourth section elaborates on the strategies of action in Project Renewal and the protest movement. Again, whereas Lazin deals with strategies within the establishment, Hasson also deals with strategies, but outside of the establishment. The final section of the chapter assesses the impact of Project Renewal and the protest movement on the growing trends of decentralization

of center-local relations and local autonomy, citizen participation and protest activities, and the narrowing of socio–
economic disparities between working-class Oriental
neighborhoods and the rest of Israeli society.

Working-Class Oriental Neighborhoods in Israel

The vast majority of the population in Lazin's and Hasson's
studies were working-class Oriental Jews (Sephardim) who
immigrated to Israel throughout the 1950s from the Islamic
countries of North Africa and the Middle East. Their absorption into the new society was problematic in three major
spheres.

Culturally, they immigrated from a traditional culture to
a relatively modern and Western-oriented culture. Economically, they were poor refugees with limited means, property,
and working skills. Politically, they confronted a centralized
and cohesive political system that was controlled by veteran
immigrants with a socialistic ideology, and that was difficult
to penetrate by newcomers. These veteran immigrants dominated all three spheres. They were largely middle-class
Ashkenazic Jews of European origin.

As noted, although both books cover the general population of working-class Oriental Jews, each focuses on a different stratum of the population. Each stratum has distinct
socioeconomic and spatial-social characteristics as well as
political behavior. Hasson targets the lowest stratum of working-class Oriental Jews, mainly from the second generation
in Israel. The youth within this stratum tended to show high
truancy rates, discharges from military service, unemployment, delinquency, and gang activity.[7] Lazin, on the other
hand, targets the upper stratum of working-class Oriental
Jews. Their rates of unemployment, delinquency, and so on
tended to be much lower. Lazin further indicates that Project
Renewal failed to address the problems of poverty in the
Israeli underclass (the stratum covered by Hasson).[8]

When working-class Oriental Jews immigrated to Israel
during the 1950s, their residential choices were limited. The

Oriental Jews in both Hasson's and Lazin's studies were located by the Israeli authorities in their respective neighborhoods. Other than that, the spatial-social characteristics of the neighborhoods described in each of the two studies are different.

The formerly Arab neighborhoods, which populated the lowest stratum in Hasson's study, formed a belt of state-sponsored housing projects in the outskirts of one large urban center—namely, Jerusalem. With many deteriorating housing units administered by the state, the neighborhoods were isolated socially and economically from their adjacent middle-class neighborhoods which represented the main stream of Israeli society. From these poor neighborhoods— and more specifically, from five of them: Ir Ganim, Katamon Alef-Vav, Katamon Het-Tet, Musrara, and Shmuel Hanavi— the protest movement emerged and operated. All five of these neighborhoods—with the exception of Katamon Alef-Vav—were included in Project Renewal. The protest movement itself was comprised of eight organizations—Ohalim (general), Ohel Yosef, Ohel Shmuel Hanavi, Black Panthers, Dai, Shahak, Tsalash, and Katamon Higher Committee.[9]

The neighborhoods described in Lazin's book were also included in Project Renewal, a national urban-renewal project which, during the period of 1977–1984 covered by the author, included a total of eighty-four neighborhoods or close to one-fifth of Israel's Jewish population. The Project began in 1977 as a coordinated effort of the national and local governments, the Jewish Agency, and overseas Jewish communities. As a comprehensive effort of physical and social rehabilitation of Israel's poor neighborhoods, the Project's aim was to improve housing, infrastructure, and utilities, as well as welfare, health, education, and job-training services. An additional goal of the Project was to stimulate citizen participation in their neighborhood affairs.

The spatial-social characteristics of the neighborhoods covered by Lazin are different than those covered by Hasson. As noted, Lazin covers neighborhoods that populate the upper

stratum of working-class Oriental Jews. These neighborhoods
are located in six towns—Ashkelon, Beer-Sheva, Beit-
Shemesh, Ofakim, Yavne, and Herzliya. Hasson covers only
Jerusalem. In addition, although Lazin's book describes a
national-level study, the focus of the fieldwork was on the
implementation of the Project in the six towns. Social programs of the Project covered all residents of four of these
towns, excluding Beer-Sheva and Herzliya. Physical renewal
programs covered a total of nine neighborhoods in five towns,
and the entire town of Ofakim, excluding two areas. According to Lazin, these six relatively small towns are not representative of the geography of Project Renewal. Absent are
neighborhoods in the northern communities, and in the large
urban centers of Haifa, Tel-Aviv, and Jerusalem. The latter
city was the site of the protest movement in Hasson's study.[10]

On the other hand, Lazin explains that the six towns
are representative of the dynamics of local-level implementation in Project Renewal.[11] Furthermore, the six towns in
center/south Israel with the exception of Herzliya, are all
development towns. The development towns have distinct
spatial-social characteristics. Most of them were built from
scratch by the government throughout the 1950s. They absorbed masses of Oriental immigrants. Although the settlement of the towns was consistent with Israel's goals of defense,
population dispersion, and immigrant absorption, the towns
lagged economically, and remained a geographic and social
periphery.[12]

The towns studied by Lazin also represent the distinct
political behavior of the general population of the development towns. Since the early 1970s, this population of mainly
upper stratum working-class Oriental Jews has demonstrated
distinct voting and leadership behaviors. With respect to voting, the residents of the development towns switched their
support from Labor to Likud. With respect to leadership,
second generation leaders quickly emerged from the ranks of
the Likud and the religious parties, as well as from local
party lists, thereby replacing the first-generation leaders of

the Labor party. These indigenous leaders were sensitive to the local interests and the cultural values of their Oriental constituents. They also enjoyed massive support from their voters, as well as an increasing amount of resident participation in local affairs. The most successful of these leaders became mayors, while a few used their positions as stepping-stones to national politics, becoming members of the Knesset and the cabinet. These leaders of the development towns held close ties among themselves. Their joint demand to share power with the central government quickly showed positive results.[13]

Despite these drastic political changes, the dominant political behavior of the leaders of the development towns continued to be characterized as "politics through the establishment." In contrast, the dominant political behavior of the leaders of the urban social movements is characterized as "politics through protest." That is, much of this behavior is radical and outside the institutions of the establishment, and includes violent demonstrations. Hasson explains that, in Jerusalem, this political behavior was territorially confined. The leaders of the neighborhood-based independent organizations of the protest movement emerged between the early 1970s and early 1980s, and, attempted at times, to cooperate among themselves. Even so, they experienced major difficulties in forming an urban coalition. They also maintained only loose ties with the branches that they helped to establish in other neighborhoods in Jerusalem and in other cities.[14]

Structures Versus Processes

The relationship between the socioeconomic and spatial-social characteristics of the protest neighborhoods, and the political behavior of their residents, is the central research question around which Hasson's theoretical framework evolves. Social movements theory argues that socioeconomic and spatial-social characteristics are structural conditions, whereas political behavior is carried out by human agents through the protest process. A heated theoretical dispute involves whether the structure from which movements emerge has a decisive influence on their protest activities, or whether the protest process is an independent behavior constructed through the interpretations of the movement's members based on their past and present individual experiences.

Structure theories were at the forefront of research during the 1960s. Process theories—influenced by Jurgen Habermas' "critical theory"—were moved to the forefront in the 1980s by Manuel Castells and Alain Touraine. The two leading process theories are "resource mobilization" and "search for identity." The former deals with pragmatic mobilization of human and economic resources. The latter deals with human search for meaning including romantic elements of the nature of the good society.

The focus of Hasson's work is on these two process theories, and also on their relations to structure theories—that is, on the independent role of human agents and their reciprocal relations to structures. He argues that human agents mobilize resources, and construct their own identities and the meaning of their movements, also shaping their surrounding structures, both intentionally and unintentionally. Hasson also maintains that structures should not be overlooked, and that they enable and constrain human agents in ways that are not always explicated by the subjects. He lends support to his arguments by emphasizing longitudinal qualitative research methods, such as participant observation, open-ended interviews, and secondary sources.[15]

Hasson's book about human agents and their interpretive experiences joins other cultural anthropology books on Israel, such as those by Virginia Dominguez, Haim Hazan, and Tamar Katriel. All of these works deal with the interpretive dimensions of ethnographic descriptions.[16] As do these books, Hasson's work also represents an early-1990s growing genre of literature on constructive meaning and symbolic communication in Israel. Because of their interpretive perspective, these anthropology books provide the most recent challenge to the structural-functional school.[17] Led by S. N. Eisenstadt, this school has totally dominated Israeli sociology since the early 1950s, and views Israel as a coordinated and stable social system based on value consensus.[18] An earlier challenge to this school came from sociologists, such as Yonathan Shapiro, who viewed Israel as a conflict-and change-oriented social system.[19]

Unlike Hasson, Lazin focuses on structures, and on the political behavior of individuals in the context of these structures. However, his structures are not the socioeconomic and spatial-social characteristics of Project Renewal neighborhoods. Rather, his structures are the administrative and political organizations that implement the Project. The political behavior of human agents is largely dependent upon these organizations.

Lazin's approach to policy implementation in these organizations represents the approach of the 1970s founders of the policy analysis discipline. The founders—among them Jeffrey Pressman, Aaron Wildavsky, Donald Van Meter, Carl Van Horn, and Eugene Bardach—emphasized formal, unidirectional, and top-down implementation, thereby reflecting their interest in the political effectiveness of organizations and procedures.[20] They departed, however, from the traditional politics/administration dichotomy by stressing the constant process of interaction between the two—that is, the interaction between policy making (or politics) and policy implementation (or administration). Indeed, Lazin's approach includes both top-down and bottom-up interaction processes. That is, it covers the changes made by human agents, who attempted to adapt to economic and political pressures throughout the implementation process. This approach, like Hasson's, uses longitudinal qualitative research methods, such as open-ended structured interviews and secondary sources.[21]

As an implementation study that covers formal organizations, their informal political processes, and their members' personal political styles, Lazin's volume represents a new genre of Israeli policy studies. Previous studies—

which attempted to penetrate the "black box" of the policy-
implementation process in Israel and describe its independent life—also focused on Project Renewal which were written
by Rachelle Alterman, and Naomi Carmon with Moshe Hill.[22]
This new genre of Israeli policy studies is close to the contemporary view of policy analysis, which was first introduced
by authors such as Martin Rein, Francine Rabinovitz, Robert
Nakamura, and Frank Smallwood.[23] The contemporary view
is that of a cyclical (rather than hierarchical) policy process
comprised of three environments—policy making, implementation, and evaluation—that are mutually interacting.[24]

Formation

The protest movement and Project Renewal both began with
a demand for a drastic improvement in social services—including welfare, health, education, and job training—as well
as in housing and urban infrastructure, both renewal and
new construction. The demand for social services aimed to
improve the socioeconomic conditions, described earlier in
this chapter. The demand for housing and urban infrastructure aimed to improve the spatial-social conditions, also described earlier.

Social movements theory argues that such concrete social service and housing problems are the very structural
conditions that nourish the emergence of urban protest. In
Jerusalem's neighborhoods, according to Hasson, informal
voluntary protest organizations were formed around concrete
demands for social services and housing. From a neo-Weberian
perspective, the organizations were formed along their consumption interests in the service and housing goods market.
This perspective on the crystallization of classes according to
their positions in the goods market departs from the Marxian
perspective on the crystallization of classes according to their
positions in the production process. Indeed, the protest of
the class in the inferior market position—the underprivileged
housing class of the lowest stratum that was located in dete-

riorating state-sponsored housing projects—was against the state rather than against the dominant class. That is, the class in the inferior position held the state, not the class system itself, as responsible for its lack of services and dilapidated housing.[25]

Less concrete—but nevertheless important—structural conditions that further reinforced the protest were the general social and economic inequalities between working-class Orientals and middle-class Ashkenzazim. These inequalities were supplemented by the cultural and political dominance of the middle class. Such class and ethnic divisions were the very structural strains that promoted the struggle of some of the protest organizations from a particularistic-instrumental level of service and housing interests—on which other protest organizations remained concentrated—to a universal-expressive level of macrosocietal values. That is, these organizations began to struggle over the nature of existing social, economic, cultural, and political systems.

A similar mix of structural conditions—poor services and housing, as well as social and economic inequalities—prepared the ground for Project Renewal. In contrast to the voluntary protest movement initiative, the Project was a mandatory government initiative. Thus, the structures within Lazin's interest are the administrative and political organizations that implemented the Project. The author provides a systematic list of these formal organizations.[26] He then analyzes the informal political processes among the major actors in these organizations.

Along these processes, the main interorganizational conflicts at the beginning of the Project were:

1. Between the central government and the Jewish Agency,
2. Among partners in the Likud-led coalition government,
3. Among government ministries,
4. Between government ministries and local governments with the mediation of the parties, and
5. Between bureaucratic and professional units in the government.

An interesting observation made by Lazin pertains to the political weakness and failure of the head of the Project— namely, deputy prime minister, Yadin. Yadin headed a minority party within Begin's Likud-led coalition government, and was frequently co-opted by his partners from the majority party. Another interesting observation made by Lazin concerns the important role played by American Jews—either as representatives from the twin communities, or as professionals in the government—in promoting the citizen participation component of the Project.[27]

Whereas Lazin analyzes the political behavior of actors only within the context of their organizations, Hasson also analyzes actors' political behavior independent from their organizations—that is, as constructed by interpretive human experience. Indeed, the historical base for the political behavior of the members of the protest movement was their interpretation of their collective experiences with respect to social background, informal ties, and their sense of identification and belonging to a unique neighborhood territory. Crucial to the formation of the movement was the members' interpretation of their relative deprivation, which they frequently viewed as interchangeable with ethnic deprivation. Deprivation with respect to culture meant that the members felt that their traditional Oriental culture was repressed by modern European culture. It also meant that the latter's history, literature, art, folklore, and custom dominated the society at large, and were formally dictated by a paternalistic state through its public schools and other socializing agencies. Deprivation with respect to social and economic status meant that the members felt that they were discriminated, which led to feelings of injustice.[28]

The interpretation of deprivation varied among the different protest organizations. When deprivation was emphasized, it was linked to the macrosocietal level, and the organization demanded a radical social and political change on that very level. The organization received support and socialization to such demands from leftist organizations with class-based Marxist approach. When deprivation was not emphasized, the organization demanded an incremental change and concentrated on service and housing problems. The organization received support for such demands from community workers. Despite the similar structural conditions, these two different interpretations of deprivation eventually determined different strategies of action of the protest organizations.

Action

The strategy of action outside the established system included violent demonstrations, destruction of property, squatting in public areas, and provision of alternative services as opposed to state-sponsored ones. This strategy was based on the interpretation of members of the protest organization that concrete service and housing problems were rooted in a deeper sociopolitical context of class/ethnic conflict and discrimination. The strategy did not reject, however, the fundamental values of the society and state. The so-called "outside" strategy—as employed by the Black Panthers and the Ohalim—included a universal expressive demand for radical reform in social services, housing, employment, redistribution of resources, political participation, and cultural recognition. This outside strategy—as employed by Ohel Yosef, Dai, and Shahak—included a particularistic-instrumental demand for specific improvement in social services, housing, and local political representation.

The strategy of action within the established system included lobbying, negotiation, and media relations. Such a strategy, according to Castells, is not employed by genuine urban social movements. The so-called "within" strategy—as employed by Ohel Shmuel Hanavi, Tsalash, and the Katamon Higher Committee—included a particularistic-instrumental demand to improve local transportation, housing maintenance, employment, and education. That strategy—as employed by Tsalash and the Katamon Higher Committee—was based on a narrow interpretation of concrete service and housing problems with no class/ethnic reference.

To confront these strategies, the state employed its own set of measures. The only state strategy before the emergence of protest has been centralized paternalism, based on "machine politics" in which there was a neighborhood boss who served as a mediator between the local government and the poor immigrant neighborhood. This strategy included an exchange of government resources and services for the neighborhood's votes for the ruling Labor party. With the rise of the protest movement in the early 1970s, the strategy of the state—or central and local governments—toward the movement was one of confrontation and repression. This involved hostile efforts by the state to weaken the movement internally, to delegitimize its leaders, to block its expansion to other neighborhoods, to neutralize its support among community workers, and to solve the problems of a few members on an individual basis.

In the early 1980s, the state strategy changed to coproduction and social exchange, based on the incorporation of the protest leaders into the existing political system, mainly through Project Renewal. That strategy included the state's support for leaders by providing them with bureaucratic positions or jobs within the Project or elsewhere, political support and legitimization, control over substantial government resources and services, and personal material aid to leaders. Thus, the state increased the within-the-established system participation of its most active citizens, while neutralizing them politically. This type of state strategy developed gradually, and was situational rather than intentional. The pragmatic collaboration between the state and the leaders marked the institutionalization of the grassroots movement. The movement adopted a pragmatic interpretation, and shifted its focus toward everyday instrumental activities within the boundaries of its neighborhood territory.

A similar lack of meaningful citizen participation in Project Renewal was also observed by Lazin. Most of the original goals and structures of citizen participation were devoid of their genuine meaning during the implementation process. Members of local steering committees—mostly moderate and compromising local activists—were appointed by government officials instead of being elected. The committees themselves were not involved in implementation, and they were restricted to planning functions. Although all the major actors of the Project—in the government ministries, local governments, professional units, Jewish Agency, and overseas twin communities—explicitly endorsed the mandated citizen participation, they implicitly supported its limited and symbolic version because of their different interests.

Most influential on this weak version of citizen participation—as well as on the rest of the local implementation process—were the mayors. Their style and personality, more than their party affiliation, dictated the process. They were at the intersection of negotiations and bargaining. They directed the power streams with minimal intervention by professionals and residents. The empowerment of the mayors, through the implementation process, was the most significant local-level departure from original planning which had viewed the mayors as part of the problem of these poor neighborhoods. Another unexpected development was the direct support given to the mayors by the Jewish Agency and overseas twin communities as a leverage against the central government. In the beginning—and interestingly—the Jewish Agency tried to maintain its monopoly on access to the overseas communities to prevent their direct contact with the mayors. The overseas communities themselves were not expected to expand their powers through direct contacts with the mayors.

There were also some significant national-level departures from original planning. Foremost among them was the political weakness of the Inter-Ministerial Professional Committee under Deputy Prime Minister Yiga'el Yadin. The Committee was virtually powerless and ineffective vis-a-vis the government ministries, which received their own budgets for the Project, and the Jewish Agency, which developed its own independent renewal organization. Most influential of the

ministries were those concerned with housing and education, as they respectively dominated the physical and social
programs. Housing, in particular, built its own powerful renewal agency for the Project, and did not cooperate with the
Committee. Its minister, David Levy, eventually took overall
responsibility for the Project after the 1981 general elections.
Unlike Yadin, Levy was a powerful actor from the majority
party in the Likud-led coalition government. He and his
deputy, Moshe Katzav, were second-generation Oriental leaders from the development towns, and each had more interest
than did Yadin in the Project. Levy moved the Committee to
his ministry, and Katzav took charge of it. Thereafter, the
Committee became less and less effective.

Impact

The protest movement and Project Renewal did not drastically change the distribution of social, economic, and political resources in Israel. They did not alter the principles of
the class/ethnic distribution of resources. The protest movement was internally divided. It did not develop long-standing
connections to other social movements—such as Peace Now
and Palestinian national groups—nor did it connect with other
segments of the Oriental working class. In the long-run, the
movement pursued particularistic-instrumental goals, and
most of its organizations were dissolved. As for Project Renewal, it lacked a clear political steering force as well as a
unified goal-oriented coordination. Its implementation was
fragmented with multiple conflicting interests. The Project
did not remove all the socioeconomic disparities between its
neighborhoods and the rest of the society.

Having said that, however, the protest movement and
the Project did have a significant impact in spearheading
several trends that are continuously re-shaping the distribution of resources, as well as gradually transforming the contents of the social, economic, and political systems in Israel.
One such important trend is the growing decentralization of
center-local relations and the growing autonomy of local com-

munities. The protest movement—especially those of the Black Panthers and Ohalim—was effective in pressuring the central government to clear slums and construct low-priced housing projects. It was also effective in incorporating the neighborhoods into planning such renewal programs. As for the Project, it expanded the power and functions of local governments and mayors. They became more involved in areas traditionally controlled by the central government. The second-generation mayors increased their political leverage, not only through massive grassroots support, but also through their direct contacts with organizations that had little access to local affairs in the past. The involvement of organizations, such as the Jewish Agency and overseas communities, introduced new ideas to local politics, and diversified its content as well as its power distribution. Thus, the mayors became the center of local politics and power. They were relatively independent from the national parties in their politics through the establishment.

Another important trend spearheaded by the protest movement and the Project was that of assertion of opinion and citizen participation. For the first time—and despite the government's paternalistic and cooptation efforts—protest and citizen participation became legitimate and wide-spread activities. Politics through protest, as introduced by the Black Panthers, also infiltrated other areas, including settlement and defense—for example, Gush Emunim and Peace Now. The ultimate legitimatization—as well as the final termination of these politics—was the election of the most famous Panthers to the Knesset through a number of small left-wing parties. As for citizen participation, it became the rule, rather than the exception, in local planning and service delivery. More local governments in Israel began to promote new forms of citizen decision making and neighborhood self-management.

Finally, the protest movement and the Project were effective in narrowing the socioeconomic disparities between working-class Oriental neighborhoods and the rest of Israeli society. This resulted in significant improvements in housing, infrastructure, welfare, education, job training, and the general quality of living.

As for cultural differences—they have remained. Such cultural pluralism, however, became more acceptable to the society at large. Not only did Oriental culture become clearly prominent, but more and more of its elements were transmitted through the state and its socializing agencies to the general Israeli public.

Notes

1. See for example: Myron J. Aronoff, *Frontier Town: The Politics of Community Building in Israel* (Manchester: Manchester University Press, 1974); Erik Choen, "The Power Structure of Israeli Development Town" in T. Clark, ed., *Comparative Community Politics* (New York: John Wiley and Sons, 1974) 179–201; Sholomo A. Deshen, *Immigrant Voters in Israel: Parties and Congregations in Local Elections Campaign* (Manchester: Manchester University Press, 1970); and Sami Mari, *Arab Education in Israel* (Syracuse: Syracuse University Press, 1978).

2. Daniel Elazar, "The Local Elections: Sharpening the Trend toward Territorial Democracy" in A. Arian, ed., *The Elections in Israel, 1973* (Jerusalem: Jerusalem Academic Press, 1975) 219–237.

3. See for example: Efraim Ben-Zadok, "The Impact of National Characteristics on Local Citizen Participation: A Developmental Research Framework Applied to Israel," *Contemporary Jewry* 7 (1986), 19–42; and Sam Lehman-Wilzig, "Public Protest Against Central and Local Government in Israel," *The Jewish Journal of Sociology* 24 (1982), 99–115.

4. For citizen participation studies of Project Renewal, see, for example: Arza Churchman, "Issues in Resident Participation—Lessons from the Israeli Experience," *Policy Studies Journal* 16 (1987), 290–299; Paul King et al., *Project Renewal in Israel: Urban Revitalization through Partnership* (Lanham, Md.: University Press of America, 1987); and Ruth Liron and Shimon Spiro, "Public Participation in Planning and Management: Criteria for Evaluation and Their Application to Project Renewal," *Society and Welfare* 9 (1988), 17–34 (Hebrew).

5. For public protest studies of the Black Panthers, see, for example: Erik Cohen, "The Black Panthers and Israeli Society" in E. Krausz, ed., *Studies of Israeli Society.* (New Brunswick, N.J.: Transaction Books, 1980), 147–163; and Shlomo Hasson, "The Emer-

gence of an Urban Social Movement in Israeli Society—An Integrated Approach," *International Journal of Urban and Regional Research* 7 (1983) 157–174.

6. Early 1990s books which integrate these subjects are: Efraim Ben-Zadok, ed., *Local Communities and the Israeli Polity: Conflict of Values and Interests* (Albany: State University of New York Press, 1993); Sam Lehman-Wilzig, *Stiff-Necked People, Bottle-Necked System: The Evolution and Roots of Israeli Public Protest, 1949–1986* (Bloomington: Indiana University Press, 1990); and Sam Lehman-Wilzig, *Wildfire: Grassroots Revolts in Israel in the Post-Socialist Era* (Albany: State University of New York Press, 1992).

7. Shlomo Hasson, *Urban Social Movements in Jerusalem: The Protest of the Second Generation* (Albany: State University of New York Press, 1993) 26, 94–101.

8. Frederick A. Lazin, *Politics and Policy Implementation: Project Renewal in Israel* (Albany: State University of New York Press, 1994) 167.

9. Hasson, *Urban Social Movements.* 12–13, 27–29, 141.

10. Lazin, *Politics and Policy Implementation.* 1–13.

11. Ibid. 47–48.

12. For more on these towns, see, Elizabeth Altman and Betsy R. Rosenbaum, "Principles of Planning and Zionist Ideology: The Israeli Development Town," *Journal of the American Institute of Planners* 9 (1973), 316–325.

13. This brief description of voting and leadership in the development towns is taken from Efraim Ben-Zadok, "Oriental Jews in the Development Towns: Ethnicity, Economic Development, Budgets, and Politics" in E. Ben-Zadok, ed., *Local Communities and the Israeli Polity: Conflict of Values and Interests* (Albany: State University of New York Press, 1993) 91–122.

14. Hasson, *Urban Social Movements,* 42.

15. Hasson, *Urban Social Movements,* 6–14, 161–164, 175. Manuel Castell, *The Urba Question.* (New York: Edward Arnold and MIT Press, 1977); Alain Touraine, *The Voice and the Eye* (Cambridge: Cambridge University Press, 1981).

16. Virginia Dominguez, *People as Subject, People as Object: Selfhood and Peoplehood in Contemporary Israel* (Madison: University of Wisconsin Press, 1989); Haim Hazan, *A Paradoxical Community: The Emergence of a Social World in an Urban Renewal Setting* (London: JAI Press, 1990); and Tamar Katriel, *Communal Webs: Communication and Culture in Contemporary Israel* (Albany: State University of New York Press, 1993). For a review article on Dominguez and Katriel, see, James Armstrong, "The Search for Israeliness: Toward an Anthropology of the Contemporary Main-

stream" in R. A. Stone and W. P. Zenner, eds., *Critical Essays on Israeli Social Issues and Scholarship* (Albany: State University of New York Press, 1994) 121–134.

17. There is no indication in Hasson's volume that affiliates the research with a specific academic discipline. It seems to be interdisciplinary social science research which is somewhat closer to anthropology than to sociology and geography. Hasson is associate professor at the Department of Geography, The Hebrew University in Jerusalem; and senior researcher at the Jerusalem Institute for Israeli Studies.

18. See, for example, S. N. Eisenstadt, *Israeli Society*. London: Weidenfeld and Nicolson, 1967.

19. Uri Ram, "From Apparatus to Populus: The Political Sociology of Yonathan Shapiro" in R. A. Stone and W. P. Zenner, eds., *Critical Essays on Israeli Social Issues and Scholarship* (Albany: State University of New York Press, 1994) 137–160. See, for example, Yonathan Shapiro, *The Formative Years of the Israeli Labor Party: The Organization of Power 1918–1930* (London: Sage, 1976); and Yonathan Shapiro, *The Road to Power: Herut Party in Israel* (Albany: State University of New York Press, 1991).

20. Eugene Bardach, *The Implementation Game* (Cambridge: M.I.T. Press, 1977). Jeffrey L. Pressman and Aaron Wildavsky, *Implementation* (Berkeley: University of California Press, 1973); and Donald S. Van Meter and Carl E. Van Horn, "The Policy Implementation Process: A Conceptual Framework," *Administration and Society* 6 (1975), 445–488.

21. Lazin, *Politics and Policy Implementation.* 7–13.

22. Rachelle Alterman, "Opening Up the "Black Box" in Evaluating Neighborhood Problems: The Implementation Process in Israel's Project Renewal," *Policy Studies Journal* 16 (1987), 347–361; Rachelle Alterman, "Implementing Decentralization for Neighborhood Regeneration: Factors Promoting or Inhibiting Success," *Journal of the American Planning Association* 54 (1988): 454-469; Naomi Carmon and Moshe Hill, "Neighborhood Rehabilitation Without Relocation or Gentrification," *Journal of the American Planning Association* 54 (1988), 470–481.

23. Robert T. Nakamura and Frank Smallwood, *The Politics of Policy Implementation* (New York: St. Martin's Press, 1980); and Martin Rein and Francine Rabinovitz, "Implementation: A Theoretical Perspective" in W. D. Burnham and M. W. Weinberg, eds., *American Politics and Public Policy* (Cambridge: M.I.T. Press, 1978). 307–335.

24. This view comes from the political science branch of policy analysis. Lazin is a political scientist. He is associate professor at the Department of Behavioral Sciences, Ben-Gurion University of

the Negev, and the Lynn and Lloyd Hurst Family of Local Government professor.

25. Hasson, *Urban Social Movements.* 4–5, 18–19, 31–35.

26. The major organizations are government ministries, Inter-Ministerial Professional Committee, Social Policy Group, local governments in municipalities, city councils, mayors' offices, municipal departments, local steering committees, local project directors' offices, political parties, Jewish agency, and overseas twin community offices.

27. Lazin, *Politics and Policy Implementation.* 1–29, 94.

28. Hasson, *Urban Social Movements.* 15–16, 24–25, 41–47.

4. Israeli Courts and
Cultural Adaptation

Samuel Krislov

Martin Edelman *Courts, Politics and Culture in Israel*
(Charlottesville: The University Press of Virginia, 1994).

I

$\mathcal{I}$n the summer of 1994, the Supreme Court of Israel
ruled that two members of the Knesset, who had broken with the party they had been elected to represent, could
not become cabinet ministers or deputies. This was an interpretation of a Basic Law: Knesset provision. (The subject
matter of Basic-Laws is a sort of constitution in parts, en-
acted to fill the role of a document too difficult to agree upon
as a single entity.) Those followers of the events who were
informed enough to know that Israel nominally does not
have judicial review—the power to declare laws unconstitu-
tional—might well be puzzled.

One of the many virtues of Edelman's comprehensive,
deft treatment in this short book is that he demystifies such
issues. The Supreme Court treats the Basic Laws as higher

law. The sum of the Basic Laws is an almost comprehensive constitution leaving gaps and ambiguities mainly in the religious arena. Looking at realities, not labels, makes a difficult and complex system understandable.

II

For a small country, Israel attracts extraordinary attention. Not surprisingly, most of the work in English deals with aspects of society that are of most concern to outsiders— namely, the policy aspects of foreign relations, or the strategic position of the country in a geographically vital and resource-rich portion of the globe. Other outside concerns feed on this central interest. Social conditions—including absorption of waves of immigrants, the tensions between ethnic identities, and the religious divisiveness—are all, in significant measure, traced back to Israel's need for stability. The institutions most studied—the military, the political parties, the electorate, and the Knesset—are all vital to Israel's capacity to defend itself, and to effectively formulate foreign policy, especially in dealing with potential peace.

These concerns have dominated less strategic issues, which are sometimes intriguing from an abstract point of view. Long ago, Judah Matras, an Israeli demographer, pointed out that Israel represented a remarkable transplant that, theoretically, could teach us much about social needs and constructed social roles.[1] One could compare, for example, the roles which immigrants had in their home countries with their new jobs in the Israeli economy, getting clues as to which roles were vital. However, no one has really attempted such a daunting task—including Matras himself.

In the political sphere, the paucity of material on the prime minister's office is surprising, although this is, perhaps, for reasons of security. The scope of Michael Brecher's volume on foreign-policy decision making in Israel published in 1972, however, suggests that something else has really impeded such research.[2] In fact, it is precisely in the area of defense and foreign-policy decision making that we have the best work on elite interaction, as Brecher's volume has been supplemented by Yehuda Ben Meir's studies, based partly upon his own experience as deputy foreign minister.[3] Israeli Cabinet affairs are among the most publicized in the world, but they are little analyzed. Perhaps this is because the cabinet is "a little Knesset" rather than a true executive-decision body. It is the so-called "inner cabinet" which each Prime Minister has constructed in accordance with his or her style that plays the normal role of cabinets. Local government has also been relatively neglected, perhaps because the national government has kept that level of governance on a short leash, thus, making its study seem trivial. This is changing. See Efraim Ben-Zadok's chapter in this volume, for example.

Similarly, the paucity of systematic English material on law in Israel is, no doubt, part of its mundaneness, and its disconnectedness from strategic foreign affairs, which are matters of life and death for the community. So, not surprisingly, a disproportionate amount of coverage of the legal order deals with Supreme Court cases on military law in the West Bank. Some wooden treatments on the Court system and stray articles of a routine sort dot the landscape. Pnina Lahav's writings are a clear exception.[4] American scholars of law—when teaching or doing research in Israel—tend to devise yet another peace plan for the Middle East. Israeli law professors have multiple roles open to them in the society, and take political or administrative jobs freely. To be immediately influential, they write books in Hebrew.

Thus, there was a tremendous need for basic hornbook treatment of virtually all subjects, and the professorate has filled this gap impressively. An excellent example, that is most relevant to this essay, is Amnon Rubinstein's magisterial constitutional law treatise originally published in 1969, and still both cited and highly respected.[5]

Additionally, there are impressive contributions to jurisprudence, including Menacham Elon's *Mishpat Ivri*, published originally in 1973, and again as a four-volume translation in 1994.[6] Others include a theoretical treatment of *Judicial Discretion* by Aaron Barak,[7] the long-time Justice who became

President of the Supreme Court in 1995.[8] What has not emerged—although Elon's work does a bit of this—is a sociological, or anthropological treatment of the legal order. This is paradoxical, for the sociology of law has been—both historically and currently—a major concern of Jewish scholars in the diaspora.

This is regrettable, because the Israeli legal system is a fascinating hybrid of many legal systems. The substantive law is a mixture of British, Turkish, German, and American traditions. Its dominating constitutional and juridical style has evolved from Eastern European to Germanic to American—all in quest of a new Sabra synthesis. Once viewed with the sense of awe that Israeli audiences bring to symphony performances—and not usually to religious services—the judiciary now occupies a less lofty position in popular esteem, although it's probably an enhanced position in the legal order.

One of the to-be-hoped-for peace dividends for Israel is that world attention will become less focused on war and peace, and Israel will be studied as something more akin to a so-called "normal society." If that happens at the journalistic level, there's no doubt that scholarly coverage will follow.

Martin Edelman's thoughtful and measured book is an important harbinger of such scholarship. To be sure, Edelman is no recent arrival to Israeli studies, having long provided the most authoritative and informative body of work in English on Israel's judiciary. Indeed, this volume is clearly the culmination of several years' effort. Even so, it is distinguished by a clear tone of dispassionate analysis, both for purposes of dealing with external issues—as in legality in the occupied territories—or internal issues—the religious issue and the rights of religious minorities in the state. Edelman writes with full awareness of American social-science methods, jurisprudence in general, and Jewish law. However, his greatest commitment is to the social sciences and the subfield of comparative judicial behavior.

The book is perhaps best described as concerned with the architectonics of the Israeli judicial system. This centers on the Supreme Court. Selection of the Justices and the Court's basic roles are the major focus, together with a good description of the Basic Laws, as a virtual constitution, and the Court's unusual role functioning as the High Court of Justice. Briefer, but highly useful, descriptions are given of the Jewish, Moslem, Druze, and Christian religious courts, as well as their selection and composition. The boundaries with the secular court system are explained, although only with respect to the Jewish religious courts is there any extensive account of the litigation involving claims of overreaching by the religious authorities.

The treatments are also asymmetrical with respect to composition of the courts. Edelman draws upon studies in Hebrew as well as his own research to tell us about the background of the Supreme Court Justices.[9] However, he describes the lower-court judges mostly in terms of required qualifications and methods of selections. Religious judges are also not analyzed. At this level, few individuals are discussed, and sociological detail is skimpy. Finally, there is a highly useful chapter on the courts and the occupation authority. This provides a picture of yet another legal-order-within-the-legal-system in Israel.

Although very briefly described (Edelman, 11–12, 34–35), the local secular court arrangements are not given full-scale treatment, nor is there any attempt to differentiate among or describe judges elevated from the District Courts to the Supreme Court from those who were not so honored. The nominations committee, while chaired by the Minister of Justice, is believed to be dominated by the three Justices—including the court President—and the two practicing advocates who serve by law. They are joined by another Cabinet member and two members of the Knesset chosen by secret ballot. By statute, the President of Israel must nominate those put forward by that process. It is clear that the legal elite have entrenched themselves, providing high-caliber choices, and resisting most political pressures, through this heavily professionalized selection method. At the same time, the elite have resisted the forces for representativeness or diversity, except for the tradition of the religious justice. Indeed, Sephardic judges themselves resisted the concept that they come to the Supreme court on ethnic grounds. Prior to 1994, only four Justices came from a Sephardic background, the first being named in 1961. When Miriam Ben-Porath was chosen a Justice, the President of the Court explicitly rejected any thought that gender could have been a factor. Whether these austere principles really serve so diverse a society is arguable. More to the point, the high professionalism of the judiciary is likely to be sorely tested in so political a polity as Israel.

While the basic arrangements involving each of those diverse systems—the Supreme Court, the various religious courts, and the West Bank occupation—and the government and citizenry are set forth, no attempt is made to describe substantive law—that is, nonconstitutional day-to-day law. Nor is there any attempt to study the court system as a whole, the flow of cases, or the handling of actual litigation including the intricacies of divorce in a two-court process. Marital status is determined by religious courts, while the financial arrangements are established by civil courts. Edelman deals with boundaries, but not, for example, how bouncing around between two systems while getting a divorce affects families and individuals.

As *halakhah* (Talmudic law) developed an extensive and complete system of family law, the bifurcation of religious status—as opposed to economics and welfare of children—is nothing like a clear or clean division, and results in great costs to divorcees contesting any part of the process. However, in contrast to Elon, Edelman does not attempt to place the burgeoning Israeli system in the stream of Jewish contributions to law, nor does he attempt to portray Israel's system in terms of the Jewish courts' historic relations to other court systems.

Of course, that would be a different book—or, more precisely, two or more other books. The present volume is a disciplined culmination of more than a decade of Edelman's fine research, and it suggests what can be done on foreign legal systems with perseverance and imagination. Some of the roads that new research might undertake, now that we have so fine a basic volume, will be adumbrated before returning to his accomplishments and findings on the road that he did pursue.

III

In a country of paradoxes, Israeli law still ranks high in its complexity. Law is almost venerated. Witness the political decision making of commissions dominated by justices, or by Torah sages based on halakhic analogies. Public opinion polls, as well, rank the Judiciary highly. Yet, courts have been poorly treated in mundane terms. Resources and enforcement mechanisms are pitifully lacking.

The image of Israeli courts that is held by knowledgeable insiders is of very able judges, with little assistance in their record keeping, sloppy files, and, on the whole, adjudicating rushed and poorly presented cases by overworked and mediocre advocates. Decorum in court is not remarkably high, and pleading is ad hoc and largely oral and uneven.[10]

It would be surprising, given what is generally agreed upon, if this description were not essentially correct, but actual observations of courts in other systems inevitably yield surprises over folklore. Essentially we are describing a levantine—or, more generously, Mediterranean—court system run by a founding generation of East European and Germanic judges, who put a stern *Rechstaat* face on a loosely obeyed structure. In a society in which everyone adds new rooms without building permits, or parks overnight on the sidewalk, the sanctity of the law seems to have special symbolic value, but relatively little practical effect. Yonathon Shapiro writes of the high Zionist functionary in the 1920s who was found to have embezzled *Yishuv* funds. He was severely reprimanded, but the investigators decided that public identification would have forced him to become a *yored* or emigrant. So, he was neither punished nor named. This superpractical approach to so-called "strict law" characterizes much of Israeli justice. In a country which once was virtually free of real crime, laxity was not much of a burden. In a society with increasingly diverse cultures and attitudes, and growing rates of what is viewed as "normal" crime, it might become a necessity.

How Israeli courts work on a day-by-day basis has some intrinsic interest of its own. How do judges manage dockets with three-year delays, and litigants with vastly distinctive notions of how to express respect? All of these factors are, perhaps, more of interest to Israelis themselves, but such studies would provide comparisons, for example, with the efforts of Italian courts under similar economic stringency and poor judicial compensation. Israel's complex social matrix adds piquancy. The tracing of cases through their paths in religious and civil courts would add factually to theoretical knowledge. Knowledge of the life of the advocate in Israel would supplement existing studies in other systems.

Even more valuable would be an exhaustive evaluation of the multiple sources of Israeli law, and their integration into a coherent whole. The borrowing of aspects of law and court institutions is quite standard, and what have been dubbed "legal transplants" are found throughout the world. The Japanese, for example, hired experts—mostly teams of Germans—to provide them with comprehensive corporation, criminal, and investments law when they decided to modernize and Westernize at the turn of the century. Those legal subsystems were adjusted to enduring Japanese law. However, Israel has an unusual amalgam of Turkish, British, German, and Talmudic law, chosen from inertia, political advantage, and history—almost anything but rational purpose.

Turkish land law was retained—at least in part—during the British mandate, and then by the new state in 1948, because it left the bulk of the land as property of the government. The traditional *millet* system of family law delegated to confessional communities was the Ottoman solution to governing one of the most polyglot and complex empires ever known. It suited the British to keep it, and it was politically imperative for Israel to do so, too. The basic religious pattern has been status quo—even in favoring the Christian community financially, by allowing bus and cable-car traffic on the Sabbath in Haifa, and by providing a financial subsidy to the Karaites, a religious minority condemned for centuries as heretics by Rabbinic Judaism. The fourteen recognized confessional communities are simply legacies or relics (Edelman, 124). The strangest heritage from the British is their corporation law of the 1930s—even then inferior to existing American and continental, especially Polish, laws of the times—which has plagued Israel's business ever since.

What is intriguing about Israel is not its targeted "system borrowing." The Japanese easily accepted German corporation law, for they had none. Some parts of the legal order appear to be more easily integrated than others. Commercial law has always been, and is increasingly, international in character, and seemingly can be transplanted easily. Family law, being socially determined, is the most distinctive and hardest to borrow or adapt.

Any legal order that contains elements of other legal orders was viewed with suspicion by advocates of the German historical school who believed that law was essentially a true emanation of a nation's soul. These theorists—also known as "political romanticists"—thought that borrowing of institutions was unfortunate, and, perhaps, even inevitably doomed. Society after society has, in practice, refuted the historicist fallacy, and extreme forms of the approach are seldom heard. However, anthropologists are fond of weak forms of that argument. Thus, Clifford Geertz has suggested that law is a way in which society structures reality—"part of a distinctive manner of imagining the real."[11] It is difficult to find this operative in a system that is so obviously jerry-built as Israel's, with a bit from here and a bit from there. A model for the study of integration of those divergent strands exists in Robert Eisenman's excellent study of the Turkish effort to

Westernize Islamic law before World War I.[12] In a sense, we need successor volumes to that work.

Over time, of course, modifications can be expected from legislation, executive regulations, or habitual practices—modifications which, at least theoretically, can be expected to move a system toward greater consistency and in the direction of dominant social values. On a day-to-day basis, the burden of accomplishing that inevitably falls on the judges. Assessing that accommodation in Israeli law is not completely without ambiguity. It could be that, as happened with the Indian civil service when the raj ended, Israeli judges are fighting a rear-guard action to preserve Western legal values in the face of an inevitably levantine, personalistic, and nonlegalized order.

One would hope that what is being forged is a unique system, combining Eastern personalism and Kadi-law with Western principled notions, a German *Rechstaat* with American Warren Court social compassion, and a blend of civil law and common law with Talmudic law and Islamic law. Just as Israeli haute cuisine is emerging as international leaders of a cuisine blending North African, Southern Europe, and Levantine and labeled "Mediterranean Rim"—implausibly enough to those who partake of its normal diet—Israeli law has the opportunity, and perhaps need, to create a new and distinctive legal synthesis.

However, opportunity is just that. It is no guarantee of success. Divergent elements might produce a chaotic botch, the sort of result that John Kennedy had in mind when he described the Washington, D.C., of the 1960s as "a place that combined Southern efficiency with Yankee charm."

The task of the Israeli judge is, then, doubly daunting. Making a motley system reasonably consistent with inadequate resources under heavy case loads is, to say the least, challenging. If, as is assumed by most observers, the system currently works only on the backs of ultracompetent judges, the question of the pipeline for judges becomes paramount. Israel has been able and willing to draw upon a supply of talented jurists from all over the world. That supply is, per-haps, not as abundant now as it was in the past, but it is still quite remarkable. However, inevitably the quest for high-quality, home-grown judges must assert itself, and filling this need will be a major test for Israel.

IV

By its very title, Edelman's volume focuses attention on the question of the relationship of culture and law. By and large, he is content to deal with this by demonstrating the utility of allowing the obviously discrete communities within Israel to keep and interpret their traditional law of the family. Essen-tially, he suggests that millet law is almost a necessity for so divided a society, although he carefully examines arguments for an alternative—perhaps civil marriage existing side-by-side with religious ceremony. Cohesiveness can be main-tained, as he notes, by options, as well as delegation and monopoly.

There are multiple advantages in recognizing subcom-munities, imparting dignity, and allocating prestigious posi-tions to Arabs, Sephardim, Druze, and others, as well as limiting friction within the religious communities. However, current arrangements deny such recognition to other group-ings—namely, the less orthodox, small, but growing, and more vocal, liberal religious groups; and the anticlerical in-heritors of the socialist builders of the society. In a sense, these, too, are recognizable cultures, and the monopoly given the Orthodox over family definition and great authority given them over *Kashruth* is a denial of what is arguably a cultural tradition of its own. The Orthodox, in turn, argue that this legal monopoly is integral to maintaining a single culture, and is necessary to avoid "two-streams," by limiting permis-sible marriages and preventing deep rifts. Edelman summa-rizes these arguments—and their opposite—very well. Those forced into marrying abroad or who live together in semi-recognized marriages could be deeply estranged from their society.

The limited legal monopoly on these matters has been kept in check by the civil courts. This can be interpreted as a tacit compromise, or a vigorously contested careful balance— and the record is really very inconclusive as to which is the correct description. In general, the secular courts' disposition of economic and child custody matters are not in consonance with Talmudic tendencies, and these have seldom been challenged by the Rabbinic courts. When they have tried to, the Rabbinic jurists were quite unsuccessful, although a new challenge emerged in 1994 subsequent to the publication of Edelman's book. It is extremely likely that this challenge will be handled as others described in Edelman, and on grounds which he makes clear—secular predominance in financial allocations have been explicitly granted to the regular courts by Knesset action.

Still, only here and there does Edelman touch on a broader sense of culture, and attempt to answer the question of whether law in a Jewish state reflects Jewish law. Obviously, Geertz's proposition—and even perhaps the stronger arguments of the Historical School—should have special application to Israel. For, if there was ever a culture centered on law and the study of law, certainly it has been that of traditional Judaism. Immersion in "the sea of Talmud" was the highest expression of the culture, and remains a popular intellectual passion in modern Israel. To what extent, then, has the society chosen to live by it, not merely be edified by it? Edelman does not address the problem directly, but provides enough to give a presumptive answer—and that answer is, "Some, but not very much."[13]

The simplest, crudest index is the fact that only one Supreme Court Justice has traditionally been chosen as knowledgeable in Jewish law. The original appointments to the Supreme Court included a Rabbinic authority without legal training. This was, presumably, not a success, because that mode was not repeated in the four decades since his death in 1953. Rather, a legalist with extensive halakhic knowledge—and one who is personally observant—has always been a member of the Court. That Judge has recognizably also been well-trained in law in the usual sense. The Orthodox, and especially the ultra-Orthodox, have not been content with this arrangement, and they have lobbied for a *dayan* on the Court, as well as other candidates sometimes successfully. Edelman reports that in 1989 four of the twelve Justices were personally observant, a percentage slightly higher than that of the general populace. However, Orthodoxy is hardly synonymous with halakhic knowledge, and some members of the secular element have also been among the more knowledgeable Talmudists on the Court.

Another index, perhaps, is the decades-old absence of Arab judges on the Supreme Court. Menacham Begin, both as an opposition leader and prime minister, sought unsuccessfully to change this. Part of the opposition was that the presidency of the court is, by tradition, a matter of seniority, and some deemed the possible ascension to that office to be inappropriate. Yet, Edelman concludes that, on the whole, what has been operative is largely an "old-boy network" that, while assuring quality in the choice of Justices, restricts, not merely Arabs, but also Sephardim and women in the process. Insulation from politics has its minuses as well as it pluses.

The most conspicuous source of Jewishness is the provision that all law be interpreted in a manner consistent with Jewish tradition. Because the bar is now overwhelmingly Israeli-trained, and the Talmud is a conspicuous part of the law-school curriculum, both at the level of advocacy and judging, this provision can be expected to become more significant with time—at least, at the margins. A Western-trained advocate remains at home in the Israeli courts—assuming fluency in Hebrew—more than does a Talmudic legalist.

One can further validate this conclusion by walking into an Israeli court. Procedurally—in tone, content, and form—it is a Western court, albeit under Israeli auspices. The judges, as keepers of that tradition, would, no doubt, have it no other way. In most areas of law, Israeli jurisprudence is seldom anti-halakhic, but largely ahalakhic, whether one looks at corporation law, security law, criminal law, or zoning law.

It is easy enough to account for this state of affairs. Strict Talmudic law is, per se, an incomplete system for a modern society. In areas other than family life and Kashruth, implementation during the diaspora period was not legally a matter of extrapolation from *halakhah*, but was regarded by the Rabbis as either delegation from the external authorities, or an empowerment from the community. Therefore their decisions were ad hoc and unsystematically derived, little recorded, and noncumulative. Talmudic scholarship is about authorized texts and commentaries on its puzzlements, not the nonsanctified practical application of its usage under millet or ghetto exigencies. Furthermore, the Emancipation era largely ended enforceability of *halakhah* among those less observant or unwilling to accept Rabbinical authority. Even in the medieval period, Rabbis usually sought consensual acceptance, emphasizing the mediational aspects of decision making. In his significant volume on courts, Martin Shapiro has argued that modern courts overemphasize established modes of decision and coercive enforcements, and, thereby, lose some of the advantages of mediation and moral suasion.[14] Traditionally, most Rabbinic Courts relied heavily on persuasion—even cajolery—both out of principle, and— in many eras—to avoid dissident appeals to outside authorities, which were often disastrous to the community, regardless of how the original decision was resolved. In the post-Emancipation era, acceptance of the very submission of a matter to the Courts was generally voluntary, and the Rabbinic Courts became ever more mediational in their approach. Even its ultimate methods of enforcement—flogging or excommunication—became obsolete, unseemly, or ineffectual—or, sometimes, all three.

Even if these historical and legal realities are easily identified, hasn't there been a steady infusion of Talmudic thought into Israeli law? Generally speaking, the evidence here is very weak. That could easily be happening without much notice. The Courts start with Knesset enactments, and these could be subtly turning to traditional modes. Here and there, laws which are clearly Talmudic in origin exist, and the rule of interpretation in consonance with Jewish law should have cumulative impact. Certainly the older socialist mode of actual hostility to religious values is diminishing rather rapidly. In certain areas abutting on those allocated to the religious community—such as Sabbath observances, or medical practices relating to cadavers—conflict does occur, but with the religious power waning. In other areas, conflict does not arise, even when, theoretically, it might.

In general, the Knesset does not automatically turn to religious or historic guidance to solve problems, but usually to practice elsewhere, to functional necessities, to logic, and to standards of efficiency. So, too, do the Courts. The ambiguities in politics and law in interpreting equity and justice modify or set limits to discussions, but seldom dictate the answers, which are usually not antihalakhic but rather ahalkhic. The fact seems to be that—to apply Geertz's formula—Israel is a Jewish version of the Western secular state—recognizably more Jewish than most Western Christian societies, but also recognizably within the range of such societies. As the society goes, so goes the legal system.

V

In the end, a book is judged by the reasonableness of its intent, and its success in dealing with its aspirations. On these dimensions, Edelman is remarkably successful, especially for a terse book of 160 pages. He is admirably succinct, unpretentious, and pithy. Major issues are laid out with dispassion and candor seldom achieved by writers with internal axes to grind or international missiles to shoot off. Edelman is descriptive and analytic, tries to avoid being judgmental, and completely avoids homilies.

This is essential in the three key chapters of the book, which establish the connections between politics and law, and community cultures in Israel. As Edelman sets out in his preface, his purpose is to see courts as part of governance. Thus, his treatment of politics and the courts outlines the lack of a constitution and the emergence of the system of Basic Laws as an effective quasi-substitute, especially with the Supreme Court's assumption of a role as the High Court of Justice. Warren-Court type precedents fit well with a loose sense of judicial review built upon broad principles of equity, nonrigorously derived from Basic Laws or even from general principles.

The unusual power which the Court acquired through expansion of its role as High Court of Justice was extremely well-received in the early years. The Court was careful to restrict its use to popular—or very basic—cases in which its check on the government was either applauded or grudgingly accepted even by unpliant leaders like David Ben-Gurion. In recent years, that picture has altered due, in part, to two factors—the influence of Justice Aaron Barak, and the adoption of the 1992 Basic Law on Human Dignity and Freedom. The result is complex, and is still unfolding. Wisely, Edelman has only outlined the matter which will ultimately produce many fascinating books. It is obviously a momentous process.

Barak came to the Court with incredible assets, and he has employed them vigorously. However, the final verdict will not be possible until his compulsory retirement at age seventy, which is ten years hence. An internationally recognized scholar—he teaches recurrently at Yale even now—a brilliant intellect, and an effective attorney general, he was also an architect of the breakthrough Camp David agreement.

In addition, he was given an even more valuable asset—appointment at an early age in a system governed by strict seniority. One of the new breed of Israeli-trained judges, Barak is among the handful of Justices who reached this pinnacle in their early forties. The others were on the court more-or-less at the same time, so Barak has been the recipient of special advantage on seniority, in addition to his vigorous and self-confident persona.

Before the 1992 Basic Law, he pursued rights mainly under doctrines of strict construction of statutes, but, with the 1992 Basic Law, he now had a quasi-constitutional basis for activism. Perhaps because of the controversy that rights decisions in recent years has generated, Barak has, in recent decisions, emphasized a balancing approach—which he has consistently advocated—and rendered more rather conservative decisions. This has alienated admirers without satisfying his chief critics—the religious groups and the government of the day. Still, it could have diminished outright institutional warfare. His advent to President of the Court in 1995 ushered in yet a new phase of his fascinating tenure.[15] Israeli law has already been drastically affected by his efforts, and a decade of his leadership will be significant.

Although Edelman does delineate well the multiple complexities of Israeli legal culture, and the utility of the Supreme Court's assumption of higher-law authority, he does not speculate on why it emerged. Given the absence of judicial review in the dominant traditions of the vast majority of Israelis—including that nation's lawyers and judges—it is, by no means, self-evident that it had to occur.

I have recently argued that the absence of a firm disciplined party majority is a necessary and probably sufficient explanation for the emergence of judicial review.[16] How does Israel measure up to that assumption? On policy matters, the Knesset as a whole—and, generally, the parties individually—are undisciplined enough. A court can reasonably expect that its decisions will not be reversed. Israeli parties are quite organized—and even outrageous—when dealing with strict party advantage. However, these are seldom sustainable in the cold light of day, when Court decision focuses attention on them.

Edelman also provides an excellent history of the Supreme Court's evolution, the differing membership, and a brief delineation of its religious courts. He discusses the tradition of the religious Justice, and provides thumbnail accounts of the actual behavior of individual justices. He notes that the relatively noncontroversial nature of the religious Judge has been enhanced by the judicial record of the recently retired Menahim Elon, a judicious and scholarly figure of international standing. His foray into a presidential contest proved a blemish, however.

The specifics of the confessional courts, Jewish, Druze, and Muslim, are largely limited to the selection process and the chief social issues addressed by the courts. Only in a limited sense do these courts address real governance, and the discussions are therefore a bit clipped. There is no attempt to assess, for example, the role of these courts in strengthening or weakening the role of the Israeli state. As there are, to my knowledge, no studies on this point in any language nor for any community, this omission is not merely wise. It was probably inevitable. Yet, it weakens the stated goal of studying these subsystems from the standpoint of governance.

Having said all that, the treatment in this book of the courts is head-and-shoulders above other treatments in English, and it is competitive with the best work on each system in any language, including Hebrew. The pattern that emerges is subtly and sympathetically nuanced, so that the book, as a whole, gives a sensitive account of the complex interactions. Even as to the constitutional order—Edelman's secondary subject—this volume seems to be as informative as are more extensive treatments recently published.[17] Edelman has provided a strong, basic book that will inform and elevate all future work in the field.

Notes

1. Judah Matras, *Social Change in Israel* (Chicago: Aldine, 1965).

2. Michael Brecher, *The Foreign Policy System of Israel* (New Haven: Yale, 1972).

3. See, Ben Meir, *National Security Decision Making* (Boulder: Westview Press, 1986); and *Civil-Military Relations in Israel* (New York: Columbia University Press, 1995). Both of these books were originally published in Hebrew by the Jaffe Center for Strategic Studies at Tel Aviv University.

4. Especially useful is Pnina Lahav, "Foundations of Rights Jurisprudence in Israel," 24 *Israel Law Review* 211 (1990).

5. Amnon Rubinstein, *Ha'Mishpat Haconstitutioni shel Medinat Yisrael* (Tel Aviv: Schoekon Books, 1969).

6. Menachem Elon, *Mishpat Ivri* (Jerusalem: Magnes Press, 1973); and *Jewish Law: History, Sources, Principles* (Philadelphia: Jewish Publication Society of America, 1994).

7. Aaron Barak's *Judicial Discretion* (New Haven: Yale University Press, 1989) is a revised version as well as a translation of his *Shikul D'aat Shiputi* (1987). It is avowedly and, in fact, a general theory, not essentially emphasizing Israeli law.

8. Shimon Shetreet's *Justice in Israel: A Study of the Israeli Judicial* (Boston: Martinus, 1994) is a culmination of considerable work on the role of judges and their independence.

9. The most comprehensive efforts remains those of Eleakim Rubinstein, *Shoftai Eretz* (Jerusalem: Schoeken Publishing, 1980).

10. See, for example, the chapter on the judiciary in Asher Arian's magisterial *Politics in Israel: The Second Generation* (Chatham, N.J.: Chatham House, 1989).

11. Clifford Geertz, *Local Knowledge* (New York: Basic Books, 1983) 175.

12. Robert Eisenman, *Islamic Law in Palestine and Israel* (London: E. J. Brill, 1978).

13. For a vigorous attempt to find more influence, see, Elon's *Jewish Law;* and Agranat, Elon, and others, "Developments in Jewish Law" reprinted from *Dine Israel,* vol. 4, 1974 (Tel Aviv: University Press, 1975).

14. Martin Shapiro, *Courts* (Chicago: University of Chicago Press, 1987).

15. See, Aaron Barak, "The Legal Revolution: Basic Rights Defended" (in Hebrew) *Law and Government Review* 9:35, and compare with his basic overview in *Judicial Discretion.*

16. Samuel Krislov, "Courts and Legislatures," in J. H. Silbey, ed., *Encyclopedia of the American Legislative system,* vol. 3 (New York: Scribners, 1994) 1559–1586.

17. The most rewarding of these new efforts is Gary J. Jacobson's *Apple of God: Constitutionalism in Israel and the United States.* (Princeton: Princeton University Press, 1993).

5. Modern Jerusalem: Politics, Planning, People

Jeff Halper

Victor Azarya, *The Armenian Quarter of Jerusalem: Urban Life Behind Monastery Walls.* (Berkeley: University of California Press, 1984).

Yehoshua Ben-Arieh, *Jerusalem in the 19th Century: The Old City* (1984); and, *Emergence of the New City* (1986). (Jerusalem: Yad Izhak Ben Zvi Institute).

Meron Benveniste, *Jerusalem: Study of a Political Community* (Jerusalem: West Bank Date Base Project, 1983).

Jeff Halper, *Between Redemption and Revival: The Jewish Yishuv in Jerusalem in the Nineteenth Century* (Boulder: Westview Press, 1991).

Eliezer David Jaffe, *Yemin Moshe: The Story of a Jerusalem Neighborhood* (New York: Praeger, 1988).

David Kroyanker, *Developing Jerusalem: 1967–75*; *Jerusalem Planning and Development, 1975–82*; and *Jerusalem Planning and Development, 1982–85: New Trends* (Jerusalem: The Jerusalem Foundation, 1975, 1982, 1985).

Arthur Kutcher, *The New Jerusalem: Planning and Politics* (London: Thames and Hudson, 1973).

Nasser Eddin Nashashibi, *Jerusalem's Other Voice: Ragheb Nashashibi and Moderation in Palestinian Politics.* (Exeter: lthaca Press, 1990).

Ali H. Qleibo, *Before the Mountains Disappear: An Ethnographic Chronicle of Modern Palestinians.* Author's publication, 1992.

Michael Romann and Alex Weingrod, *Living Together Separately: Arabs and Jews in Contemporary Jerusalem* (Princeton: Princeton University Press, 1991).

I. Zilberman, "Change and Continuity Amongst Muslim Migrants in a Suburb of Jerusalem." Doctoral thesis. Cambridge University, 1988.

I. Introduction

Jerusalem is undoubtedly one of the most written-about cities in the world. Between the 1840s and the early twentieth century, some five thousand books were written about the modern city, or how it has supposedly "degenerated" from its biblical glory. Indeed, it seems that every tourist, traveler, and missionary considered it to be a self-imposed requirement to write a book setting forth his or her impressions.

The pace of publishing has hardly slowed over the years, making the range of literature on Jerusalem extremely rich and diverse. In this review, I will restrict myself to books in English which I consider to be the most valuable for scholars and interested lay people wishing to examine the complex field of conjunctions, conflicts, interactions, historical developments, politics, cultural geography, and urban planning that characterizes modern Jerusalem—although I stay close to the ground, rather than enter into the vast literature of regional and international politics in which the issue of Jerusalem plays such a central role. Most of the literature reviewed, therefore, comes from anthropology, historical geography, planning, and social work. However, several important autobiographical and polemical works are included. By necessity, many valuable books are omitted, including guidebooks, impressionist and literary works,[1] polemics, poetry (Yehuda Amichai, Dennis Silk), straightforward history,[2] anthologies,[3] religious tracts and "coffee table" books, to mention just a few.

I have also limited myself to works published in English, partly because the bulk of studies on modern Jerusalem, published primarily by historians and historical geographers, deals more with the development of the contemporary city than with its current realities. Much of this literature has been nurtured—if not actually published—by the Yad Ben Zvi Institute, in addition to publishing scholarly books on the entire history of Jerusalem and the Land of Israel before 1948, this Institute also issues the most important academic journal on these subjects—*Cathedra*, now almost twenty years old. Professor Yehoshua Ben-Arieh at the Hebrew University, and his students—now mature academics in their own rights—together with several key historians of the pre–1948 Yishuv have virtually created the field of modern Jerusalem studies. Because this literature is, nevertheless, important for understanding contemporary Jerusalem life, I include in this review two works that have been published in English: Ben-Arieh's seminal volumes on the city's physical development in the nineteenth century, and my own cultural history of the same period.

I should also mention the Jerusalem Institute for Israel Studies, which has sponsored much of the research on contemporary Jerusalem. Although most of its publications are in-house reports and booklets, I include Michael Romann and Alex Weingrod's study as an example of this literature. As I am not insufficiently versed in works in Arabic on modern Jerusalem, one should note the work of the Bir Zeit University sociologist Salim Tamari. I have included only a couple of books that have been published in English—those by Nasser Nashashibi and Ali Qleibo. I would refer readers to major journals of Middle Eastern studies for English sources of on-going scholarship on this subject in Arabic.

This review begins, then, with books on the evolution of modern Jerusalem in the nineteenth century, because this is the period in which its contemporary physical and social

structure—not to mention important ideological currents—
first emerged. We will then consider the ways in which
Jerusalem's planners dealt with the momentous demographic
and political changes that came about after 1967, and their
impact upon the nature of Jerusalem life. Turning to local
ethnic and religious communities, we will examine a number
of ethnographic studies and, subsequently, descriptions of
general cultural life in the city. Finally, we will briefly mention political studies on Jerusalem's future. In conclusion, I
will indicate areas of study which might form a research
agenda for the future.

II. Early Modern Roots of Jerusalem Life: Historical, Geographical, and Anthropological Approaches

To understand contemporary Jerusalem, one must return to
the last century when the long-isolated and insular city began its incorporation into the wider religious and political
conflicts of its own region, and of Europe and Russia beyond. This is the period of rising European hegemony, of
immigration of many of Jerusalem's contemporary groups,
and of incipient Jewish and Arab nationalism. Physically,
too, much of the modern city we know today emerged at that
time.

Jerusalem's modern urban development is the subject
of Ben-Arieh's comprehensive and seminal two-volume work—
the first on the growth of the Old City and its environs in the
century preceding World War I; and the second on the emergence of the New City during the same period. A historical
geographer, Ben-Arieh marshals a vast array of data, mainly
from archival sources, to set out, quarter by quarter, neighborhood by neighborhood, and occasionally street by street,
the physical growth of the city. What emerges from the mass
of contemporary accounts and documents is a systematic
and coherent description of Jerusalem's urban development.
Nonetheless, Ben-Arieh stays so close to developments on
the ground and to written records that no analytical model—
or even theoretical questions—emerge. Instead, the reader is

left to infer how the wider political, social, and cultural context affected the city of Jerusalem's urban growth.

As a result, Ben-Arieh's book offers an implicit paradigm that fits comfortably with post–1967 Israeli views, which highlights Jewish life in Jerusalem as a part of Eretz Israel. Based on the Old City/New City dichotomy, Jerusalem emerges as an essentially Jewish city in which the Jewish "new" steadily overtakes and finally dominates the Arab "old," which is presented as fundamentally static. With only physical building and population growth as evidence—and little cultural, economic, or political context—one might infer, for example, that late-nineteenth-century Jerusalem was an overwhelmingly Jewish city. In fact, most building was initiated by Jews from abroad—mostly philanthropists and investors who had no intention of settling in the city—or by foreign churches and missionary organizations. For all of these reasons, Ben-Arieh's book has had a great influence on both academic and popular views of the city—an influence that has taken the form of an explicit paradigm.

As one of the few social scientists engaged in examining the development of contemporary Jerusalem, I was trying to bring some theoretical order and analysis to the mass of descriptive studies that had accumulated during the 1970s and 1980s. My own book, *Between Redemption and Revival*— came about as a result of that work. It focuses on the culture and society of the Jewish pre-Zionist "Old Yishuv," and particularly its role in shaping modern Israeli culture. However, my book takes pains to place that culturally and ideologically diverse society of the nineteenth and early twentieth centuries within its wider regional and international contexts. As my goal was to ask anthropological questions of the material presented by historians and geographers—leading eventually to the outlines of a cultural/political paradigm which might help make sense of modern Jewish Jerusalem history—I relied mainly on previous historical research, complemented by selected primary sources and informed by interviews and fieldwork in old Jerusalem neighborhoods. I also chose as my format a narrative style, keeping the story, the characters, and the chronology "up front," and the analysis embedded within the text. This approach, I am aware, has been justly criticized as giving a privileged voice to one point of view—in this case a secular Israeli academic of American origin. Nevertheless, as Said points out, narratives are a necessary first step for constructing a coherent identity and history.[4]

What had been mere background in Ben-Arieh's study became the foreground of my book, namely

1. The impact upon the city's development of broader international and regional political events, both general and Jewish;
2. The cultures and ideologies (primarily religious) of the communities which came to constitute the Old Yishuv, and the interactions among them;
3. The roles of prominent individuals;
4. Sources of ideological change and their relationship to changes in Jerusalem's demography, economy, political situation, and the varied process of cultural change to which it was exposed;
5. The relation of culture to settlement patterns, architecture, and the use of space; and
6. more—much more.

This broader conceptual frame gave rise to a more complex picture of Jerusalem Yishuv life. Activities, constraints, and ideological views of different communities were linked to regions of origin and the contemporary political context. For example, why did the formally dominant Sephardis quickly lose their financial and political edge to the Ashkenazi newcomers? How did patterns of ethnic stratification—which were clear until today—emerge from parallel Old Yishuv colonial economies? This also explains, to a point, the preponderance of Jewish over Arab building during the pre–1948 period.

In the end, I argue that a knowledge of the Old Yishuv is essential for understanding modern Israeli society. While it is true that the State of Israel would not have arisen from the Old Yishuv, that community did not simply disappear, as the triumphant secular leaders of the Zionist state assumed it would after 1948. Instead, it went through a prolonged period of dormancy beginning with World War I, but has emerged again as a powerful social, cultural, political, and economic force in Israel, skillfully navigating between right and left.

A contrasting paradigm of Jerusalem life—entitled, tellingly, *Jerusalem's Other Voice*—is found in the political biography of Ragheb Nashashibi, a Palestinian mayor of Jerusalem during the fourteen years of Mandate rule (1920–1934). Here, one finds strands common to Palestinian writings on Jerusalem. The Muslim view, as gleaned from the biography of Nashashibi by his nephew, is, briefly put, as follows:

Jerusalem is essentially a Muslim city and has been since its conquest by Omar in 638. Its heart is the "Old City," which is Arab Muslim in design and culture. Jerusalem has always been characterized by tolerance toward its Christian and Jewish inhabitants. Jews living in Jerusalem from before 1917 and selected Jewish individuals from the Mandate period—such as Judah Magnes, who was Nashashibi's neighbor and friend—are differentiated from Zionist Israelis of the wider society, who are generally seen as insensitive conquerors who ruined relations among the religious communities. Jerusalem had become cosmopolitan in the nineteenth century, as opposed to the Israeli view of the city as an exclusively Jewish "fortress." Its urban scale, character, integrativeness, and charm has been destroyed by massive Israeli building and intolerance. Palestinians are the victims of conquest and occupation. They have been made homeless in a physical and metaphorical sense, but will persist—perhaps even compromise with the Zionists—and will eventually see Jerusalem reemerge as an Arab city.

Benveniste's book, briefly mentioned later, also contributes to an understanding of the ways in which Palestinian and Israeli paradigms and claims underlie the whole range of intercommunal relations.

III. Planning, Economics, Urban Policies, and Development

Because of the fundamental religious and political contests over hegemony in Jerusalem—in the past, as in the modern period—there are few cities as deliberately constructed. Without a thorough grounding in the religious ideologies, cultural backgrounds, and political aims of Jerusalem's diverse communities, it is impossible to understand where neighborhoods were established and why, what buildings were erected and where, or what sites have become contested venues and why.

Seldom have ideology and politics been so explicitly translated into physical form as in post–1967 Jerusalem, when Israeli planners and politicians worked together to refashion the city as thoroughly and unambiguously as possible as a historically Jewish city, which is also modern Israel's undivided capital, to the virtual exclusion of other populations and tradition as anything but historical remnants. Beyond the larger issues of religious and political hegemony lie lesser—yet, for Jerusalemites, still important—questions, including preservation of the "Little (Jewish) Jerusalem" of pre–1948 that does not have the historical legitimacy of older periods, and the degree to which Jerusalem can be transformed into a major Western metropolis similar to Tel Aviv.

There are several books on planning in Jerusalem, each examining in particular the post–1967 period of rapid urban growth and development. Kutcher leads the reader on a fascinating tour of Jerusalem from the point of view of historical aesthetics, comparing it to other historic cities and illustrating essential principles of urban preservation with a plethora of instructive drawings. Having educated the reader in the first half of the book about what is essential in preserving Jerusalem—including an appreciation of its site, and the architectural integrity and details of its unique buildings—he delivers an angry indictment of post–1967 planning policy and decision making in the second half. By 1973, it was already becoming apparent that both East and West Jerusalem were threatened by a planning process in which financial interests took precedence. Massive high-rises and extensive road systems were preferred to more modest forms of development, and the public had little say. Surveying key projects, Kutcher concludes that, for the city fathers and government officials, Jerusalem

> ... does not look imposing enough to be the capital of Israel. They of course realize that Jerusalem can probably never rival Manhattan. So they have set their sights a bit lower. Their dream of Jerusalem is a sort of copy of Kansas City.

David Kroyanker's series of illustrated books—actually more public reports of the Jerusalem Committee, a body of prominent architects and planners from around the world whose views were solicited in annual meetings with Mayor Kollek—attempt to review issues of planning in considerable depth without, however, openly criticizing the municipal administration. In the first volume covering the years 1967–1975, Kroyanker, a Jerusalem architect, sets out the parameters of the planning process.

One the one hand, between 1948 and 1967, Jerusalem had been a divided, even marginal city. Economic and urban development had been severely restricted on both sides of the Israeli-Jordanian border. In 1967, with reunification under one Israeli municipality, the urban area suddenly grew from 8,500 to 25,000 acres, and the population from that of two small cities—about 200,000 in the Israeli Western side, and about 65,000 in the Palestinian Eastern section—and not including the semirural surroundings), to one rapidly growing—although still socially and ecologically divided—urban population. In terms of infrastructure and housing, both sides were woefully inadequate.

On the other hand, certain political rather than planning-based principles guided Jerusalem planning. Kroyanker notes that government policy was—as it still is—to maintain a two-thirds/one-third ratio of Jews over Arabs, despite the fact that Arab population growth outpaced that of the Jews (p. 20). While not mentioning the gerrymandering that, in 1967, incorporated vast tracts of empty, unbuilt, but not unowned land, he does touch upon urban development policies designed to boost the Jewish population and "create facts" on the ground at the expense of local Arabs. Thus, for example, in 1971, ten-thousand housing units were built by the government in the Jewish sector. There were only 450 in East Jerusalem, an increase from only 50 the year before, Kroyanker points out (1975, pp. 20–21).

But Kroyanker's book is primarily one of an urban planner, and politics figures in only to the degree that government agencies are able to dictate urban projects opposed by the relatively powerless municipality itself. Kroyanker sets out the major themes of planning that emerged in these heady years following the physical reunification of the city. According to him, the thrust of planning policy in those years was to preserve the historical and spiritual character of the city, along with its natural topography, open vistas and distinct skyline, open spaces, modest urban scale, and limited road network—yet should also develop Jerusalem as Israel's capital and major administrative center.

In terms of social planning, a key aim of the government and municipality was to limit the numbers of Arabs in Jerusalem. Besides higher birth rates, significant numbers of Palestinians from the West Bank were being attracted to the city by job opportunities in construction and services. This was done, says Kroyanker, in the oblique professional language of a planner close to municipal officialdom, by keeping East Jerusalem unplanned, thereby making it exceedingly difficult for Arabs to obtain building permits. Nor were any government funds made available to Arabs for building or infrastructural purposes. Kroyanker's last report, covering the years 1982–1985, indicates little change in policy. By then, the desired proportion of Jews to Arabs had risen to 70 percent to 30 percent, and the main problem of the Arab sector had shifted from inadequate housing to illegal construction. Kroyanker relates plans to build a north Jerusalem Arab neighborhood, which never materialized (1985, 85).

Kroyanker's reports contain a great deal of information of relevance to urban researchers. (For a statistical portrait of Jerusalem's modern development, however, see Schmelz[5].) Kroyanker mentions the fact that Jerusalem had long been a marginal, underdeveloped, and generally low-income city consisting largely of ultra-Orthodox and immigrants from Middle Eastern countries, and that a central aim of the municipality after 1967 was to strengthen its inadequate tax base by constructing massive middle-class housing projects, such as those of Ramat Eshkol and French Hill (1975, 22–24). This led to controversial urban renewal projects, such as those of Yemin Moshe and Mamilla, in which working-class immigrant populations of Jews from Muslim countries have been relocated in distant housing projects to make way for higher-income newcomers of Western origin.

Eliezer Jaffe's book on the history—but more so on the process of transforming the working class slum into a high-income artists colony in the decade between 1967–1977—brings out the impact of abstract urban planning on the lives of people in a particular community. Jaffe is a professor of social work and not an anthropologist. While his study of the Yemin Moshe quarter is not an ethnography per se, it does survey many of the areas of community building, social life, and, eventually, urban renewal of interest to anthropologists. He uses extensive interviews with residents and municipal officials, historical records, and official reports—all compiled from the knowledgeable point of view. Jaffe was the head of the Municipal Welfare Department during part of the evacuation process. "We do hope," he writes, "to sensitize both ordinary citizens and government officials to the issues involved and considerations that have to be taken into account when tampering with people's lives and with neighbourhood change" (p. 12).

Social controversy surrounded Yemin Moshe from the start. Even before it was built close to the walls of the Old City, it had been a site where poor Jewish immigrants from Yemen and Persia had squatted. The first battle over the nature of the neighborhood took place in 1889, when the Montefiore Foundation decided to build houses for a more established population, and had the squatters evicted. Between the 1920s—when the first serious violence broke out between Arabs and Jews in Jerusalem—and 1967, Yemin Moshe was a border neighborhood, and the well-to-do vacated their space in favor of a poor population. When, in 1967, Jerusalem was again reunited, the neighborhood suddenly became prime real estate. It was a quaint historic quarter overlooking the Old City walls that had turned into a slum of working-class Jews from Middle Eastern countries. The process by which the municipality evacuated them in favor of what it described as "desirable and tasteful people," how it impacted upon the evacuees, and what the implications are for future social planning in Jerusalem is discussed in depth by Jaffe. "We will not be another Yemin Moshe" is a popular slogan of residents of other historic quarters.

IV. Ethnic, National, and Religious Communities

Turning to anthropological works per se, one cannot help but notice how thin the ethnographic literature is on such a culturally rich city. Victor Azarya, a sociologist at the Hebrew University, has written an ethnography of the Armenian Quarter in Jerusalem, and, in particular, on the Armenian monastery of St. James, where a secular lay population of about fifteen hundred people shares residential space with a small number of clergy.

Azarya has two main theoretical concerns: What is the nature of the monastery community? And how do the clergy and laity adapt to each other's lifestyle and social roles?

After a useful introduction to Armenians in history, and to the history of Armenians in Jerusalem—where approximately twenty-five thousand continued to live by the late

1970s, mostly in middle-class neighborhoods in the Eastern part of the city and outside of the walls—Azarya takes us inside the monastery for a closer look at the religious and secular communities. As he tells us in the introduction, his research involved interviews with knowledgeable informants and periodic observations, rather than prolonged residency in the monastery. Because of this, his discussion is somewhat descriptive and removed. The reader emerges, however, with a clear picture of monastery life.

Azarya characterizes the monastery as a kind of intentional community based on strong, common national and cultural ties, in which the clergy provides the lay population with a range of services from education and employment to housing and affordable commercial properties. Overall, he sees the monastery as a "modern defended residential neighborhood" with clear ethnic boundaries, internal organization, and regulated in-group interactions. Within the monastery walls, the Armenians maintain an overall group identity, the clergy preserves a special "virtuoso" role as religious figures, and members of the laity are able to carry on a voluntary existence with a minimum of interference.

Besides Azarya's study, little of an ethnographic nature has been published on the populations of East Jerusalem. Zilberman's doctoral thesis (1988) concerned the immigration of Palestinian immigrants to an East Jerusalem suburb from Hebron, and a book is forthcoming. After describing the historical background of Hebron and its conservative, cohesive, and highly Muslim population, Zilberman traces the immigration to Jerusalem of thousands from that city, especially in the 1950s to 1970s. Although they suffered low social status as both conservative Hebronites and as immigrants, they succeeded—in contrast to most other immigrant communities in other Middle Eastern cities—in becoming a dominant force in East Jerusalem commerce, politics and religious life. This Zilberman explains by the preservation of their religious traditions and institutions, and a cohesive family and community life still oriented to Hebron, and in tandem with the decline of once-dominant Jerusalem Palestinian families. This form of adaptation, he contends, is well-suited for the East Jerusalem situation, in which Palestinians possess no formal political or municipal institutions under Israeli rule.

An anthropological work of a very different kind is the personalized account of life in Muslim Jerusalem during the first years of the Intifada, written by Ali Qleibo, a native Palestinian and an anthropologist. Although not concerned with Jerusalem alone, Qleibo's book dwells on life in the Muslim Quarter where he lives. It is, perhaps, too much to expect of an anthropologist/native to approach his or her own culture with the same objectivity of an outsider—and certainly during a period as wrenching and formative as the Intifada. Qleibo does not pretend to any objectivity, nor is his book, a series of vignettes, meant to be a descriptive or analytical account. Instead, he presents his book as "a personal journey through the Palestinian *wijdan*, the cultural and emotional aspect of Palestinian society" (p. xix). Yet Qleibo cannot keep from viewing events and situations with an anthropological eye, and his position as an informed insider only adds depth to his experiences. In terms of anthropological literature on Jerusalem, perhaps the most important contribution of Qleibo's work is to bring out the inner thoughts and realities of a portion of the local population of whom much has been written, but little of it from their own viewpoint.

Overall Arab-Jewish relations in Jerusalem are the subject of the collaborative work of an urban geographer (Michael Romann) and an anthropologist (Alex Weingrod), appropriately entitled *Living Together Separately*. Although their research predates the Intifada, it nevertheless offers useful insights into the subtle dynamics of local life that often betray a more complex reality than the overt conflicts and apparent polarizations might indicate. Romann and Weingrod's Jerusalem is, of course, a contested city, and, in part, an occupied city—one characterized by the antagonistic segregation of the two national communities. However, it is also a functioning city in which considerable intercommunal inter-action takes place—in commerce, in offices and hospitals, in the workplace, in parks, and the boundaries between neigh-borhoods, as well as in other settings examined by the au-thors. Rather than imposing a grand theoretical scheme on a complex urban reality, Romann and Weingrod explore in con-crete situations "on the ground"—or how people negotiate their daily activities in close contact with one another.

The collaboration works well. After jointly reviewing Jew-ish-Arab relations in Jerusalem, both before and after 1967, each describes and analyzes an aspect of intercommunal life from his own discipline's perspective. Thus, Romann de-scribes, in general, the spatial division of the city into Arab and Jewish sectors, followed by Weingrod's investigation of life on the so-called "ethnic borders" between neighborhoods. Romann's statistical analysis of labor relations between Ar-abs and Jews since World War I is complemented by Weingrod's intimate look at Arabs and Jews working together in a local bakery. Romann compares the distribution of pub-lic services to each community, while Weingrod presents a study of the complex relationships of the two groups in an Israeli hospital.

Frequent—and sometimes surprisingly intimate—inter-actions aside, the authors admit, in their joint conclusion, that voluntary segregation constitutes the essential fact of Jewish-Arab relations in Jerusalem. Because, in the end, it is the wider conflict that defines inter-national relations—aggravated (or, at times, relieved) by urban events and reali-ties—the varied daily interactions carry little potential for true intercommunal harmony and understanding. Still, Romann and Weingrod's descriptions of the contemporary urban context and its complex skein of communal relations, uncovers the many layers of what might otherwise, appear to be merely (and simplistically) conflictual situations.

Benveniste, a former deputy mayor and scholar of Jerusalem history, also describes Jewish-Arab relations in Jerusalem of the early 1980s, but he presents them much

more starkly—and politically—than do Romann and Weingrod.
Benveniste, who made a study of divided cities, argues that
segregation in Jerusalem exceeds that of Belfast because, in
the former, there are virtually no crosscutting ties between
the contesting communities. In an interesting chapter on the
different levels of intercommunal/national conflict, he contrasts the Israelis' attempts to symbolically assert their dominance over the city—through memorials, flags, placing of
neighborhoods and public buildings, holiday celebrations such
as "Jerusalem Day," and the naming of streets—with Palestinians' attempts to resist the occupation through "illegal"
demonstrations and strikes, tire burnings, minaret loudspeak-
ers, graffiti, and the commemoration of defeats. In the end,
he concludes that "Jerusalem is a city held together by force.
Take away Israeli coercive powers and the city splits on the
ethnic fault line" (p.102).

Caplan also writes about Jewish-Arab interactions, but
from the perspective of a community health mediator.[6] His
discussions of patterns of interactions in such settings as
municipal offices, markets, and schools is interesting. However, his conclusions deal with the possibilities of community
mediation rather than more theoretical issues. Finally, Layish
and Tsimhoni have also written on Arabs in Jerusalem and
the West Bank.[7]

In terms of ethnography on the Jewish communities of
Jerusalem, I can point only to five dated doctoral theses.
Handelman's (1974) study of interactions in an old-age home;[8]
Zenner's (1965) on the ethnic identity of Syrian Jews;[9] Shai's
(1978) work on folklore and ethnic identity among Kurdish
Jews;[10] Berger-Sofer's (1979) fieldwork on ultra-Orthodox
women;[11] and my own research (Halper 1978) focused on
ethnic identity, education, and social mobility in an inner-
city neighborhood settled in the pre-state period by immigrants from Kurdistan, Iran, Syria, and Yemen.[12] The last
three describe particular communities in Jerusalem, as Zenner
and I did our work in the same neighborhood, but some
eleven years apart. However, they deal less with Jerusalem

per se than with more general issues, with the city serving primarily as the research location. Shilhav and Friedman (1985) have written on the Jewish ultra-Orthodox population—which today constitutes almost 30 percent of the total Jerusalem population—but they wrote Hebrew with a brief English summary.

V. Conclusions

The preceding review, based on selected books of anthropological interest in English, is necessarily incomplete. However, even if we include works in Hebrew, and the more limited Arabic literature, as well as articles in academic journals, we still confront an extremely spotty, thin, and somewhat dated literature on modern Jerusalem. This is true especially in the areas of ethnography and cultural theory.

Despite the considerable attention that nineteenth-century Jerusalem has received in recent years, it has, as yet, to be researched and analyzed by social scientists, whose approaches might complement and enrich those of geographers and historians. Especially because of important carryovers from the pre-state period—in terms of the cultures and dynamics of urban communities, neighborhoods, and other urban patterns including the nature of the local economy, religious attachments, and perceptions of hegemony among the city's contesting populations—this prelude to contemporary Jerusalem deserves to move beyond the descriptive stage to analysis and theory. Certainly there is no dearth of important issues in Jerusalem's many-faceted cultural and urban history.

In terms of the contemporary city, basic ethnographic studies are obviously missing, including those—such as by Romann and Weingrod—which deal with interactions among different populations. Of course, Jerusalem cannot be isolated from the rest of the country and region. Ethnographic works on a broad range of issues done in other parts of Israel and Palestine have direct bearing on the Jerusalem scene, although they fall outside the parameters of this review.

The voice and analyses of anthropologists on Jerusalem per se is faint as compared to that of other disciplines. This is a pity, because the increasingly trenchant discourse among Israelis, and between Israelis and Palestinians, could benefit from the sense of proportion, elucidation of the issues and conflicts, and articulation of the perspectives of the other side or sides, that anthropologists could bring to the conflict—not to mention the wealth of analytical subjects that await beyond the level of description. However, let this serve as an invitation rather than a criticism.

Notes

1. Amos Elon, *Jerusalem: City of Mirrors* (London: Weidenfeld and Nicholson, 1992); and Samuel Heilman, *Walker in Jerusalem* (New York: Summit Books, 1986).

2. Martin Gilbert, *Jerusalem: Rebirth of a City* (Jerusalem: Domino Press, 1985).

3. Alice Eckardt, *Jerusalem: City of the Ages* (Lanham, Md.: University Press of America, 1987); Joel Kramer, ed., *Jerusalem: Problems and Prospects* (New York: Praeger, 1980); Lee Levine, ed., *The Jerusalem Cathedra*, 3 vols (Jerusalem: Yad Izhak Ben-Zvi Institute, 1981, 1982, 1983); and John Oesterreicher and Anne Sinai, eds., *Jerusalem* (New York: American Academic Association for Peace in the Middle East, 1974).

4. Edward Said, *The Politics of Dispossession: The Struggle for Palestinian Self-Determination* (New York: Pantheon, 1994).

5. Uziel O. Schmelz, *Modern Jerusalem's Demographic Evolution* (Jerusalem: Institute of Contemporary Jewry, 1987).

6. Gerald Caplan, *Arabs and Jews in Jerusalem: Explorations in Community Mental Health* (Cambridge: Harvard University Press, 1980).

7. Aharon Layish, *The Arabs in Jerusalem* (Jerusalem: The Jerusalem Institute for Israel Studies, 1992); and Dafna Tsimhoni, *Christian Communities in Jerusalem and the West Bank Since 1948: A Historical, Political and Social Study* (New York: Praeger, forthcoming).

8. Don Handelman, *Work and Play among the Aged: Interaction, Replication, and Emergence in a Jerusalem Setting* (Assen, The Netherlands, Van Gorcum, 1977).

9. Walter P. Zenner, *Syrian Jewish Identification in Israel* (Ann Arbor: University Microfilms, 1965).

10. Donna Shai, *Neighborhood Relations in an Immigrant Quarter* (Jerusalem, Israel, Henrietta Szold Institute, 1978).

11. Rhonda Berger-Sofer, *Pious Women* (Ann Arbor: University Microfilms, 1979).

12. Jeff Halper, *Ethnicity and Education: The Schooling of Afro-Asian Jewish Children in a Jerusalem Locality* (Ann Arbor: University Microfilms, 1978).

Part III

Religion

Continuing the theme of decentralization or a return to local-level issues, the three essays in this section all deal with aspects of Judaism as revealed in the works and lives of a single scholar (Zvi Zohar), a single community (Walter Zenner's Aram Soba—Aleppo—transplanted to Israel), or small groups within larger (but still localized) communities (Kevin Avruch). There is also a Sephardi bias in these essays—although Avruch considers, as well, the Ashkenazi *haredim*—reflecting an increasing awareness among students of Israel that emergent Israeli Judaism is not synonymous with Ashkenazi practice nor, as Avruch's essay indicates, with simply *male* practice.

The essay by Zohar—exploring the published works of an influential contemporary Sephardi *hakham*, Rav Haim David HaLevi—is especially important in this regard. Zohar shows HaLevi as fully engaged with searching for halakhically defensible solutions to very modern problems—in politics, governance, and polity—facing Israel, including such controversial ones as Jewish settlement on the West Bank, and the character of the peace process. This makes an interesting counterpoint to the usual religious-nationalist pronouncements on

these issues by, for example, rabbis (mostly Ashkenazi) associated with Gush Emunim. Zohar shows us that there is a
plurality of voices among Orthodox (and Sephardi) rabbis, as
there is among other segments of the population.

6. Sephardic Religious Thought in Israel: Aspects of the Theology of Rabbi Haim David HaLevi

Zvi M. Zohar

I. Introduction[1]

In recent years, the electoral successes of Israel's SHAS party have drawn attention to the resilience of Sephardic ethnic religiosity—or religious ethnicity?—in Israel. This resilience is all the more remarkable, in that it has emerged despite what many writers have seen as a determined establishment policy, in Israel's early years, to follow a melting-pot ideal, and to forge a new Israeli identity based on a modern secular, national—but not ethnic!—ethos. Yet, focus on SHAS threatens to exact a price—namely, the conflation of Sephardic political and religious spheres of action and thought—not only in the eyes of broad sectors of Israeli society, but also in the minds of academic observers. Indeed, the personality of SHAS leader Rabbi Ovadiah Yossef has contributed greatly to this conflation. Born in 1920, Rabbi Yossef is rightly regarded as one of the world's greatest post-World War II rabbinic scholars. His halakhic creativity is both broad and original, and his impact on Israeli society in general—and on the life of Sephardic/Oriental Israelis in particular—has been great. During the past decade, however, Rabbi Yossef's personality as a Torah scholar has become—perhaps inextricably—entwined with his personality as a charismatic leader of the SHAS religio-ethnic political movement. As time progresses, the task of differentiating between his activities in the capacities of master halakhist and political leader has become increasingly difficult—arguably, even for Rabbi Yossef himself.

Yet, behind the shifting sands of politics, religious thought and creativity, remain mainstays of human life, even in postmodern Western societies—and, with greater reason, in Israeli-Jewish life, located as it is in the intersection of Western and Middle-Eastern cultures. Delving beyond ethnic politics, a student of Israeli society might choose to focus on the Judaism of Sephardic Jews in Israel since 1948. From an anthropology-of-religion perspective, important and illuminating work has been done by such scholars as Shlomo Deshen, Moshe Shokeid, and Yoram Bilu. However, the same cannot be said with regard to research on intellectual and philosophical aspects of Sephardic religious life. What has happened in the intellectual world of Sephardic/Oriental *hakhamim* or rabbis in Israel, since 1948?[2] What have they written? What have they created? What is the content of their halakhic work? What are their theological-philosophical perspectives on major Jewish issues?

Although almost half a century has passed since 1948, little research seems to have been done on these topics. For those engaged in Judaic Studies outside of Sephardic *yeshivot*, the entire intellectual domain of Sephardic/Oriental rabbinic culture in Israel is virtually unknown territory.

Any move to engage in study of this realm must begin with recognition of the fact that, quantitatively, the field is vast. According to a preliminary survey which I have conducted, Sephardic/Oriental rabbis writing in Israel since 1948 have published *at least* several hundreds of volumes, and thousands of articles, in various genres of "Torah literature," such as legal responsa, original interpretations

(hiddushim) to the Talmud and Codes, Biblical commentary,
ethics (mussar), kabbalah, theology/philosophy and others.
At this point, no overview of the contents of this tremendous substantial body of work exists, and—with great reason—no serious discussion of trends, developments, or
schools of thought can be conducted. Therefore, I attempted
to locate an outstanding Israeli Hakham, who could in some
way, be considered as representative of Sephardic religious
intellectual creativity in Israel—and whose realm of activity
is clearly religion, not party politics. Such a Hakham—no
less a representative Sephardic scholar than Yossef, and
perhaps more wide-ranging and original in creativity—exists in the person of Rabbi Haim David HaLevi. A close
personal disciple of the great Sephardic Chief Rabbi Ben-
Zion Uzziel (d. 1953), HaLevi is unquestionably both a link
in the grand tradition of Sephardic rabbinic scholarship,
extending back to pre-expulsion Spain, and a Hakham active as a nexus of contemporary Israel. As a prolific author,
HaLevi's *Meqor Hayyim* is the standard textbook of *halakha*
(Jewish religious law) in all Israeli State religious schools,
and his articles appear frequently in the Israeli press. Not
affiliated with any political party, HaLevi has been Sephardic
Chief Rabbi of Tel-Aviv since 1973.

In this article, then, I focus on Haim David HaLevi.
Beginning with a brief biographical sketch, I then present an
overview of his published works. Next, present and analyze
HaLevi's theological views on history, providence, and human freedom.[3]

II. Haim David HaLevi—A Brief Biography

Haim David HaLevi was born in Jerusalem on 24 January
1924. His father was a devout layman, who, after a day's
labor, would devote time to study of Torah, especially of the
Zohar. HaLevi studied in Jerusalem's traditional Sephardic
schools, eventually entering the great *yeshiva* of Porat Yosef,
and was ordained by the head of the *yeshiva*, Rabbi Ezra
'Attiyah.[4]

In his seventeenth year, he married Miriam Ouaqnin,
daughter of an illustrious rabbinic family of North African
provenance.[5] After continuing his studies for several more
years, he was appointed as Rabbi of Jerusalem's Rommemah
neighborhood, and taught at several Sephardic *yeshivot*, including the Sha'arei-Zion *yeshiva* founded by Rabbi Uzziel,
and the center for rabbinic training called "Even-Shmuel."
He was very close to Rabbi Uzziel, who also gave him *semikha*
(or rabbinic ordination), and with whom he seems to have
enjoyed a master-disciple relationship. HaLevi served as Rabbi
Uzziel's personal assistant and secretary for several years.[6]
In 1951, HaLevi was chosen as Sephardic Rabbi of Rishon
LeZion. Since 1964, he has served as a member of the High
Council of Israel's Chief Rabbinate. In 1973, he was elected
to the post of Sephardic Chief Rabbi of Tel-Aviv, a title which
he continued to hold as of 1994 when this chapter was
written.[7]

III. HaLevi's Substantial Body of Work

HaLevi has written some twenty-five volumes, and published
more than one hundred articles. His published books, all in
Hebrew, include:

Bein Yisrael La'Ammim (Between Israel and the Nations),
Jerusalem, 1954. HaLevi discusses and analyzes Judaic attitudes toward other nations, both in the context of foreign
policy and of internal policy—that is, policy toward non-Jews
living in Israel.

Devar HaMishpat (Matters of Justice) three volumes.
1963–1965. This work includes commentary and analysis of
Maimonides' Laws of Sanhedrin. In many places, HaLevi not
only explains the Maimonidean position, but also explicates
its implications for courts in Israel today.

Dat uMedinah (Religion and State). Tel Aviv, 1969. This
work contains several seminal essays by Rabbi HaLevi, dealing with the significance and function of Jewish religious
tradition in the context of a modern Jewish polity.

*Maftehot haZohar uRa'ayonotav (Annotated Index to the
Zohar's Ideas)*. Tel-Aviv, 1971. In this work, HaLevi presents

significant concepts of the great mystical work, the Zohar, in alphabetical order. He notes where the Zohar deals with each concept, and frequently quotes salient passages, adding brief translations or explications.

Meqor Haim HaShalem (*The Complete "Meqor Haim"*) five volumes. Tel-Aviv, 1967–1974. In this work, HaLevi simultaneously undertakes two major projects. First, he presents a comprehensive but clear and practical guide to halakhic norms relevant to Jewish life today, in a manner accessible to any Hebrew-reading layperson. Second, he presents and explains all these norms in the context of a religious philosophy and theology that is understandable to today's reader, thus enabling the reader to appreciate and identify with the significance of halakhic norms. Other works, which are based on this opus, include:

• An abridged version, *Qitsur Shulhan 'Arukh Meqor Haim*, which is currently a standard textbook in the Government Religious (*mamlakhti dati*) school system of Israel;
• *Meqor Haim li-Vnot Yisrael* (*Meqor Haim for Jewish Women*). Tel-Aviv 1977. According to classic *halakha*, women are not required to perform certain of the halakhic norms. This work is written for women, and is designed to explicate which halakhic norms are binding upon them;
• *Meqor Haim laHattan ve-laKalla* (*Meqor Haim for the Bride and Groom*). Tel-Aviv, 1979; and
• *'Aseh Lekha Rav* (Make Yourself a Teacher/Rabbi), nine volumes. Tel-Aviv, 1975/6–1988/9. A collection of responsa composed by Rabbi Haim David HaLevi. The questions posed to HaLevi reflect an extraordinarily wide range of issues, in both halakha and religious thought. His responses are written in a very lucid, deceptively simple style, deliberately refraining from halakhic casuistry (*pilpul*). In consonance with his philosophy of *halakha*, he is quite open to recognizing the need for innovative halakhic rulings, and to respond accordingly.[8]

As noted, *'Aseh Lekha Rav* includes both *halakha* and religious thought. After 1990, Rabbi HaLevi decided to cease adding new volumes to that series, and to divide his published work into two series, which are categorically differentiated as

1. *Mayyim Haim*—Halakhic responsa. Tel Aviv, 1991– ; and
2. *Torath Haim*—Religious thought. Tel-Aviv, 1992– .

To date, two volumes of the first, and one of the second have appeared.

Characteristically, and despite HaLevi's intention to categorize his body of work, the halakhic responsa in *Mayyim Haim* continue to integrate *halakha* and religious thought. *Torath Haim* contains materials on a variety of topics, organized as essays on the weekly Torah portion.[9]

Moreh laRabim (Teacher to the Public). Pardes-Hannah, 1991. These are responsa and halakhic norms in matters of education and pedagogy, collected from HaLevi's major halakhic works and arranged topically by Rabbi M. 'Awwami of Pardes-Hannah.

IV. Haim David HaLevi's View of History

In his first published work, HaLevi explains that the study and contemplation of history are a central spiritual and religious task:

> Humankind bereft of history would not know or under-
> stand its true worth, and would not attain its proper and
> worthy place in the universe. Similarly, a nation without
> history would lack all moral and national responsibility,
> and an individual human being [with no sense of history]
> would lack all feeling of worth or significance.[10]

Subsequently, HaLevi devotes an entire essay to a discussion of the value which the Torah places upon history. That essay is called "History as Ground for Faith [in general] and as as Ground for Belief in 'The Beginning of Redemption' ".[11] He writes that the Biblical text is replete with calls for attention to historical matters, and that the true and valid goal of quite a few of the commandments is to create and preserve awareness of historic events.[12] Indeed, HaLevi proceeds to determine that the Torah includes a commandment—albeit not cited in conventional lists of the 613 *mitzvot*—

to contemplate the events of history, and, thereby, to comprehend the significance and nature of God's relation to Israel.[13] The prophets grounded their calls to Israel in the context of their times' historic events, and historic consciousness was a salient characteristic of the Israelites in Biblical times.[14]

True to this vision, HaLevi alludes frequently to history and to historical matters, in the course of his writings. Sometimes, he attempts to unravel, and to interpret, the sense of Biblical passages and narratives, in the light of modern research on ancient history.[15] Elsewhere, he seeks to derive from history lessons for contemporary life.[16] Contemplation of history also leads HaLevi to conclude that Jews may and should adopt advanced sciences and sociopolitical structures developed by the nations of the world.[17] In addition, his writing reflects interest in ideas of history, as expressed by modern historians.[18]

In this essay, I shall focus less on specific issues which HaLevi discusses, in order to concentrate on his general view of history, providence, and human freedom.

V. Haim David HaLevi and His Theology of History, Providence and Free-Will

In an essay written in the early 1950s, HaLevi discusses the notions of history and historical determination.[19] Referring to unnamed philosophers of history, he notes two different extremes.

On the one hand, there are those who hold that human reality consists of essentially discrete, separate events, unconnected but for the creative imagination of historians. On the other hand, others—primarily theologians of various religions and nations—who hold all of history to be a web of causally linked events, susceptible to rigorous scientific analysis and—in principle—predictable in the end. HaLevi rejects both views, for several reasons.

First, he believes that it is impossible to characterize current history with the precision required for valid prediction because that history consists, not of events, but of processes whose boundaries in time, and whose fullness, can only be known after the fact. Second, even action planned and initiated by human agents is rarely performed according to the original blueprint. This is due, in no small part, to innate lack of consistency even in the mind and thoughts of the actors themselves, as well as the confounding effects of contradictory actions undertaken simultaneously by several human individuals.

While holding that history is scientifically unpredictable, HaLevi does not concede it to be completely indeterminate. Rather, he argues, a central tenet to be gleaned from the Bible is that history has a final goal whose attainment is assured by a hidden hand. According to HaLevi, all historical phenomena, from creation onward, relate to one over-arching process which shall ultimately lead humanity to manifest the high and noble vision. "For then I will convert the peoples to a purer language, that they may all call upon the name of the Lord, to serve him with one consent." (Zeph. III:9)

VI. Jewish Particularity and Universal Redemption

Thus, history's goal is universal, and inclusive of all humankind. It is only in the context of this universal vision that significance can be attributed to the Jewish people. They were chosen to fulfill the function of "a kingdom of priests and a holy nation," enabling humanity to realize its spiritual potential. Indeed, a basic characteristic of HaLevi's thought is his consistent refusal to accept any version of Judaism—religious or secular—which attaches to Jewish existence a validity unconnected to humanity's joint spiritual quest. Thus, in an Independence Day address delivered soon after the founding of the state, HaLevi stresses to his audience that Israel's independence must be seen as only a stage in a much broader drama.

> We daily hope for our complète redemption, which shall be a redemption for all time and for the entire world in the universal sense of that word, a spiritual redemption which shall redeem the spirit of all human beings per se. . . .[20]

Writing in the early 1950s, HaLevi sought to outline for the new State of Israel a diplomatic strategy commensurate with the Jewish people's authentic historical role. Thus, while acknowledging that his suggestion might well be at odds with raison d'etat, he maintained that Israel should follow a policy of complete nonalignment, and refrain from identifying with either of the two Cold-War blocs. It is true that initial expectations from the United Nations had been dashed by its member-nations' collective unwillingness to rise above narrow self-interest in order to advance the world's joint good. Nevertheless, Israel should not follow suit. Rather, Israel should utilize the forum provided by the United Nations' General Assembly (and other entities) to speak out on international affairs in a spirit of morality, justice, and human brotherhood, and in a manner consistently unconnected to any immediate advantage for itself. By doing so, Israel would be making use of the opportunity which God's "hidden hand" had created for the furtherance of Israel's mission—and, as an inevitable result, humanity's spiritual well-being—via the formation of the United Nations.[21]

VII. Divine Providence and "Windows of Opportunity"

The idea, that the function of God's "hidden hand" is to provide windows of opportunity for the realization of His design for history appears both in HaLevi's earliest and latest writings, although, in what might be termed his "middle period" (circa 1967–1980) he seems to have tended to a more interventionist and necessitarian view of providence as manifest in contemporary Israeli history.[22] In many of his writings—especially, but not solely, in more recent years—the notion of divinely provided opportunity turns out to be crucial for HaLevi's conception of the essentially unnecessary character of human history.

This notion is directly linked to HaLevi's theological position on the primordiality of human freedom-of-choice.[23] In his view, man's ontological uniqueness and status lie in his power of free choice. Indeed, man's similarity to God is primarily in the capacity for free choice. This capacity was not caused by Adam's eating from the Tree of Knowledge. To the contrary, it was due only to his primordial possession of free choice that he could eat of that fruit.[24] Thus, writes HaLevi,

> It is self-evident that all human beings are created in the Divine Image, and therefore all persons from all nations of the world can become righteous men and attain high spiritual degrees, by virtue of the spirit of life that God instilled in Adam, father of all humanity. This is why Ben-'Azzai held . . . that the verse "This is the Book of Adam's descendants" is of greater significance than the verse "Love thy neighbor as thyself."[25] Clearly, Ben-'Azzai sought to indicate not the opening words of the verse, which in themselves are meaningless, but rather its conclusion: ". . . in the Image of God was he made."[26] [Note references added.]

The assumption that humans are created with the power of free choice is logically crucial for the notion of Covenant, which is so central to Biblical—and, indeed, all Jewish—theology. Not only Jews, but also all humankind, are engaged in a Covenental relationship with God, through the Sinaitic and Noahide Covenants respectively, writes HaLevi. Covenant also assumes an agreement and mutual commitment of two sides, each of which is a moral agent. As a human being, HaLevi writes,

> . . . [Y]ou are jointly responsible [with God] for the well-being of His creation . . . just, as He created you out of His free will, so did He create you with the power to freely choose at will to do evil or good.[27] [Material added]

Because freedom of choice lies at the very core of the Divine Image of man, history is inconceivable as a simple "guided performance" by human actors performing according to some Divine telekinesis. Rather, the basic mode of history, as theologically viewed, is, Divine contrivance of opportunity for humans to choose action leading to advancement of His plan. Ultimately, in the fullness of time, enough "right choices" will be made to enable the completion of God's program for history.

VII. HaLevi's View of Twentieth Century History

According to HaLevi, some periods in history are "denser" than others, with respect to the quantity and quality of opportunities provided. He is deeply convinced that the ingathering of exiles, the Jewish rebuilding of the Land of Israel, and the founding of the State of Israel are all facets of progression toward history's goal. However, he stresses, time after time, the very contingent aspects of these processes. Thus, he writes in his earliest work,

> Our period is one of the most wonderful phenomena in the golden chain of our people's existence; a period of the restoration of our national independence and of the ingathering into her of Israel's dispersed exiles—which had been the object of our souls' desire during centuries of exile. Yet it is a difficult period for religious Jewry, which is engaged in a difficult struggle to fulfill its role: shaping the face of the state in the spirit of Torah. It is our duty not to miss this wonderful historic opportunity, for we do not know for how long the effects of the state's formation shall continue, and how much time may be required to shape its spiritual character after which this page in history will be closed.[28]

After the Six-Day War, HaLevi was deeply moved and exhilarated—as were most Israelis—by Israel's sudden emergence from the shadow of Egyptian and Syrian threats upon its very existence into the light of victory and conquest of Biblical territory, especially of Jerusalem. He recognized these events, not as a hidden, but rather as a manifest action of God in history. He also called for bold halakhic acknowledgement and radical liturgical expression of their Providential character.[29] Yet, even at that time, he continued to regard the effects of these events as contingent.

In early November 1967, HaLevi composed a responsum on the topic of Jewish entry to the Temple Mount.[30] He explained that all rabbis in all generations concur in differentiating between the Temple Mount and the Temple Precincts. Entrance to the Temple Precincts proper is forbidden,[31] but only part of the Temple Mount was covered by these Precincts.

The remaining area of the Mount may be entered by Jews after proper purification rites.[32] Now that Israel has regained possession of Jerusalem, archaeologists and other experts should be directed to determine which areas of the Temple Mount are enterable, and Jews should be permitted and encouraged to pray there. A year and a half later, HaLevi published the responsum, with the following postscript:

> Now, after almost two years have passed since the lib-
> eration of the Temple Mount from alien rule, it is clear to
> us beyond doubt that we have lost a great hour of oppor-
> tunity, by not creating a [political] fait accompli immedi-
> ately after the conquest. Had a house-of-prayer been
> established in the halakhically permitted area of the
> Temple Mount . . . we would have set a foundation for
> [the realization of] the Jewish people's right to the Place
> we were the first to sanctify. . . . But, due to our shocking
> failure during the first two years after the conquest, the
> Holy Place remains— at least at this stage [until when?!]—
> in the sole control of another religion, who sanctified the
> site after the destruction of our Temple.[33] [Material added]

A similar vein runs through his assessment, in 1979, of Israel's hold on the territories liberated or conquered in 1967. Citing passages from the Talmud and Midrash, he points out that the rabbis of antiquity had observed that lack of Diaspora response to the opportunity provided by Cyrus's decree had foredoomed the second temple to destruction.

> There are periods in history that offer the nation an
> opportunity that is unique, or that shall re-occur only
> after thousands of years. In the first years of the second
> temple, the Jewish people missed a great historic oppor-
> tunity. . . . the Jewish people committed a fateful error in
> adhering to life in exile, instead of returning to the Land
> en masse in the days of Ezra, and this error led to the
> destruction of the second temple . . . it was an historic
> hour of grace—forfeited![34]

At present, HaLevi continues, such an opportunity re-
appeared—yet, is once again, on the verge of nought.

> Immediately after the Six Day war, there was an hour of
> grace. . . . had Jewish multitudes "ascended" then from the

rich Diaspora communities, and settled in Judea, Samaria and Gaza and in that part of Sinai which we then thought never to return, we would today possess the "Complete Land of Israel." If a million Jews were living in Judea and Samaria, no one would imagine that "the wheel could be turned back." All of this could have been done with ease immediately after the Six Day war. Today [in 1979] it is very difficult, although still possible. . . . I'm afraid that these are perhaps the last hours in which it is still possible to repair twelve years of historic failure.[35] [Material added]

As the final example of HaLevi's contingental view of providentially offered opportunity, I shall cite his assessment of the Jewish people's behavior during the 1920s. As we shall see later in this chapter, HaLevi holds that World War I opened up radical possibilities for Jewish history. At that time, he writes,

[God] created and prepared the conditions required for the redemption of His people. There were some who "understood" the hour's greatness and put themselves at Providence's disposal, knowingly or not; of these, some were righteous Gentiles and some were Jews, observant or rebellious. Most, however, did not understand—and thus, the vast majority of Jews remained in the lands of Exile. Had the Jewish people chosen to return to the Land when its gates were wide open [that is, during the 1920s when Britain did not significantly restrict Jewish immigration to Palestine], perhaps they would have been able to ascend "in song and everlasting gladness," and who knows how the people's redemption would have then been completed by the Contriver of all causes, and how the face of history would have looked, during these past decades? But man is a creature of free choice, and God cannot force him against his will and his free choice.[36] [Material added]

In other words, recent Jewish history provides a glaring example of the Jewish people missing Divinely provided opportunity—with dire consequence.

To recapitulate, HaLevi is deeply committed to two tenets which appear to be contradictory: human freedom of choice, and Divine plan for history. He integrates the two by explaining that Providence operates primarily as a "hidden hand" providing windows of opportunity which—if chosen by humans—enable the progression of humanity towards the fulfillment of history's goal. In addition, HaLevi is convinced that important aspects of modern history, especially (but not only) of modern Jewish history, represent clear stages in the realization of that universal goal. His reading of the relevant aspects of modern history is explicated most fully in an article he published in January 1990.

VIII. The Year 5750 [1989–1990] and the Beginning of Universal Redemption[37]

In an article which appeared in the newspaper, *HaTsofe* in 1990,[37] HaLevi reminds his readers that the messianic age has a dual character. It involves both the national restoration of the Jewish people, and the universal spiritual redemption of humankind. In 1977–1978, HaLevi had written that, according to Kabbalah, the years 5748 (1987–1988) and 5750 (1989–1990) should see the realization of significant further stages in the unfolding of the Messianic Age, although the substantive nature of those stages could not be known aforetime. The significance of 5748 (HaLevi writes in 1990) had since become clear. In that year, the Arab world, which had initially greeted Israel with "blood, fire and pillars of smoke," agreed, in principle, to accept the existence of Israel in its ancient patrimony. This acceptance of Israel by its Middle Eastern neighbors—for example, in the convening of the Madrid peace talks in 1987—represented the opening of a new stage in the Messianic Age.[39] Now, HaLevi writes, the significance of the year 5750 was beginning to crystallize.

The vision of Israel's Prophets had been that Israel's redemption would take place in the context of Universal redemption. One of the reasons for this, explains HaLevi, is

> simple and logical: True redemption entails peace, and it is impossible to guarantee stable peace to any single point on Earth.

Thus, it is nonsense to conceive of Israel enjoying messianic tranquility, except in the context of global peace. Indeed, the *midrash* rhapsodizes on the importance of peace, or Shalom. Peace is the central task of the Messiah; and, according to the second-century sage, Rabbi Yosse haG'lili, the very name of the Messiah (reflecting the essence of his role) will be Shalom.[40] HaLevi points out a concrete halakhic consequence of the Torah's devaluation of warfare. While Rabbi Eliezer maintained that the wielding of arms was a manly virtue—and, thus, allowed men to bear swords, bows and shields as adornments on the Sabbath, even when not in mortal danger—the prevailing majority of sages held otherwise. Basing themselves on Isaiah's words—"They shall beat their swords into ploughshares, and their spears into pruning-hooks; nation shall not lift up sword against nation, neither shall they learn war any more," (II:4)—they rejected the very notion of weapons as adornment, and ruled that one who so dresses on the Sabbath can incur severe punishment.[41]

In another chapter Isaiah symbolizes future relations between nations as the wolf dwelling with the lamb, and the leopard lying down beside the kid. (XI)[42] HaLevi suggests that these two chapters represent two different stages. First, humanity will reach a level in which capacity for warfare and destruction will continue to characterize nations, but the more powerful will refrain from employing their strength to conquer and tyrannize the weak (XI). Later, in eschatological reality, the very capacity and preparedness for warfare will be eliminated (II). Having thus outlined major aspects of Jewish messianism, HaLevi proceeds to relate these aspects to concrete historical phenomena.

In the ancient and medieval world, the conquest and subjugation of the weaker nations by the stronger was a universal commonplace, accepted and practiced by the Egyptians, Assyrians, Babylonians, Persians, Greeks and Romans. In more recent centuries, such conquest often took the form of colonialism, which was regarded as natural and positive by European nations until World War I. However, writes HaLevi,

> The First World War led to a great change in the redemption of the world from domination of man by man (as

it also led to the creation of the political grounds
for the redemption of Israel, qua the famous Balfour
declaration) . . . after the war, the principle of [national]
self-determination was accepted by the victorious powers, which is why they did not take the conquered lands
as colonies but rather undertook to administer them
(including Eretz Israel) as mandates under the newly-
created League of Nations. . . . After the second World War,
the "United Nations Organization" was established, and
its moral goals were set out in the preamble [to its Charter—which HaLevi proceeds to quote]. [Material added]

Both the League of Nations and the United Nations represent, then, the universal human recognition of the pro-
phetic vision "the wolf shall dwell with the lamb." (Isaiah
11:6) Indeed, writes HaLevi,

Since that time [of the United Nation's founding] subju-
gated and conquered nations began to attain sovereign
independence, one after the other, and many examples
can be given (also the People of Israel then established
its own independent state, thanks in no small measure
to the help and support of the UN).

However, the ideal of nonsubjugation of nation by nation was marred by the existence of the two Blocs—which, in
fact, prevented true independence of the smaller nations. In
the West, superpower dominance was subtle and indirect,
allowing weak and small states a large measure of dignity
and self-respect. In the East, Soviet dominance was explicit
and iron-handed. Harsh was the fate of those nations that
attempted to extricate themselves from Russia's embrace.
However, a major change is occurring in 5750, writes HaLevi,

The Soviet Bloc is crumbling, and opportunity for real
sovereignty has thus opened up for many additional nations. Before our very eyes, the vision of our holy prophet
"the wolf shall dwell with the lamb, and the leopard shall
lie down with the kid," is in the process of realization.
Thousands of years passed until the world understood
the great values of peace and equality between nations
envisioned by Israel's prophets of old, and sincerely strives
[sic!] to concretize those values in praxis. This is the first

vision, of "wolf dwelling with lamb"— the powerful [still retaining military might but] aside the weak. This encourages belief in the more distant, eschatological vision: "They shall beat their swords into ploughshares, and their spears into pruning-hooks." . . . [B]efore our eyes, and in our very own days, we behold the victory of the messianic vision of Israel's spirit.

Rabbi Haim David HaLevi thus expresses a most striking historical-theological outlook. Of especial interest is his tendency, and ability, to read both "general" and Jewish events in tandem, as reflecting the realization in history of Biblical values. Thus, the Balfour declaration, the mandate for Palestine and the United Nations vote to partition Palestine and to create the state of Israel—major events in Israel's redemption—are, at the same time, but particular manifestations of the Wilsonian principle of national self-determination, of the rationale of the League of Nations' mandate system, and of the principles of the United Nations' charter—all central expressions of universal progress toward Isaiah's vision of peace on Earth. Note should also be taken of HaLevi's dual perspective on providence and human freedom of will, as expressed in this article. On the one hand, the year 5750 was known (via Kabbalah) to be predestined for dramatic progress toward messianic realization—while, on the other hand, it was (much belated!) free human recognition and acceptance of Biblically advocated values, and not Divine fiat, which enabled that progress.

IX. Postscript

Having read through this paper, the reader might understandably feel some degree of confusion. How, after all, should one characterize Haim David HaLevi? Perhaps he is some kind of mystic, for he certainly relies greatly on Kabbalah? On the other hand, his rationalistic tendencies are quite prominent—as in his explanation of Isaiah's prophecy as metaphorical, and in his use of modern historical data to interpret Biblical texts. He shows great respect for tradition—

yet, the reader will have noticed that, throughout the detailed exposition of his philosophical/theological interpretation of history, HaLevi never cites rabbinic views in order to
silence debate or shut out rational inquiry. Rather, he feels
intellectually and religiously able to relate to previous writers
and interpreters as engaged in an on-going discussion—in
which he, too, participates, respectfully but unawed. HaLevi's
deep concern with history—both Jewish and general—and
his raising of history and historical inquiry to the degree of a
religious precept, seem to reflect internalization of modern
concerns with history and historiography. Yet, his belief in a
hidden, providential hand operating in history seems quite
pre-modern.

If Haim David HaLevi seems to defy categorization, perhaps this reflects something about the biases of our categories. Perhaps he represents a Sephardic tradition which does
not sense sharp dichotomies between Kabbalah and rational-
ism, between modernity and traditionality, between contingent historical actuality and providential care? In any case,
one thing seems to be clear: accounts of modern Judaism (or
Jewish theology) would do well to beware of glibly assimilat-
ing contemporary Sephardic/Israeli religiosity to the class of
folk-religion, superstition, or quaint traditionality. Rather,
scholars and intellectuals must realize, that characterization
of modern trends in Judaism—and especially, but not only,
in Israeli Judaism—is seriously biased, so long as Sephardic
creativity is neglected. It is time for researchers and students
of Judaism to embark beyond the charted waters of European Jewish thought, and to initiate study of hundreds of
twentieth-century Sephardic/Oriental religious works. While
many of them might be no more than spiritually pedestrian,
others could significantly enrich our vision of what Judaism
is today—and what it might become in the future.[43]

Notes

1. Several persons—including, among others, Professor Shlomo
Deshen and Dr. Avi Sagi—read an earlier draft of this paper, and
provided me with illuminating and helpful comments. Special thanks

are due to Professor Norman Stillman, whose close reading of that draft, and many specific substantive and stylistic suggestions, were of great value. Whatever mistakes remain are, of course, the fault of none but the author. My ability to devote a significant amount of time to research on Sephardic rabbinic creativity in Eretz Israel the modern era has been facilitated during the past two years by my receipt of the Eliashar Foundation Fellowship established at the Ben-Zvi Institute by Toni and Oded Eliashar. My continuous research activity at the Shalom Hartman Institute's Center for Halakha, and my interaction with other members of SHI's Institute for Advanced Judaic Study, have provided an in-depth context for all of my writing over the past fiften years.

2. In the course of my research on the religious-intellectual creativity of Sephardic rabbis in modern times, I have devoted some articles to the thought of Sephardic rabbis in pre–1948 mandatory Palestine. See (in European languages), *"Un grand decisionnaire sepharade defend les droits de la femme," Pardes* 2 (1985) 128–148; *"La Tradition sepharade sur la galout et le sionisme politique: La position halakhique de R. Yaakov Moshe Toledano," Pardes* 15 (1992) 169–184; "Traditional Flexibility and Modern Strictness: A Comparative Analysis of the Halakhic Positions of Rabbi Kook and Rabbi Uzziel on Women's Suffrage," in Harvey Goldberg (ed.), *Sephardi and Middle Eastern Jewries: History and Culture.* Bloomington: Indiana University Press, 1996. In all fairness, however, these articles cannot be said to paint a comprehensive picture of the intellectual and religious world of Sephardic rabbis in Palestine before 1948—although they might indicate the surprises in store for researchers, in this area.

3. While collecting material for this paper, I found that Rabbi Marc Angel has already published a most interesting article, in which he compares and contrasts the halakhic positions of Rabbi HaLevi and Rabbi Moshe Feinstein, with regard to several important contemporary halakhic issues. See, Marc D. Angel, "A study of the halakhic approaches of two modern 'posekim'," *Tradition* 23:3 (1988) 41–52. Correspondence with Rabbi Angel has also enabled me to obtain, as this article goes to press, a second article "Rabbi Haim David HaLevi, "A Leading Contemporary Rabbinic Thinker," in *Jewish Book Annual, 1994–1995* 52. (New York: Jewish Book Council 1994) 99–109. Both of these articles provide an empathic and sensitive reading of important issues in rabbi HaLevi's thought.

4. See paean to Porat Yosef and to Rabbi 'Attiyah in introduction to HaLevi's *Bein Yisrael La'Ammim* (Jerusalem, 1954). *passim.*

5. A major branch of the family had moved to Eretz-Israel in the nineteenth century, and settled in Tiberias.

6. See Rabbi E. Waldenberg's preface to HaLevi, *Bein Yisrael La'Ammim,* 12–13.

7. This biographical sketch is based on several sources, including, among others, a one-page mimeographed precis provided upon request by Rabbi HaLevi's office.

8. See Angel, A study of the halakhic approaches, of two modern posekim, for descriptions of several such decisions. I hope to discuss HaLevi's philosophy of halakha in a future work. (See note 3.)

9. Volume 1 covers Genesis and Exodus.

10. *Bein Yisrael La'Ammim*, 112–113.

11. *'Aseh Lekah Rav* 4, 53–77.

12. For example, the eating of unleavened bread on Passover, or dwelling in a booth during Succoth. Ibid., 55.

13. Ibid., 55–56.

14. Elsewhere, HaLevi explains that this should not be understood as interest in history per se, but rather as interest in those aspects and events which the Bible—and, later, the Rabbis—saw as theologically and religiously significant. See, *'Aseh* 4:85, 274–282.

15. See, for example, "The politico-historical context of our Forefathers' descent to Egypt," *HaTsofe*, 28 Dec. 1990. *HaTsofeh* is a daily newspaper, published and funded by the Israeli National Religious Party.

16. See, for example, "National Unity Can Enable the Realization of National Goals," *HaTsofe*, 9 March 1990.

17. See, Cf. "Israel possesses Torah—Gentiles possess Wisdom," *HaTsofe*, 1 Feb 1991.

18. For example, the extent to which individual leaders influence history versus the extent to which they, themselves, are products of their times. See, "On the Character of Leaders of the Jewish People," *HaTsofe* 13 July 1990.

19. *Bein* 86–89.

20. Ibid., 116. More than thirty-five years later, HaLevi continues to hold this position, writing that the founding of the State of Israel is significant "not only for the sake of providing sovereignty for the people of Israel in their Land . . . but, as an important station on the road to universal redemption, which shall surely come." *HaTsofe* 11 May 90.

21. It is worthwhile at this point to note the difference in outlook between HaLevi and Rabbi J. B. Soloveitchik, with regard to the significance of the United Nations from a Jewish-theological perspective. According to Soloveitchik, the United Nations is, in general, lacking in theological value or purpose. Its sole reason for existence, from a Judaic perspective, was the role it played in enabling the establishment of the State of Israel. See, J. B. Soloveitchik, *Qol Dodi Dofeq*. Jerusalem: Mossad HaRav Kook 5748/1988. 78. In

other words, the creation of the State was the value which bequeathed significance to the United Nations. According to HaLevi, however, the General Assembly's 1947 vote in favor of Palestine's partition was, at most, one aspect of the United Nation's theological significance, which is nothing less than the advancement of all nations toward brotherhood, dignity, and ultimate spiritual fulfillment. Also, compare HaLevi's further exposition of the United Nation's universal value in his article "The Year 5750 [1989–1990] and the Beginning of Universal Redemption," (*HaTsofe*, 19 January 1990.

22. See, for example, his article "M'qomah shel Milhemet Yom haKippurim b'Ma'arkhot Geulat Yisrael" ("The Yom Kippur War in the Context of the Struggles for Israel's Redemption"), in *Torah she-Be'al Peh*, 17, 1975 63–68, where he adopts a near-deterministic analysis of the Redemption process, relying heavily on kabbalistic sources. See, also, *'Aseh* 4:6, where he writes, on page 60, "A Providential Hand guides the moves of humankind, and humans are but instruments toward the realization of the final goal." Yet, in that same volume of *'Aseh* on page 28, he stresses that "There are periods in history that offer the nation an opportunity that is unique, or that shall re-occur only after thousands of years." In my writing of this article, I attempt to provide what seems to me to be the best possible overall reading of HaLevi, without claiming that all of his writings consist of an integrated—or integratable—"seamless web."

23. Explicated most fully in his articles "Adam and Abraham," *HaTsofeh*, 10 November 1989; and "He Created Man in the Image of God," ibid., 12 October 1990.

24. It is for this very reason, explains HaLevi, that, although all other creatures were designated by God to be "good," man was not so designated, for Adam and Eve were *ab initio*, both "good" and "bad."

25. HaLevi refers to *midrash Sifra* on Leviticus 29:45.

26. *HaTsofe*, 10 Nov '89. By way of clarification, it should be noted that the verse "Love thy neighbor" has been understood in Rabbinic tradition as referring to intra-Jewish relations; that is, one owes fairness to all humans, but is commanded to love fellow followers of the Torah. Rabbi 'Aqivah indicated this verse as the Torah's most basic notion. Ben-'Azzai, however, considered that, by doing so, Rabbi 'Aqivah was downplaying the Torah's universal validation of humanity, as expressed in the statement that every human being is in the Image of God.

27. *HaTsofe*, 12 Oct. 90

28. *Bein*, p. 89.

29. See, at length, *Dat u-Medinah*, 82–113.

30. Ibid., 114–117.

31. As all Jews today are in the category of ritual impurity of "Tmeh-Met." See, *Encyclopaedia Judaica*, 13:1413–1414.

32. Maimonides' Code of Law, *Hilkhot Beit ha-Behira* 7:15–16; Code of Law, *Hilkhot Biat ha-Miqdash*, 3.

33. *Dat*, 117.

34. *'Aseh* 4:1, 28. HaLevi repeats this assessment elsewhere, as in *HaTsofe*, 9 March 1990.

35. *'Aseh*, 28–29. HaLevi continues by saying that, should the Jews of the Diaspora fail to seize this opportunity, they will, nevertheless, ultimately return to the Land in far less comfortable ways, as prophesied by Ezekiel (See, Ezekiel, 20:34). Note that this essay in *'Aseh* 4 is based on an address HaLevi gave in 1979 at a conference at Jerusalem's Mossad HaRav Kook. The address was also published in the volume of the conference proceedings. See, *Torah she-Be'alpeh* 5740, 39–51.

36. *HaTsofe* 11 May 90. Here, HaLevi hints that, had all Jews emigrated to the Land of Israel at that time, perhaps the Holocaust would not have occurred. Due to the complexity of the issue, I shall not deal in this paper with HaLevi's treatment of the Holocaust.

37. *HaTsofe*, 19 January 1990.

38. *'Aseh* 2, postscript, 256.

39. HaLevi notes that he had already pointed this out in his postscript to *'Aseh* 9, 395–396.

40. HaLevi refers his readers to the last chapter of the rabbinic tractate *Masekhet Derekh Eretz Zuta*, known as "The Chapter of Peace."

41. HaLevi refers to BT *Shabbat* 63; Maimonides' Code *Shabbat* 29; *Tur* and *Shulkhan 'Arukh Orah-Hayyim*, sec. 301.

42. Here, HaLevi follows Maimonides' rationalistic reading, rejecting the alternate, literal interpretation anticipating a radical change in natural zoological reality in messianic times.

43. For an attempt to characterize salient aspects of Sephardic rabbinic response to modernity, and to briefly reflect upon the implications thereof, the reader is referred to my recent article in Hebrew, "Herut 'Al HaLuhot—'al meafyeneha shel hatarbut hahilkhatit hasefaradit hamizrahit ba'et hahadasha" ("Freedom on the Tablets—An essay on characteristics of Sephardic/Oriental Halakhic Culture in modern times"), in *Dimui* 10 (Fall 1995), 14–23. Many of the matters which I discussed there are presented in English in my forthcoming article "Sephardic Rabbinic Response to Modernity: Some Central Characteristics," in S. Deshen and W.P. Zenner, eds., *Jews Among Muslims: The Anthropology of Communities in the Pre-Colonial Middle East*. (London: Macmillan and New York University Press, forthcoming.)

7. Remembering the Sages of Aram Soba (Aleppo)

Walter P. Zenner

Ya'akov Choeka and Hayyim Sabato. *Minhat Aharon: Me'asef Torani LeZikhro shel HaRav Aharon Choeka z"l (A Torahitic Collection of Essays Dedicated to the Memory of Rabbi Aharon Choeka, of Blessed Memory).* Published by the family. 5750 (1989–1990).

Rabbi David Zion Laniado. *Sefer LaQedoshim asher baAre's (Book for the Holy Men Who Were in Aram Soba).* Privately published by the sons of the author. Jerusalem: 5740 (1979–1980).

H. Makover. *Hakhme Aram Sobah* (Rabbis of Aleppo). (Jerusalem: Yeshivat Hod Yosef, 5752 (1992–1993).

Introduction

*A*mong the biases have which marked the social scientific study of Israeli ethnicity and religion have been

1. The tendency to treat these aspects as separate phenomena;
2. The neglect of texts by group members; and
3. Little concern with small ethnic groups, which did not present Israeli society with social problems.

The appearance of two Sephardic religious parties on the Israeli political scene—first, the short-lived TAMI party, and then, the more durable SHAS party—has shown how distorted the first two biases have made us. The third bias is the one of which we should always beware.

Some small groups have influenced certain sectors of Israeli society disproportionately. One of these groups were the rabbis from Aleppo or [of] Aleppian descent. One of their number was, for many years, the head of a major Sephardic yeshiva, Porat Yosef. The militant conservatism of the Aleppian rabbinate prefigured the *haredi* orientation of the SHAS party. In addition, rabbis of Israeli Aleppian origin have been important leaders of Sephardic communities in the Americas.

The various books under consideration here, while different from each other, give us some insight into the mentalities of the Aleppian and related Sephardic rabbinic circles through how they relate the rich traditions of the Aleppian rabbinate to present-day Israel. The production of these books also reveals the web of connections between different groups of rabbis and laymen in Israel and the Diaspora.

I

Books have, for a long time, been used as ways of honoring and remembering other human beings living and dead. Books are dedicated to family and friends, as well as teachers and scholars. For a long time, scholars would honor their mentors by writing papers in their honor as gifts on their jubilees (*Festschriften*) or after their deaths (*Memorschriften*). For Jewish communities—which were destroyed or abandoned, in Europe or elsewhere—the memory book (*zikhronbikh*) serves as a portable memorial for a community which is no longer in the place where it once was.[1]

As a result of Zionist ideology, there has been a tendency in Israel studies to draw a sharp line between Diaspora Jewry and Israel. Yet, a considerable number of books are published in Israel which show that there is continuity between the past abroad and the present in a variety of ways. These books, which feature remembrance of sages, represent this aspect of the relationship between Israel and the diaspora birthplace and hometown, especially with regard to the books by Laniado and Makover. Some simply want to remember their roots, while others—especially among the Orthodox—look for role models among and guidance from their forbears. The publication of such books reveals much about the values and social relationships of the people who have produced these books in both previous [and] contemporary contexts.

In a notable article, Shlomo Deshen described the publishing ventures in Israel of Jews from Jerba in Southern Tunisia.[2] In this article, Deshen sees publication of books—as well as pilgrimages to the tombs of saints—as a substitution for traditional religious practices, which have been abandoned by these Jews during their period of immigration and acculturation. For the many of the publishers and buyers of these books, their contents are of less account than their talismanic value as a quasi-magical protection of the home against evil, and as a memorial to the past. The contents of the books, which often are works of Talmudic learning, are unlikely to appeal to most buyers simply as readers. Rather, their purchase and possession by themselves are considered as meritorious.

Deshen's analysis of the "ritualization of literacy" makes sense when applied to the traditionally minded laity of many Jewish groups, including American Reform Jews. The *sefer*—the holy book—just like other ritual objects, such as *mezzuzot*—or Passover plates—has a value only partly related to its contents. Even for those who have broken with tradition, residues of guilt and pride in a heritage, from which the individual has some distance, make them display sacred objects as a way of assuaging guilt and of asserting pride.[3]

Private publication of works by rabbis is not limited to the Jews from Jerba, but can be found among other groups of Jews, whether of European or Afro-Asian origins. Among Jews of Aleppian origin, the type of works published range from rabbinic manuscripts—such as sermons, commentaries, and legal responsa—to *Memorschriften* and serial publications. The latter are not by the rabbis being remembered or honored, but by younger, contemporary scholars. While, for many of the purchasers, the contents might be irrelevant, the contents themselves reveal something about the changing nature of the descendants of Aleppo Jews, and their particular orientations in Israel and elsewhere in the world.

If the books published are reprints or previously unpublished manuscripts—such as many books of rabbinic legal responsa—they will often reveal much about the society in which they were originally written.[4] We will not deal with these publications here. Each of the books which will be analyzed here are examples of different kinds of genres. Despite this, they share a number of characteristics.

1. They all remember rabbis from Aleppo (identified traditionally with the biblical *Aram Sobah*), or of Aleppian origin;
2. They represent an Orthodox religious orientation; and
3. They were privately published.

II

Hakham David Laniado's *LaQedoshim Asher BaAre's* is a good starting point in this regard. The author was a native of Aleppo, and a longtime resident of Eretz Yisrael. He lived in Hebron until the 1929 massacre, and then moved to Jerusalem. The heart of the book consists of brief biographies and bibliographies of rabbis of Aleppian origin, but it also contains other materials. The 1952 edition of the book was printed in Jerusalem on cheap paper and in a volume that was less than seven inches by five inches, without illustrations. There evidently was an earlier edition, because Part Three of the 1952 edition begins with a title page, indicating that this book was published by the press of Rabbi Hayyim Zukerman in Jerusalem and in 5695 (1934–1935). The next edition came out in 1980, and contained numerous photographs of the rabbis whose lives are recounted.

The table of contents of the 1980 edition includes most of the material from the 1952 edition. The table of contents of the latest edition includes a forward by one of the sons of

David Laniado, an introduction to the second edition, and a brief biography and description of Laniado. Then, it proceeds to a short overview of recent history (as of 1952) by Rabbi David Laniado. Appended to this survey are pieces written by others, including a plan of the Old Synagogue in Aleppo, followed by a compilation of references to and descriptions and chronicles of Aleppo as they appear in Hebrew literature from early times on, including Sa'adia Gaon and al-Harizi to the nineteenth century. Part of that chapter is taken from a nineteenth-century book.[5] This is followed by a prayer, and the encyclopedic section on "Sages and Rabbis of Aram Sobah."

After these, we find legal decisions, praises of the rabbis of Aram Sobah, a list of Aleppian rabbis' books, dates of death, a glossary of abbreviations, and an index to the sages. In addition to a change in format and the inclusion of photographs, the expanded edition is organized somewhat differently. There is a table of contents. In the 1952 edition, one finds epitaphs from gravestones, rather than biographies. In the 1980 edition some of the brief epitaphs have been augmented by brief biographies. Whereas in 1952, David Laniado included epitaphs from places other than Aleppo, such as personalities in Damascus, these are omitted in 1980. In the earlier book, the names of rabbis were organized in alphabetical order, on the basis of the rabbi's first name, while in the expanded edition it is alphabetized by surname. When rabbis bear the same personal and family names—which is quite common among Sephardic Jews, because the oldest grandchildren are generally named for grandparents living or dead—the order is chronological.

One fairly typical biography (Entry 423) is that of Avraham Antebi, a well-known rabbinic scholar who lived between about 1765 and 1858. The biography begins with the date of his birth in 5525 (1764–1765). It then lists his father, and goes on to discuss his display of brilliance as a young man. While listing the books which he wrote, Hakham David also quotes from encomia written in his books while he lived, as well as quotations from eulogies. As in most of the biographies, the biography ends with the text of the engraving on the tombstone of the rabbi. The emphasis on this material of praise befits the hagiographic nature of the book. In the folklore section of the book, there is no legend of this rabbi, but there are legends of other rabbis.

Biographies of twentieth-century (including contemporary) figures also appear, which help us to see the continuity in many rabbinic dynasties, including that of the Laniado family itself. The biographies include those of Aleppian communal leaders, including Isaac Shalom of New York City and Joseph Shamah of Jerusalem, who were not rabbis. Some of the biographies were probably included or updated by the sons of Hakham David.

The survey of recent events by the author is one of the most personal documents in the book. It was written for the 1952 edition in the wake of the War for Independence, and it was not revised in the later edition, even though that edition came out after the Six-Day War. Much of the prose is taken directly from scriptural passages, which fit the author's interpretation of the situation of the Jews in Eretz Yisrael and Syria during that period. He begins the survey by thanking the Holy One for the miracles which permitted the Jews to survive and to establish their state, despite the cruel powers against them and the savage Arab states which surround them. He takes a Biblical verse with the word, *ELeH*, which he then interprets as standing for the three Jewish armies of the Independence period: *Irgun, Lehi* and *Haganah*.

Still, the greater part of his survey deals with what has been lost as a result of the war, including access to Hebron and the Old City of Jerusalem, as well as what was destroyed in Aleppo in 1947. He lists buildings in the Old City which fell into Jordanian hands, such as the Porat Yosef yeshiva building and the synagogue of Rabbi Yehuda HeHasid. This survey expresses a viewpoint which is simultaneously that of a traditional pious Jew and that of a modern nationalist. To him, the particular ethnic heritage of Aram Sobah is intimately linked to the fate of Eretz Yisrael. It is a holy city, and its desecrated synagogues are comparable to those of the Old City and of Hebron, where he had lived until driven out during the anti-Jewish pogrom of 1929.

Although this book has many traditional and ritualistic characteristics, it is also a product of the contemporary Aleppian diaspora and of Israel. The social environment in which Hakham David lived shows this. I discovered this book when I first began to do work on Syrian Jews around 1959–1960. I wrote a letter to Meir Benayahu—then director of the Ben Zvi Institute and son of Rabbi Nissim—who was the Sephardic Chief Rabbi at that time. He wrote to tell me to get in touch with Hakham David to get a copy of the book. When Hakham David was collecting pictures of rabbis, I showed him pictures of rabbis at work taken by an early twentieth-century Protestant missionary of Jewish origin, the Rev. Joseph Segall. Hakham David viewed his work at the Hebrew University. The second edition was published with contributions from Syrian Jews throughout the world, with a special role played by the São Paulo community where Rabbi Ephraim Laniado, son of Hakham David, is Rabbi.

Between the early part of Hakham David's life—and his later life, as well as that of his children—important changes in mentality are occurring. The sources for this book, the earlier editions, and the last edition all illustrate this. In the nineteenth century, there was little concern for either local or general history among Syrian Jews, although historical study was launched in Europe at this time. Except for Abraham Dayan's brief chronicle, most rabbis in Syria did not record history directly. By the early twentieth-century, when Hakham David began to record epitaphs, the need to preserve old local traditions must have been felt. Still, the format is traditional. The book itself shows this with the importance of prayers and imprimaturs. By the 1960s and 1970s, however, consciousness of other formats, including the use of photographs, encyclopedias, and historiography in general, has spread. Even the most traditional can see that these can aid remembrance.

We also find significant interaction between the university-based scholars and those who work out of the yeshivot. A similar interaction is taking place in Israel in general and, in Jerusalem, among folk performers, folklore scholars, and the media. Singers of traditional synagogue and secular music are asked to perform on television, as well as recording for musicologists. In daily life, the influences of modern schools and universities come out in subtler ways. Although not used in traditional literature, terms like the *Byzantine empire* or *giz'anut* (racism), are heard in sermons and conversations with many *haredi* (ultra-Orthodox) rabbis and yeshiva students. Despite the fact that Sephardic haredim discourage television-watching and try to insulate themselves and their families from secular influences, they do communicate in twentieth-century Hebrew, and they interact with the university world in significant ways.

III

Makover's book is clearly for children. The Hebrew text is vowelled. Each chapter has a picture of the rabbi, although most pictures have a stereotypic flavor with a picture that looks like it is drawn from a photograph. Only a few real photographic portraits appear. The stories about the rabbis are often legends. So, instead of the straight treatment which we find in Laniado, Makover starts the story of Avraham Antebi with a long legend. A Talmudic scholar in Safed at Shavu'ot tells the story of how a young ruffian who had no interest in the Torah was angry at Rabbi Antebi for trying to restrain him and his life. He then lay in wait to attack the Rabbi with a stick, but, instead, his hand was frozen. As a result he "returned" to the Torah. The teller of this tale turns out to be that ruffian. He then proceeds to narrate the life of Rabbi Avraham, reviewing many of the same details found in the Laniado biography.

While the story of Avraham Antebi and the young ruffian has some excitement, it is very difficult to create stories with dramatic interest for the other rabbis. Rabbi Ovadia Hedaya was a very prominent rabbi in the Jerusalem

Sephardic community from the 1930s until his death in 1969. He had served in the councils of the Chief Rabbinate and rabbinic courts, as well as being an author of numerous books and articles. As a halakhic authority, he was one of the leading kabbalists of his day. He was known for practicing mystical rituals on a daily basis, such as praying with the special *kavanot* of Rabbi Isaac Luria, which are long additional meditations added to the prayers, and purifying himself in the *mikveh* (ritual bath). After the destruction of the Kabbalistic Bet El yeshiva in the Old City in 1948, Rabbi Hedayu founded a new Bet El yeshiva in West Jerusalem, and restored it to the Old City after 1967 (Laniado, 131:36–37). Makover, however, simply repeats these facts, albeit simplified. He does not even bother to explicate what some of the mystical practices which marked Hedaya's way of life were (pp. 190–193).

The longest article in Makover's book is accorded to Rabbi Ezra Atiyeh, head of the Porat Yosef yeshiva in Jerusalem from 1925 until his death in 1970. His picture is also the central one on the cover of the book. While Laniado (419: 139–140) devotes about two columns including a photograph to this rabbi (a little less than he devotes to Ovadia Hedaya), Makover devotes forty-one pages (pp. 220–260) to this rabbi, while the stories of others are approximately between seven and twelve pages. This difference in treatment is compatible with the haredi view, which sees study of the Law in the yeshiva as one of the highest Jewish ideals.

In the book by Makover, the treatment of subjects is more dramatic as befits a children's book, although what age group this book is for is not indicated.

IV

A very different book is the *Memorschrift*, *Minhat Aharon*, prepared by Ya'akov Choeka and Hayyim Sabato, in memory of Rabbi Aharon Choeka (pronounced "Shweika"), an Aleppo-born rabbi who made his mark in Egypt. In many ways, Choeka fits more the model of the so-called "modern Orthodox rabbi" than of a traditional hakham. During the 1930s and 1940s, he set up a yeshiva in Cairo to deal with the needs of Sephardic Jewish youth in the very secular cosmopolis of Cairo. He tried to synthesize modern intellectual streams with those of the tradition.

Rabbi Shimon Alouf, who had studied with Rabbi Choeka in Israel, saw him as one who combined the openness of Sephardic rabbis before the Expulsion from Spain with the traditionalism of typical Halebi *hakhamim*. Choeka, for instance, read Maimonides' *Moreh Nevukhim* ("Guide to the Perplexed") in Arabic, and learned German in order to read Kant. In his approach to the Talmud, however, he remained true to the methods of Rabbi Ezra Atiyeh, who was, according to Alouf, his teacher at Porat Yosef. He also continued to favor the biblical account of Creation over modern scientific theories.[6]

During the 1940s, he traveled to Syria and Iraq, and was considered for rabbinical posts in both countries. Ultimately, he was either not chosen for or chose not to take these positions. During his visit to Aleppo, he was sympathetic to a small religious Zionist youth group there, which, however, faced fierce opposition from militantly conservative rabbis who had dominated the religious institutions of that city since the mid-nineteenth century.[7] It is possible that Choeka's moderation was one reason for his decision not take the post of Chief Rabbi there.

Unlike David Laniado, whose appearance was generally traditional with beard and traditional caftan, a photograph shows a mature Aharon Choeka as beardless and wearing a tie and suit, albeit with his head covered by a fez, as was common in pre-Nasser Egypt. The caption to this picture describes him as being at the peak of his activity as head of the yeshiva (p. 352). Makover does not devote a chapter to Choeka, even though he is a notable figure of the Aleppian diaspora. Perhaps he was not considered traditionalistic enough for Makover's audience. He would be the wrong kind of role model for the more haredi public.

The contents of the *Memorschrift* also shows the different milieu connected with Rabbi Choeka. This genre of publication is associated more with how the work of the individual remembered is being carried on by his intellectual heirs, rather than simply recounting his deeds or reprinting his words, although these volumes might do some of that, too. Most of the articles are by rabbis. Among them is Rabbi Ovadia Yosef, the spiritual leader of SHAS, who had been associated with Rabbi Choeka early in his career, when he served as a rabbi in Cairo. Rabbi Yosef was the Sephardi Chief Rabbi between 1972 and 1982. Ovadia Yosef's article deals with the problem of the sabbatical year when, according to Levitical law, planting is restricted, and, therefore, Jews are forbidden to use the produce of the land. One way to get around these restrictions was to follow a legal fiction by selling the lands of Eretz Yisrael to a Gentile for the year as Gentiles are not subject to the sabbatical year. This practice is offensive to Zionists, but is pragmatic in terms of permitting observant Jews the use of local produce.

The final decision of the article veers in favor the more lenient and pragmatic position. Rabbi Simha HaKohen Kook, who has been associated with *Gush Emunim* ("The Bloc of the Faithful"), contributed a piece in which he stresses the holiness of Jerusalem and the inviolability of the Holy Land, in opposition to those who would cede territory to the Palestinians. These articles reflect the two political approaches to the Arab-Israeli conflict found among Orthodox Jews, conservative pragmatism, and militant irredentism. Other articles are less politically charged. Most are written in a traditional halakhic—or legal—or homiletical mode, such as Rabbi David Hayim HaLevi's sermon on the three books of destiny, which are said to be open on High before Rosh Hashanah, the annual Day of Judgment. (See, Zohar, in this volume, chapter 6.)

Another article, by Rabbi Zvi Ilani, which is salient to Orthodox Jews in Israel, deals with switching from one's ancestral customary practices—for example, Moroccan Sephardi to other customary practices, such as those of Polish Ashkenazim.

Several articles are written in a modern scholarly vein.
An example is the article by Professor Avner Shaki who wrote
on who has the authority to deal with the status of a pros-
elyte as a Jew, which is a question of great importance in
Israel. A piece by Zvi Gotthold deals with the formulation—
"Next Year in Jerusalem"—in prayers.

Toward the end of the book, a number of letters written
by Rabbi Choeka are published, including several to Israeli
newspapers on the issues of the day in 1960. Two of these
deal with provocative statements made by Prime Minister
David Ben Gurion. One was Ben Gurion's assertion that the
Pharisaic interpretation of the Biblical verse, "an eye for an
eye," was to be understood as meaning monetary compensation for an eye, not removing the eye of the perpetrator, was
not Scriptural. Liberal Jewish interpreters would probably
agree with Ben Gurion, but would defend the Pharisaic view
as being progressive and humane for its time. Choeka, however, is a staunch traditionalist in seeing the Oral Tradition
as co-equal, both legally and chronologically, to the written
text. The second letter deals with Ben Gurion's fairly dogmatic statement that only six hundred Israelite families (not
six-hundred thousand) left Egypt. This interpretation drew a
response from the cartoonist Kishon at the time, who showed
only six Israelites leaving Egypt led by the doughty Prime
Minister. In this case, Ben Gurion was sticking his neck out,
because it is always difficult to project statistics historically.

In these letters, Choeka's tone is respectful of the Prime
Minister and of democratic principles. He shows respect for
the right of people to hold unorthodox views, although he
does appear to want the right of officials to express such
views restricted. Both the portrayal of Choeka and the contributions to the *Memorschrift* give us a sense of a more
direct confrontation between modernism and traditionalism
than we see in the other two volumes.

V

In conclusion, these three books show us how ethnic groups
and religious orientation are used in presenting role models

for Middle Eastern Jews in Israel. They show us different uses of memory for the sake of continuity, and for particular religious and political programs. Laniado and Makover utilize an old image which stresses the saints and scholars of Aleppo, and suggests that Aleppo's Jewish community was a closed sacred society. Interestingly, Avraham Antebi, a nineteenth-century hakham had already portrayed the Aleppo of his day as having departed from this idealized image of the city.[8]

Still, among Sephardic and Middle Eastern Jews, the Aleppian rabbis are noted for their militant conservatism (*shamranit lohemet*), as Zohar has termed it.[9] This image of the Aleppian rabbis fits very well with the programs of contemporary groups, such as SHAS, and, thus, can provide Sephardic precedents for such policies, which are usually associated with Ashkenazi haredim.

The militantly conservative saints and scholars, however, are not the only role models. While this feisty conservatism was dominant in Aleppo, and among Aleppian rabbis elsewhere, it was only one of several reactions to modernity found among Aleppian Jewry, although laymen and rabbis could not always express more favorable views of new developments openly, and these more moderate rabbis were never as visible as their more strident counterparts.[10] Rabbi Aharon Choeka's accommodation, which resembles that of modern Orthodoxy, represents an alternative—albeit by a rabbi who was able to maintain his position with his more militant colleagues.

These books, however, also show us an Aleppian Jewry which is in the process of merging with the other Jews of Israel. They are not necessarily interested in remaining a separate enclave. I interviewed Aleppian leaders—both secular and rabbinic—in 1993, including those who lead the World Center for the Heritage of Aram Sobah in Aleppo.[11] All indicated to me that they were not interested in separatism. Most of their own children had married with non-Aleppians. At the same time, they wanted the heritage of Aram Sobah to be represented in the Israeli mosaic. Providing role models for the religious community would certainly fit this goal.

The books themselves suggest this, especially the one by Makover, and the Choeka memorial volume. Makover's book is one of many such volumes telling stories of rabbis from different Middle Eastern communities, which are displayed in religious Jewish bookstores in Israel side by side with Hasidic stories. The Choeka volume puts the biography and works of this Aleppian-Egyptian-Israeli rabbi into the context of a broad spectrum of Orthodox rabbinic thought, including Ashkenazim, Sephardim, modern Orthodox nationalists, and conservative non-Zionists. Taken together these volumes show us the internal diversity of religious Sephardim in contemporary Israel.

Acknowledgment

I would like to thank the Memorial Foundation for Jewish culture, which gave me a grant to continue my research on Syrian Jewry. I would also like to thank members of the Laniado family, Professor Ya'akov Choeka, Rabbi Shimon Alouf, and a number of active members of the world center for the Heritage of Aram Sobah for their assistance, and Kevin Avruch for his comments. I am solely responsible for the views expressed here.

Notes

1. See, Jack Kugelmass and Jonathan Boyarin, *In a Ruined Garden* (New York: Schocken Books, 1983) *passim.*

2. Shlomo Deshen, "Ritualization of Literacy: The Works of Tunisian Scholars in Israel," in *American Ethnologist* 2 (1975): 251–260.

3. See Samuel Heilman, "Jews and Judaica: Who Owns and Buys What?," in Walter P. Zenner, ed., *Persistence and Flexibility: Anthropological Perspectives on the American Jewish Experience* (Albany: State University of New York Press, 1988) 260–279.

4. See Walter P. Zenner, "Censorship and Syncretism: Some Anthropological Approaches to the Study of Middle Eastern Jews," in Frank Talmage, ed., *Studies in Jewish Folklore* (Cambridge Mass.: Association for Jewish Studies, 1980) 377–394. Also see, W. P. Zenner, "Jews in Late Ottoman Syria," in S. Deshen and W. P. Zenner, eds., *Jewish Societies in the Middle East* (Lanham, Md., University Press of America, 1982) 155–210.

5. Rabbi Avraham Dayan, *Holekh Tamim vFo'el Sedeq* (Livorno: 1850–1851).

6. Interview with Rabbi Shimon Alouf in Brooklyn, March 1995.

7. Zohar, Zvi, "Shamranit Lohemet: Qavim LeManhigutam HaHevratit-Datit shel Hakhmei Haleb BaEt HaHadashah" ("Activist Conservatives: The Socio-Religious Policy of Aleppo's Rabbis, about 1865–1945"). *Peamim*, 55. (1993) 57–78.

8. Rabbi Avraham Antebi, *Hokhmah u-Musar*. (Jerusalem: 5721 (1960–1961). 3–5.

9. Zohar, 1993.

10. See, Yaron Harel, "Tesisah Ruhanit BaMizrah—Yesodah shel Kehillah Reformit BiHaleb BiShnat 1862," Hebrew Union College *Annual* (1993). xix–xxxv; and Zohar, "A 'Maskil' in Aleppo: 'The Torah of Israel and the People of Israel' by Rabbi Yitzhak Dayan (Aleppo, 5683 or 1923)," in Y. K. Stillman and G. K. Zucker, eds., *New Horizons in Sephardic Studies* (Albany: State University of New York Press, 1993) 93–107.

11. The World Center is led by Menahem Yedid, a former Likud member of the Knesset. Its aim is to preserve the memory and selected features of Aleppian culture, such as sacred melodies and books by Aleppian rabbis. Ya'akov Choeka, Rabbi Aharon Choeka's son, is also on its board.

8. Localizing Israeli Judaism

Kevin Avruch

Tamar El-Or, *Educated and Ignorant: Ultraorthodox Jewish Women and Their World* (Boulder: Lynne Reinner Publishers, 1994).

Susan Starr Sered, *Women as Ritual Experts: The Religious Lives of Elderly Jewish Women in Jerusalem* (New York: Oxford University Press, 1992).

I

$\mathcal{R}$eferring to the study of Muslim society, Ernest Gellner wrote,

> Orientalists are at home with texts. Anthropologists are at home in villages. The natural consequence is that the former tend to see Islam from above, the latter from below. I remember an anthropologist specialising in a Muslim country telling me of his first encounter with an elderly and distinguished Islamicist. The old scholar observed that the Koran was interpreted differently in various parts of the Muslim world. The young anthropologist remarked that this was indeed obvious. "Obvious? Obvious?" expostulated the old man angrily. "It took *years* of careful research to establish it!"

Gellner's anecdote points to what is arguably the major contribution made by anthropology to the study of so-called world religions—that is, the ethnographic documentation of religious diversity in the face of scriptural unity, and the importance of studying locally manifested historical and cultural variations in belief and practice. Even when Gellner published the story, in 1973, this insight was widely accepted. Thus, we could smile indulgently with him at the old orientalist.[2]

Robert Redfield's delineation of the Great and Little Traditions[3]—a way of connecting literate and elite centers with illiterate and peripheral village peasantries—already had been applied productively to Hindu India by Milton Singer,[4] and critiqued and refined by McKim Marriott. Melford Spiro explored the distinction between what he later called "religion-in-doctrine" and "religion-in-use" in a Theravada Buddhist society in Burma.[5] And Clifford Geertz "observed" Islam as an expression of differing historical and cultural exigencies in two very different Muslim societies, Moroccan and Javanese.[6]

Each of these writers meant slightly different things by their distinctions. Spiro, for example, was interested in the psychological uses of Buddhism by Burmans, which lead them to cognitive and behavioral reconfigurations of normative, nibbanic doctrine. However, all were agreed that the relationship between a literate, normative, religious doctrine and the ways in which the religion was *lived* by the often semiliterate or illiterate "folk," was neither transparent nor unproblemmatical. The very nature of the relationship was, indeed, an area richly deserving of study.

II

There is no reason to suspect that Judaism, as a world religion, is immune from this insight. Both of the books under discussion here also deal with Judaism's local manifestations among specific folk and their communities. Moreover, both extend the insight differentiating normative, text-based "religion-in-doctrine," to use Spiro's terms, and the locally lived "religion-in-use," to focus on women's religious lives in particular as another form of in-use local variation—a form especially deserving of analysis as it had been, hitherto, largely ignored.[7] Finally, both authors focus on Judaism in Israel—and this is worth noting because most of the earlier discussions of localized Judaism have emphasized the influence of diasporic conditions.

What of the diaspora? On the one hand, Jacob Katz, for example, has long argued that what is impressive, given the immensity and duration of the Jewish dispersion, are the basic and underlying similarities among Jewish communities—or at least among traditional ones.[8] Where striking dissimilarities occur, Katz maintains, they are the results of disruptive and differentially experienced modernizing processes. Premodern Jewish communities—be they Yiddish-speaking or Ladino or Judeo-Arabic speaking—were more fundamentally alike than they were different. Modernity, Katz asserts, sundered the essential unity of Judaism and Jewish life.

On the other hand, Katz espouses a more generic and monodimensional sense of what modernization consists of, and its apparently metacultural properties, than is perhaps warranted.[9] Looking around at Judaism in different Jewish communities one is also impressed by the variations—especially at the folk or popular level—and the ways in which these variations align with and mimic the religious practices of the non-Jewish, as well as culturally dominant, majorities. Many have commented on the distinctive Judaism of the Maghreb, for example, with its thaumaturgical, maraboutisitic, and pilgrimage-oriented beliefs and practices[10] that closely mimic and overlap with North African Islam.[11] A world away, and on the other side of the traditional/modern scrim, Sklare described, some time ago, the emergence and popular appeal of Conservative Judaism as reflecting a uniquely American civic and religious—a "denominational"—culture and practice.[12]

What all of these varieties of Judaism shared—besides, of course, the crucial scriptural base of the Torah in its extended sense, and the concomitant ideal of adult male literacy, which are foundational to Judaism's unity despite its diversity—is that they existed as part of Jewish diaspora cultures. Everywhere, Jews were a minority, practicing a marked and minority religion. In different host societies— and in different historical periods—Jews might be esteemed, or tolerated, or despised. However, in all cases, Judaism was practiced as an alternative to some other culturally and sociologically dominant religious form.

It might be practiced underground in utter secrecy (the *Marrano* model), with *dhimmi*-discretion as a separate and recognized confessional entity, as in the Ottoman *millet* model. Or it might be practiced openly, even sharing the same building with another denomination, but using it on different days and times. This is a not uncommon form in newer American suburbs. It's a church on Sunday, and a synagogue—or "temple"—on Friday night.

In its millennial dispersion, perhaps the closest that diaspora Judaism has or can come to a distributive cultural empowerment is in the United States, where many—but not all—Americans speak self-consciously of "Judeo-Christianity" as a cultural and ideological entity. Here, Judaism achieves an honorific equality in one public version—essentially a liberal one—of the society's civil religion.

The range of diasporic environments in which Jews have practiced their religion—and the varieties of praxis—have, thus, been very great. However, notwithstanding America, diasporic Judaism is a marked, minority form. There has been but one environment in which Jews constitute the majority, and Judaism is the dominant religious form—since 1948, in Israel. Now just in its beginning, the study of Israeli Judaism is especially important for exploring the relationship between "doctrine" and "use." For now, Judaism is realigned to a state—a hugely important development. With the advent of the state, it was once thought, all the local varieties could be ingathered into a single center. The periphery would collapse, conjoining in the center. But has it? Both Sered and El-Or address this issue, and explore problems around the distinction between "doctrine" and "use" that stubbornly remain, even at the center—around problems of recalcitrant marginalities inherent within emergent Israeli Judaism and society.

III

In both books, the marginality devolves, first and foremost, on gender, and, secondarily, on literacy. Both focus on women and, for my purposes, the contrast between the women makes their comparison fruitful. Sered's book is about old women of Middle Eastern background (mostly Kurdish), who are illiterate. El-Or writes about younger women, beginning their married lives or their lives as mothers, Ashkenazi, and not merely functionally literate, but highly educated. Both groups of women are very religious, and both books end up by illuminating the form and nature of women's religiosity within the confines of a normative and patriarchal Judaism that either does not take women's religion very seriously, or views it—when it aspires to connect with learning and textual expertise—with uneasy ambivalence.[13]

Sered's ethnographic locale is a senior citizen's day center in Jerusalem, and the ethnographic present is between 1984 and 1985. The center is mostly frequented by women—it is "women's space;" the few men who show up feel uncomfortable and soon leave—of Yemeni, Iraqi, Moroccan, Persian, and mostly Kurdish provenance. The women range in age from the late 50s to 90. Most are widowed, and have never worked outside the home. They came to Israel as adolescents or younger. Many learned to speak Hebrew imperfectly, and almost none reads it. They are often marginalized by their age, in a society that celebrates youth; by their ethnic origins, in a society founded and originally dominated by Ashkenazim; and by their illiteracy, poverty, gender, and religiosity, in a modern, materialist, patriarchal, and secular Israel.

Yet, Sered tells us, they live rich and meaningful lives—and fundamental to the richness and meaning in their lives is their religiousness. They invest deeply in Judaism, and, in turn, are invested by it. Yet—and here is Sered's paradox—their religiousness seems "to have little in common with what most of us mean when we talk about Judaism" (p. 3). This is because traditional, normative Judaism is androcentric and patriarchal, focused, as it is, on rituals practiced almost entirely by—and for—men. Its epitome is a life devoted to learning Torah and Talmud, goals which are denied these women ideologically by their sex and functionally by their illiteracy. (The latter becomes important when we turn to El-Or's work.) How then can these women be "ritual experts in Judaism" (Sered's teasing title) when they are normatively denied any expertise?

This is the question that Sered sets out to answer, and what she ends up describing is how these women fashion *their* Judaism, a "religion of the illiterate," a "domesticated" world religion which celebrates and sacralizes the female experience. This experience includes the idea of nurturing or safeguarding the health and well-being of their families and kinfolk. However, with their own families grown and independent, the notion is expanded to include all of their ancestors and descendants, the people of Israel, and the soldiers of the IDF who defend it—even, indeed, the non-Jewish Druze. They seek to invoke this protection by dint of intensely personal relationships forged with God, with the prophet Elijah, and with a panoply of Jewish saints (*zaddikim*), whose tombs they visit on pilgrimage, when the day center can provide transportation. A host of elements from normative Jewish ritual—the raising of the Torah in the synagogue service; the festival of the new moon; the lighting of shabbat candles; the giving of charity—are appropriated by the women, reinterpreted, and given over to the modality of nurturance. Sered draws the comparison with normative male practice in this eloquent passage.

> When a literate Jewish man listens to the Torah reading in synagogue, he is obeying a divine law, learning about the history of the Jewish people, and participating in the

> life of the community. When an illiterate Middle Eastern
> Jewish woman listens to the Torah reading in synagogue,
> she is seeking the most efficacious moment, the moment
> when the channel of communication between human and
> God is most open, to ask God a personal favor for a
> particular, loved person. (pp. 32–33)

These women are able to live in a parallel Jewish universe—but a noneuclidean one, since it touches normative Judaism at many points and draws its symbols from it. Take the normative emphasis on text, scripture, and learning. The women are illiterate, and so cannot partake directly in these. However—in the manner described by Shlomo Deshen in another context—they ritualize literacy by contributing money to the center's Kurdish rabbi for the purchase of books for his yeshiva.[14] They mystify the written word by obsessively kissing *mezuzot* or holy books, and they sacralize literacy by visiting the places where young men study Torah and blessing them. Yet, Sered argues, the women's religion cannot be merely reduced to the men's. Its valences are different, based, not so much on orthopraxis or the punctilious concern with ritual and *halacha* characteristic of Orthodox Judaism, as on faith and belief—orthodoxy proper. To these women, "being religious" is not (as for Jewish men) a matter exclusively of halachic observance, although they are observant. It is much "more a matter of belief in God, of 'having a clean heart'" (p. 79).

The freedom these women have to create a "radically gynocentric" Judaism is a fragile one. Sered relates it to modernity, but, here, her analysis seems forced. It is based partly on their age—they are freed from the burdens of childcare and husbands, able to visit the synagogue as they rarely could in their youth—and partly on the protected space that the day center provides them. It is based also—and perhaps paradoxically—on the very strict sexual segregation, with its attendant different norms and expectations, that traditional Judaism imposes. Simply put, men are for the most part ignorant of what these women believe and do. They take very little notice of it.[15] This ignorance is precisely what is not true of other patriarchal societies undergoing modernization. There, men might monitor much more closely—and label as truly deviant and heterodox—innovations in religious practice or belief initiated by women. There might also be heavy costs for women to bear in these cases. Finally—as we shall see when we turn next to El-Or's work— these elderly women are also *protected by* their illiteracy, which removes any threat to orthodoxy that their innovations might potentially present.

Without challenging or actively opposing the masculine rendition of Judaism—indeed, the women support it; they are not revolutionaries, hardly even unself-conscious subversives[16]—the women superimpose their own glossess and adroitly maneuver upon the stage of patriarchal religion. They live rich religious lives—but ones that they themselves are unable to articulate. Here, then, is Sered's project: as ethnographer to describe these lives, as feminist, as amanuensis to these unarticulated lives to celebrate them, and as comparativist to use them "to challenge preconceptions about the very nature of such concepts as the sacred, the holy, and human spirituality" (p. 3). Sered is a skillful ethnographer and a committed amanuensis. However, the book is less of a grand challenge to previous religious studies than it is another contribution to the, by now, long-established ethnographic study of localized forms of practice and belief—to the study of so-called "little traditions," here refracted through gender, generation, and life cycle,[17] rather than region, caste, or class.

IV

Modernity—at least in the form of the Jewish state and its founding ideology of Zionism—is, in fact, hardly present for Sered's old women. They view their own immigration to Israel as part of a miraculous, eschatological drama—in many ways, they preferred life in the old country—not as part of nationalism or politics. In keeping with their intense ritual focus on saints, ancestors, and the interventionary powers of the dead, they make of the Israeli Memorial Day (*Yom HaZicaron*) an important holiday, but hardly celebrate Independence Day (*Yom HaAtzmaut*). They plant trees (on *Tu b'Shvat*, the Jewish Arbor Day), which is a Zionist activity, but they assimilate it to the gaining of *zechut*, or religious merit, with God. They consider their relationship to the IDF—praying for the welfare of the soldiers—in the same way. They have almost no interest in politics, and except for their old-age pensions, the state of Israel is a distant entity.

Modernity—Zionism and the state—is, on the other hand, not at all distant for the women of Tamar El-Or's world. These are *haredi* or ultra-orthodox women of the Gur Hasidic community. El-Or's ethnographic locale is the Development, a housing project on Tel Aviv's periphery, and, to a lesser extent, also the Gur communities in Bene Brak and Jerusalem. The almost four-hundred Gur families who live in the Development—nonharedi Israelis, mostly of North African and Middle Eastern origin, also live there—are there because the former Gur rebbe decided to disperse his followers around the country. He directed newly married couples to spend at least five years in places like the Development before they could return to the Gur's centers—Bene Brak or Jerusalem. Although the former is just a short bus-ride away, many Gur in the Development feel that it is a sort of exile to be endured, and count the days before they can move. The ethnographer El-Or travels to the Development, also with a sense of going into exile from her middle-class and secular life in the university and in Tel Aviv. The book is a perfect example of the possibilites for doing truly foreign fieldwork in one's own backyard, enhanced by El-Or's evocative portraits of her informants and her self-reflexivity in the ethnographer's role. The latter is especially done with grace, humility, and, to my mind, great effectiveness.[18]

Like Sered, El-Or deals in paradox, but hers are multiple, darker, and more problematical. For Sered, the main paradox lay in claiming ritual expertise for illiterate women in a normative religion based on literacy and the mastery of texts. However, the women about whom El-Or writes are hardly illiterate. In fact, these haredi women go to school from the age of five (in *ulpanot*) to twenty (in a Beit Ya'akov women's college). After marriage, they continue in evening classes near their homes. They are, in one sense, extremely well-educated—but to what purpose? It is hardly to produce female scholars to sit beside men in the yeshivot. The Talmudic edict forbidding a father from teaching his daughter the Torah—better to burn than to teach—is known to the Gur, as well. The paradox of El-Or's title—"educated and ignorant"—is illuminated by specifying the linking preposition. These women are in fact "educated *for* ignorance." How this is done—and for what reasons—are the main concerns of El-Or's work. She sets forth the paradox by quoting the late Rabbi Avraham Yosef Wolf, founder of the Beit Ya'akov College for Girls in Bene Brak.

> If we succeed in instilling in our girl students that the purpose of their studies is to aspire to emulate our matriarchs, who did not study, then we have succeeded in educating our daughters. (p. 65)

The origins of female education among the haredi can be seen as a delayed effect of Emancipation and Haskalah— that is, of the advent of the modern era for European Jewry, which gave rise also to the very notion of an Orthodox Judaism as distinct from Reform and other alternatives. "The haredi women's intellectual world is of recent make," El-Or writes. Only in 1917 is the first Beit Ya'akov College established in Krakow. Very soon, some ten thousand girls throughout Eastern Europe are enrolled in them. By 1929, at the Third Congress of the Agudat Yisrael in Warsaw, the girls' colleges are formally approved—after much opposition—as "the only solution to the question of education for girls, which is a difficult and painful problem" (p. 68). The first college in Palestine is begun in Tel Aviv in 1936. By the eve of World War II, there are about 250 Beit Ya'akov schools in Europe and the United States, serving almost forty thousand women.

Female education was conceived explicitly by haredim as a way to compete with the corrosive effects of public or secular, and Zionist education, both of which were becoming widely available to both boys and girls, and men and women. It was thought that it was better to set up, direct, and control educational opportunities from within the haredi community than lose souls to the lures of secularism, socialism, and worse. By carefully tracing the public debate within the haredi community through time—using conference proceedings, journals, magazines and newspapers—El-Or convincingly shows, moreover, that haredi education grew, and, in Israel, was relatively more open and innovative in times of haredi weakness—namely, from the 1950s to the 1970s. By the mid–1970s, as haredi self-confidence and institutional strength grew apace, the female educational system was reined in more tightly. Once again, an apparent paradox appeared. The more vulnerable the community, the more open was the system to self-examination. However, the openness was always, in fact, defensive, and crafted to allow the community to "fight for the souls of their girls and women with the same weapons used by their opponents" (p. 68).

An entire literature in sociology and anthropology argues that acquiring literacy brings to subaltern groups empowerment, autonomy, and social change.[19] El-Or shows how much more complicated the situation is. Knowledge or learning are never acquired in a social vacuum. They are always implicated in wider contexts of social inequality. Thus, an ideologically driven literacy—such as with the haredim—does not so much serve to "blur class, sexual, ethnic, and racial divisions," as it serves "to reproduce them in other, complex ways" (p. 73). Just how complex these ways are is shown in a series of vivid depictions and deconstructions of adult classes and lectures attended by El-Or. This is the heart of the book.

Among other things, El-Or demonstrates how the women are taught to avoid substantive issues—such as those dealing, with respect to Torah and Talmud—with speculation, critical inquiry, hermeneutics, or understanding of the sources of the Law. All are considered to be negative and dangerous for women to engage in. The ideal life for a young man (an *avrech*) is to devote all his time to the study of Torah. These young women, by contrast, are exposed to their teachers saying the Torah "is what defines all our life," and then posing the puzzle—worthy of any Zen master—"And what [then] about woman? After all, she is not required to study. How does the Torah become hers? First, not by study!" (p. 103). Or they are admonished about the proper way to approach their studies.

> Given that we are women . . . We will be like poor people given permission to walk through the court of a king. We will gather up the leftover food, enjoy the splendor and beauty of the garden, pick up what we find in the courtyards. . . . (p. 101)

Or, in a class studying the laws governing the Shabbat, they are told outright that "We do not study in order to make rulings. That's for men. . . ." (p. 123).

In place of substantive issues, the women are taught and encouraged to engage with the practical, such as laws relating to or techniques for housekeeping or childraising— anything that touches directly on their daily lives as women, wives, and mothers. When discussion strays to substantive matters, the women are discouraged by their teachers, and, for the most part, the women discipline themselves (and each other) to avoid straying into forbidden areas. When confronted with the substantive—say, in a lecture on Maimonides by a rabbi and scholar—they transmute it into matters of homemakers' techniques and womanly praxis. Where Sered's old women sacralize their world, El-Or's young women pragmatize it.[20] Sered's women are illiterate, El-Or's educated. However, in their thinking, the latter resemble nothing so much as Levi-Strauss' famous formulation for so-called "savages"— untrained and unwilling to think abstractly, they are "scientists of the concrete."[21]

V

Ultimately, El-Or argues, we must refine our notion of literacy to encompass two sorts, as in a "dual literacy." "Know-how" literacy allows the women to connect to the praxis of their female role expectations. The more loaded "knowledge" literacy brings them into freighted contact with the textual world of Judaic scripture and doctrine—but also, through the media and beyond, with the larger world of secular Israeli society. This latter, of course, is the world that the Gur Hasidim and other haredim (men and women) fear the most. A good deal of El-Or's analysis then concerns the uses of education and literacy in the definition and maintenance of social boundaries between Jew and Gentile (rarely experienced first-hand by these women); and between haredi and *hiloni* (secular); and even between Hasid and Misnagid.

Because the maintenance of these boundaries is so crucial to haredim, these women are not left alone to fashion their own "radically gynocentric" version of Judaism. Again and again in El-Or's narrative we get the feeling that she and her women friends and informants are being watched very carefully by the Gur menfolk—and with no apparent bemusement or indulgence. In fact, taking Sered and El-Or's analyses together in the same frame shows even more that easy generalizations about women's religious lives are just as likely to be as faulty as are generalizations about men's religious lives. In both cases, we need local knowledge—knowledge about the localizing strategies and experiences of lived religions in use.

VI

Turning at last from ethnography to cultural critique, El-Or's final paradox concerns the very existence of the haredim in Israel—or, more precisely, their views of secular Israelis, and the secular Israelis' views of them. Haredim view secular Israelis as "captive children," imprisoned against their will in the false values of Zionism, materialism, and secularism. Secular Israelis, on the other hand, view the haredim with a mixture of contempt or revulsion, and nostalgia or respect. Trusting—perhaps wrongly?—in the modernity of a secular, national identity, and trusting in their state, secular Israelis thought they left questions of Jewishness behind them. Actually, they only left them by default to the Orthodox and ultra-Orthodox. In the book's conclusion, El-Or leads to us to believe that the secularists abdicated the struggle for an authentic Israeli-Jewish identity, and that, therefore, the final and costly paradoxes will remain for them to be resolved.

Notes

1. Ernest Gellner, "Post-Traditional Forms in Islam: The Turf and Trade, and Votes and Peanuts." *Daedalus* 102 (1973), 191.

2. Although it is less clear who has had the last smile; the irony here is that Gellner's story appeared in *Daedalus* a year after Clifford Geertz published "Deep Play: Notes on the Balinese Cockfight," also in *Daedelus* 101 (1972) 1–37. In that epochal essay, Geertz revealed the semiotic nature of anthropology and declared, "The culture of a people is an ensemble of texts . . . which the anthropologist strains to read over the shoulders of those to whom they properly belong." So, just as Gellner proclaimed the epistemological gains to be made by forsaking texts for lives in the village— or at least supplementing the study of one with the other—Geertz had already sounded the opening gun of a revolution in anthropology that would turn village life—indeed, all life as we know it—into the study of texts.

3. Robert Redfield, *Peasant Society and Culture* (Chicago: University of Chicago Press, 1956).

4. See for example Milton Singer, ed., *Krishna: Myths, Rites and Attitudes* (Chicago: University of Chicago Press, 1968).

5. Melford Spiro, *Buddhism and Society* (New York: Harper & Row, 1970).

6. Clifford Geertz, *Islam Observed* (New Haven: Yale University Press, 1968).

7. See, also Lynn Davidman, *Tradition in a Rootless World: Women Turn to Orthodox Judaism* (Berkeley: University of California Press, 1991); and Debra Kaufman, *Rachel's Daughters: Newly Orthodox Women* (New Brunswick: Rutgers University Press, 1991), which treat women's "return" (as *ba'alei teshuvot)* to Orthodoxy. For a look at gender in a very different construal of Judaism (localized here in the United States), see Riv-Ellen Prell, *Prayer and Community: The Havurah in American Judaism* (Detroit: Wayne State University Press, 1989).

8. For example, see Jacob Katz, "Traditional Society and Modern Soceity," in ed. Shlomo Deshen and Walter Zenner, *Jewish*

Societies in the Middle East (Lanham, Md.: University Press of America, 1982) 35–47.

9. But such ideas have resonated particularly strongly in the sociology of Israel. See, S. N. Eisenstadt, *The Absorption of Immigrants* (London: Routledge & Kegan Paul, 1954), for a classical statement of them. For a critical review of this orientation, see, Kevin Avruch, "The Emergence of Ethnicity in Israel," *American Ethnologist* 14:2 (1987), 327–339.

10. For example, Issachar Ben-Ami, *The Folk Veneration of Saints among the Jews of Morocco* (Jerusalem: Magnes Press, 1984), in Hebrew; and Norman Stillman, *The Jews of Arab Lands.* (Philadelphia: Jewish Publication Society, 1979).

11. See, Dale Eickelman, *Moroccan Islam* (Austin: University of Texas Press, 1976).

12. Marshall Sklare, *Conservative Judaism* (New York: Free Press, 1955).

13. To take one pole of the traditional ambivalence, Sered cites the tosafot on the Talmud "Sotah," 21b, where it is written that is preferable to burn the Torah, than teach it to a woman.

14. On the ritualization of literacy, see Shlomo Deshen, "The Ritualization of Literacy: The Works of Tunisian Scholars in Israel," *American Ethnologist* 2:2 (1975) 251–260.

15. Sered writes about the Kurdish Rabbi Hacham Benyamin, who visits, advises, and teaches the women in the center, as a man who views them and their deviations from Orthodoxy with apparent understanding, respect, and indulgent bemusement—but not essentially seriously, as a valid *alternative* form. She also writes about the way in which the women are frustrated at saints' tombs by new regulations of the Ministry of Religious Affairs that now prevent them from throwing lit candles at the tomb, a traditional women's practice.

16. Contrast the unreserved respect the women hold for the male Kurdish Rabbi Hacham Benyamin, with their ambivalence toward female Rabbanit Zohara, who also teaches, visits, and advises them.

17. Sered tells us a little, but not nearly enough, about the adult children—especially the daughters—of these women. Some, we learn, are no longer very observant. And the others? These daughters, mainly born in Israel, are presumably not illiterate. What are their religious lives like? Are they also involved in reconfiguring normative Judaism to a gynocentric perspective? Or is this creative achievement limited to their mothers and grandmothers—a fleeting moment enjoyed only by the often marginalized "generation of the desert"—to use that infamous locution of Zionist *klita*—as that generation waits, finally in Zion, for the end?

18. The book was originally published in Hebrew by Am Oved in 1992. The translator, Haim Watzman, has done a fine job.

19. In anthropology, see Jack Goody's work, *Literacy in Traditional Societies* (Cambridge: Cambridge University Press, 1968); *The Domestication of the Savage Mind* (Cambridge: Cambridge University Press, 1977); and *The Logic of Writing and the Organization of Society* (Cambridge: Cambridge University Press, 1988).

20. In both books we can compare the respectful attention the women pay to male teachers with their ambivalent (sometimes bordering on defiant) feelings toward female teachers. In both books, the male instructors also come across as self-assured, while the females seem given to moments of self-doubt about their roles.

21. Claude Levi-Strauss, *The Savage Mind* (Chicago: University of Chicago Press, 1966).

Part IV

Literature and Culture

In some ways, this final section of *Books on Israel, volume 4,* contains, as a group, the most "critical" of all the critical essays. Are we to be surprised that it is in some of the arts—literature, memoir, and cinema—that critical attitudes are expressed, as in the films described by Gertz)—or brought forth, as in Lahav's rather cutting reading of the generals' memoirs?

All three essays in this section deal in some manner with the past, or with memory, and with reconstructions of both. Pnina Lahav's analysis of the memoirs—and self-apologies—by three important military figures touches on a number of important themes in Israeli culture and society. For example, she reveals much about the division in Israeli society between sabras and immigrants, as well as the manner in which these figures have tried to present themselves. She reveals much about attitudes toward the IDF, and how these were affected by the Yom Kippur War. She also suggests ways in which the generals' deluded themselves, and Israeli society—at a crucial moment in history.

Nancy Berg's review of *sifrut HaMa'abarah*—literature of the transit camp period of the late 1940s through the early

1950s—depicts an alternative—and much less rosy—view of the process of "ingathering of the exiles" and, by extension, of the basic, Zionist values of the state. This literature forms an interesting counterpoint to the recent and controversial revisionist historicizing about the early years after independence. As with several of the essays in this volume, the ethnic dimensions of Israeli society, the Ashkenazi-Sephardi divide, are also stressed.

Similarly, Nurith Gertz, focusing on cinema, underlines how Israeli films and literature of the 1980s and 1990s often returned to themes that were treated in earlier films with a new critical and skeptical eye. There has been much talk of late about Israel's entrance into a so-called "post-Zionist" era—as with "post-modernism," the term itself means different things to different people—talk that invariably invites passion and controversy. (See, also the essays by Tamar Katriel, Aliza Shenhar, and Eve Jacobson, in volume 2 of this series.) However, whatever that term means, the engagement by Israeli artists, poets, novelists and film-makers, with a revamped vision of Israel's key institutions, its past—especially the War of Independence and the IDF, for example—will surely form a crucial part of that debate.

9. Israeli Military Leadership During the Yom Kippur War: Reflections on the Art of Reflection

Pnina Lahav

Gen. (res.) Eli Zeira, *The October 73 War: Myth Against Reality.* (Tel-Aviv: Edanim Publishers, Yediot Aharonot, 1993) (Hebrew).

Brig. Gen. (res.) Arie Braun, *Moshe Dayan and the Yom Kippur War.* (Tel-Aviv: Edanim Publishers, Yediot Aharonot, 1992) (Hebrew).

Brig. Gen. (res.) Yoel Ben-Porat, *Ne'ila: Locked-on.* (Tel-Aviv: Edanim Publishers, Yediot Aharonot, 1991) (Hebrew).

Shortly after the Six-Day War, Elie Wiesel interviewed Colonel Mordechai Gur, commander of the paratroopers who liberated the Western Wall in old Jerusalem. The following exchange took place between the Jewish intellectual and the Israeli commander:[1]

WIESEL: What did you feel?
GUR: I don't think I can put it into words.
WIESEL: Try.

171

GUR: No, I don't think people should discuss their feelings.
WIESEL: What should people discuss?
GUR: Who says you've got to discuss anything? You don't have to.
WIESEL: I beg to differ. It's a duty—and a privilege—to talk . . .

Gur and his comrades-in-arms were not big talkers, neither in private nor in public. Between 1967 and 1973, little deliberation concerning military policy took place in the upper echelons of the military and security establishment. To these men—victors of the Six-Day War and mostly in their forties—the surprise of the coordinated Egyptian-Syrian attack in 1973 was a shattering trauma. Terrible Israeli losses in the first two weeks of the war destroyed their self-confidence. Growing public accusations and recriminations within the military establishment exacerbated their condition.

After the war, public outrage forced the government to appoint a Commission of Inquiry to investigate what came to be called *ha-mechdal* ("the Mishap"), and the lack of preparedness for the war. The Agranat Commission found Chief of Staff David Elazar (Dado), and his Chief of Intelligence, Eli Zeira, personally responsible for the Army's initial failure to foresee and respond adequately to the mounting military threat. The Commission also found that the Minister of Defense, Moshe Dayan, was not personally responsible, and it declined to take a stand concerning his political or parliamentary responsibility. The Commission also declined to measure the political responsibility of then-Prime Minister Golda Meir. Dado and Zeira handed in their resignations, and Gur replaced Dado as Chief of Staff.

Their lives were never the same again. Disgraced and psychologically wounded, the men directed their rage at the Commission for singling them out as culpable. They felt the Commission not only failed to hold accountable the political leaders, but also unfairly exonerated them. Golda and Dayan also paid a price. Indeed, they won the general elections of December 1973, and stayed in office for a short while, but public pressure compelled both to resign. Yitzhak Rabin, the hero of 1967, became Prime Minister. His ascension launched a new era. While Israel talked to its enemies, the disgraced officers took their stories to the publishers.

This review discusses three memoirs published in Israel by the military officers who experienced the Yom Kippur War: Arie Braun, who served as Dayan's adjutant; Eli Zeira, who was the IDF's chief of intelligence; and Yoel Ben-Porat, Chief of Intelligence under Zeira's command.[2]

The books are self-serving accounts of the war's events. Braun rationalizes Dayan's activities prior to and during the war. Zeira tears this version to shreds, insisting that both Dayan and Dado acted irresponsibly before and during the war, and that they were the main culprits. Zeira himself takes no responsibility for the debacle. In Zeira's version of the events, the Intelligence branch met the highest standards of performance, and both it and its chief survive scrutiny. Ben-Porat, Zeira's subordinate, does not share this rosy vision. His book opens a window onto conflicts inside the Intelligence branch. Ben-Porat claims that some, including Zeira, failed to read the writing on the wall and even misled their superiors. Ben-Porat recalls that he, and others, understood the enormity of the Egyptian-Syrian threat, but were prevented from communicating their views to those in the upper echelons.

That the books recount conflicting versions of the same events is an interesting phenomenon in itself. More important, however, is the quality of the discussion and the collective portrait that emerges from between and beneath the lines of the best and brightest of this generation, the elite of Israel's defense forces.

First, a few words about the curiosity of publication. The fact that the officers are engaging in any self-disclosure, albeit self-serving, and that these men have found publishers eager to publish, suggests a perception that there is an audience for information about this war. Indeed, Israelis widely recognize the Yom Kippur War as a watershed event in their history, and they thirst for more discussion of it.

Furthermore, the war shook the consensus that military discourse is best held behind closed doors and is inappropriate for open debate. Openness has slowly been gaining more and more legitimacy. Israelis no longer perceive challenges to prevailing dogma as being disloyal or subversive. Another question, however, is whether this public discourse goes so far as to question the paradigm within which the Zionist enterprise has been unfolding.   Openness of discourse, however, is not enough. Even if a national trauma such as the war could dissolve a culturally based aversion to discussion, a culture of discourse would not automatically replace it. One thing which all three books share is the poor quality of the authors' presentation. The officers cannot write. The books are jammed with inarticulate, repetitive prose. At best, they read as a stream of consciousness. At worst they descend into incoherence. Perhaps our literary expectations of military personnel ought to be low—high command included—particularly given the authors' inexperience as writers. Self-revelation and analysis of close events comes uneasily to them.

One is reminded that Israel's Army always expected itself to be different—not a professional army, but rather a collection of men (women were irrelevant) who consciously decided to sacrifice in service of the State.[3] To generalize from the Wiesel/Gur exchange, this generation was not skilled in articulating thoughts, particularly when the fullest expression of those thoughts bordered on an iconoclasm that soldiers found to be intolerable. Furthermore, military leaders of the era were so intent on "doing" rather than talking,[4] that they never developed an ability to meditate on the meaning of the events which they precipitated. In addition to their lack of reflection in military matters, the officers appear to be out of touch with their feelings. We shall discuss this further within this chapter.

The poor editorial quality of the three books also leads the reader to wonder about Israel's publishers and editors of the early 1990s. The books—all published by Edanim Press—would have benefitted greatly from an experienced editorial hand. All three accounts read like draft manuscripts rushed to publication without prior review.

The narrative structure of all three books displays a formal distinction between objective reportage and value-guided analysis. The authors declare that they are merely recounting so-called "facts" as they actually were, leading the reader to the correct conclusions—that is, the conclusions that served the same political motive that compelled the authors to publish. This rigid separation between facts and values is designed to cloak the authors in objectivity. Their goal is to lure us into thinking that this authoritative account of facts finally sets the record straight as to who really caused "the Mishap." The hidden agenda is promotion of the authors' version in which each one alone escapes responsibility for Israel's unreadiness.

The premise of this approach is disturbing. The authors' devotion to facts—and their refusal to reflect on the moral significance and political consequences of those facts—reveals a serious deficiency in Israel's military elite. Twenty years after the war, the authors still conceive of themselves as pawns on the chessboard. One searches in vain for an acknowledgement that this war was a part of a larger historical process, initiated by the staggering victory of 1967 which engendered confusion, paralyzed thinking, and entrenched the status quo. There appears to be no awareness that this stagnation, rooted in the ambiguity of the Zionist project from its inception, affected everything—foreign affairs, security policies, and the psychological climate. However, rather than situate the war in this historical context, the authors confine themselves to a technical discussion. The result is dry, detailed accounts that proceed from the premise that some mistakes were made in the few months prior to the war. The authors very carefully attribute these errors to others. Had these mistakes been avoided, the authors conclude, Israel would have repeated its glorious performance of 1967.

A good example of this genre is Arie Braun's book, *Moshe Dayan and the Yom Kippur War*. Braun, a retired Brigadier General, served as Dayan's adjutant prior to and during the war.

Dayan was one of Israel's most charismatic and controversial leaders. One always welcomes more information about
this extraordinary man who stood at the helm of Israeli Security since independence, served as Minister of Defense from
1967 to 1973, and played a crucial role in shaping Israeli
policy. What was Dayan's leadership style? Did he surround
himself with sycophants, or did he welcome a broad spectrum of views?

These questions are of extreme importance in this context, because the most important post–1967 phenomenon in
Israeli politics was Israel's self-image as a regional superpower that could comfortably enjoy the status quo until the
Arabs accepted its conditions for peace. Dayan encouraged
this new self-satisfied state of mind. Did Dayan's lieutenants
contribute to this new world view by challenging his authority? Or did Dayan, alone, transform Israel?

Braun opens his book with a description of his very first
meeting with then-Defense Minister Dayan, who

> ... emphasized ... that he expected complete candor. I
> should tell him my opinions, he said, in every subject
> and every area—without fear. He promised to "descend"
> on me if I suppressed my views ... because of shame,
> fear or any other reason." (p.10)

In spite of this exhortation to be candid, the entire book
describes no blunt encounters between Dayan and Braun.
Only on the last page (p.363) are we told that

> On the second day of the war, I used the order Dayan
> gave me to speak to him candidly, and I proposed that
> he take over as direct commander of the armed forces,
> instead of the Chief of Staff who lost control of the army.

Dayan declined to act on Braun's suggestion.

Here are the seeds of a fascinating story about Dayan's
relationship with Dado—an equally elusive figure—and about
Dayan's rapport with Braun. What circumstances prompted
Braun to advocate this maneuver? Was Braun alone in feeling that Dado had lost control? Did Dayan have good reasons for acting contrary to Braun's recommendation? What

did Dayan really think of Dado and why? The reader is told none of this. Instead, the book dryly rehearses details widely known, with virtually no effort to give them color or depth.

Take, for example, the famous allegation that Dayan's confidence collapsed on the third day of the war and that he began talking of "the destruction of the Third Commonwealth."[5] Some accounts suggest that he had sunk so deeply into pessimism that Golda Meir asked him not to address the people on television and, instead, assigned the task to Zeira's predecessor, General (res.) Aharon Yariv.[6] Braun denies that Dayan ever foretold the destruction of the Third Commonwealth (p.98). Braun concedes that Dayan did not anticipate unqualified success, but explains Dayan's pessimism as the inevitable result of a conservative strategist's cynical evaluation of the military situation (pp.98–99, 129, 133).

Given the abundance of stories about Dayan's loss of heart, however, it is a disappointment that Braun—who was, after all, Dayan's adjutant—does not offer a more substantial account than this. From a person who stood with Dayan during these moments one would expect insight into Dayan's state of mind, his private comments, and his reaction to the fact that the military command perceived him as a defeatist. Braun simply recounts already well-known exchanges and instructs the reader to deduce no defeatism.

Braun also fails to enlighten us about Dayan's position regarding the so-called "war of the generals"—that is, the quarrels among Dado, Gonen, and Sharon as the army desperately tried to contain the Egyptian invasion. Shortly before the war, General Shmuel Gonen replaced Gen. Arik Sharon as chief of the Southern Command. As a result, Sharon, who in the Yom Kippur War led a military division, found himself subordinate to Gonen. In their contests, Chief of Staff Dado tended to side with Gonen, while Dayan supported Sharon.

Furthermore, Braun presents Dayan's failure to resign from the government as evidence of Dayan's integrity and sense of responsibility. Surely the picture is more complex:

How responsible did Dayan feel? How much personal responsibility did he take for the years of glory and conceit, between 1967 and 1973? Could it be that he hastily embraced Golda Meir's refusal to accept his resignation because he could not face his own guilt? Did he fail to resign because he was terrified of conceding responsibility? Was he hoping to make amends, to show the people that he could still be worthy of their trust? The rich undercurrent beneath Dayan's public persona still waits to be explored.

Retired General Eli Zeira's book, *The October 73 War: Myth Against Reality,* effectively destroys Braun's version. Brilliant and able, the Israeli-born Zeira had a meteoric military career, a career squashed in the aftermath of the 1973 War. Zeira's reputation within the political and military leadership skyrocketed in May 1973, when he speculated—accurately, as it turns out—that war was unlikely, even in the face of Egypt's massive concentration of troops on the border. Zeira repeated his prediction in October 1973, but, this time, he was wrong. For this error he paid dearly, losing more than his high military position and reputation. Public opinion targeted Zeira as the one man whose failure to sound the alarm made Israel's defeat inevitable. As a result of Zeira's abdication, Israel was unable to defend herself properly. Because Israeli military men expected complete sacrifice to the State to be a defining aspect of service, Zeira's failure to protect Israel from the Egyptian threat must have weighed heavily on him.

Zeira depicts himself as hurt, misunderstood, and betrayed. The book reveals a determination to prove that others were responsible for failing to sound the alarm. Thus, the book reads like the monologue of an obsessed and wounded soul, desperately yearning for exoneration. Perhaps it is an apologia to himself.

The narrative oscillates between the first and third persons. At times, he simply recounts events from his own perspective, as a diarist. At other times, he plays the unbiased reporter, referring to himself in the third person. This might be yet another device to persuade the reader of the inherent objectivity of his version. The text is full of unnecessary exclamation marks, impressing upon the reader the flaws in competing renditions of the events, rhetorical questions designed to underscore his own infallible logic, and repetition of the main points, as if he simply cannot restrain himself or hopes that repetition will persuade. All of these flaws, one suspects, signify not only bad writing skills and a lack of editing, but, rather, an emotional turbulence that still torments him and that he does not permit himself to confront emotionally.

Zeira insists that Israel's unpreparedness be attributed to a disregard for time-honored Israeli military doctrine. Military tradition holds that, regardless of the enemy's intent, Israel should activate the military reserves each time the enemy amasses troops on the border, no matter how expensive or frequent the action might be. Zeira asserts that even this would not have helped, because the Air Force failed to account for the possibility of missile technology in Egypt and Syria. The presence of missiles, Zeira observes, neutralized the Air Force, and prevented it from performing its expected role as "flying artillery." Zeira further maintains that the nature of the Intelligence's obligation to warn did not encompass a responsibility to provide information as to the enemy's intent. Rather, "warning" required Intelligence to supply information about actual preparations for war. Zeira claims that Dado, Dayan, and Meir had this information in abundance. Dado, Dayan, and Meir's failure to interpret the facts is theirs alone, not his.

Zeira also condemns Dayan for failing to follow up on his own declaration in the summer of 1973 that war was imminent. Finally, Zeira attacks the Agranat Commission and Israel's Supreme Court for favoring the politicians, for failing to interpret the facts correctly—meaning, as Zeira sees them—and for reaching erroneous conclusions as to accountability.

Zeira's main arguments are thoughtful and interesting, even though many of them have already been aired in the available literature. His intended "scoop" is that King Hussein personally informed Golda Meir of the impending war, which is information that he suggests she withheld from the Agranat Commission. Nevertheless, Zeira's strategy of presenting himself as a small cog in the military machinery is not credible. His repetitive assertions that he took no part in the Mishap are, at best, unpersuasive. Here is a high-ranking general, widely acknowledged for his sterling abilities, with access to the Prime Minister, the Minister of Defense, and the Chief of Staff. Why did he not raise his voice when he realized that, despite ominous warnings about heavy military concentration on the border, Meir, Dayan, and Dado were flouting Israeli military doctrine? Why did Zeira not sound the alarm, or even resign, in an effort to draw public attention to the gravity of the situation? Similarly, if he understood that the Air Force was ill-prepared to fight the war, why did he keep silent? Zeira might claim either that he understood this only in a hindsight, or that the atmosphere at the time discouraged dissenting views. Either interpretation would give us important insights into the Israeli elite just before the war. Instead, Zeira merely shifts responsibility to his superiors, avoiding reflection on his own contributions. His claim that the business of Intelligence is merely to supply facts is ludicrous. Zeira would have done better to meditate on the central question: Why did an officer as bright and able as he was fail to see the writing on the wall? What factors in Israeli political culture and military organization facilitated ignorance of President Sadat's strategy since 1971?

Yoel Ben-Porat's book *Ne'ila: Locked On*, does not provide any insights into this question. It does, however, cast doubt on Zeira's claim that Israel's military intelligence performed its role adequately in the weeks preceding the war. Ben-Porat, Zeira's subordinate and Chief of Intelligence prior to and during the war, chose the title of his book from the final chapter in the Yom Kippur services—Ne'ila—when Jews pray for mercy before the gates of heaven close. While Ben-Porat's text suffers most from the lack of editing, his prose is rich and frequently draws on Jewish sources. By contrast, Braun and Zeira's prose display no reference to Jewish culture.

The title—Ne'ila—is a playful double entendre. "Locked On" aptly describes the terror that seized Israel as she confronted her own vulnerability. The title also alludes to the leadership's state of mind—that is, locked into the misconception that the Arabs did not have a military option and would never challenge Israel's self-perceived invincibility (p. 16).

Ben-Porat's book develops two principal objections to Zeira's account. First, he argues that the Intelligence had the capability and the responsibility for interpreting data as to the enemy's intent. Second, he disputes Zeira's factual argument that adequate warning was not within Zeira's capabilities. Not only was Zeira culpable for shirking this responsibility, but he was also guilty of obstructing the channels of communication. Ben-Porat claims that Zeira felt so confident in his assessment of the low probability of war that he refused to credit—and even censored—all information to the contrary (pp. 54, 64–668, 100, 115).

Although Ben-Porat is more perceptive and introspective than either Braun or Zeira, a disturbing image emanates from his prose. Through Ne'ila we see a man on the edge. Perhaps Ben-Porat has never recovered from the shock of the war, or from his guilt over his part in failing to give adequate warning. One wonders if the persistent denial and suppression, so characteristic of Braun and Zeira, is rooted in some flight from self-awareness.

The Holocaust pervades the dispute between Zeira and Ben-Porat. The two books reveal the profound effects which the Holocaust has had on the Israeli psyche, and, more importantly, on the dynamics of the relationship between survivors and Sabras.[7] Ben-Porat is a Holocaust survivor. He tells us about his background while attempting to explain his lifelong obsession with "intelligence." Ben-Porat was eight years old when the war began. An early recollection has his father arguing that disaster was imminent. Ben-Porat remembers his father urging the Jews to leave their native

Galicia. Ultimately, the father succumbed to family pressure to stay, and only Ben-Porat survived the Holocaust.

Ben-Porat became obsessed with "intelligence"—data-gathering about the enemy—and with "warning"—divining in advance the enemy's intent. He wrote about

> ... wars, bombings, strategic surprises, partisans and everything that soaked into my personality. The Great Carnage [a term he prefers to the Holocaust] and everything before and after ... all of these ... made me into an intelligence officer, cautious and dedicated to a single issue—advanced warning. (p.46)

Given Ben-Porat's near-obsession with ascertaining the enemy's intent, it is not surprising that he faults Intelligence for Israel's lack of preparedness thirty years after the Holocaust.

In this drama, Zeira is the protagonist. Born and raised in Haifa, Zeira was a typical product of Zionist dogma, which held that Jewish life in Israel was superior to life in exile and that native Israeli children epitomized that superiority. Zeira's story reads like a Zionist textbook. In 1935, at the age of seven, he took a trip to Lodz, Poland, to visit his mother's family. In a summer home in the Polish countryside, the Sabra and his Jewish/Polish cousins encountered local Polish boys armed with sticks, and eager for a fight. The cousins became frightened and ran away, signalling to Zeira to follow suit. However, the Sabra stayed and fought. Zeira recounts the story's aftermath.

> They [his mother's family] were struck by fear, since from experience they knew that the parents of the local boys will come to take revenge. That night we packed our belongings and by the morning the entire family ... returned to Lodz (p. 243).

The moral of the story is clear. Jews in Galut, or exile, were meek and fearful, and they did not stand up for themselves. Zeira next remembers saying farewell to his mother's family at the Lodz train station. The family urged his mother to stay. What was the point in living in the desert of Palestine? The moral of this story is a reminder. In the great battle between the Zionists, who chose the desert, and the non-Zionist middle-class Jews of Lodz, the Zionists won. Zeira never saw his cousins again.

> A few of them probably left on their final way to the death camps from that same Lodz train station. Only in order to ensure that such a Holocaust will not recur was it worth to establish the Jewish State! (p.15)

A part of Sabra culture was profound disdain for anything associated with Galut, or exile. Sabras stereotyped Holocaust survivors as meek and obedient, the antithesis of the courageous and daring Sabra. Israel's Army elite consisted of men such as Dayan, Zeira, Gur, and Braun, all quintessential Sabras. The prerequisite to joining that elite was not necessarily birth in Israel, but rather assimilation of Sabra culture. For example, Dado was born in Sarajevo and immigrated to Palestine with a youth group in 1941 when he was sixteen years old. Dado's biographer tells us that, within six months of arrival in Israel, Dado's youth group, staying in a kibbutz, held a ritual of "burning the Yugoslav language," and, henceforth, spoke Hebrew alone.[8] By purging the attributes which tied him to "there," Dado had the good fortune of earning acceptance into Sabra culture.

Men such as Ben-Porat were not so fortunate. Once branded a "Polish officer"—an Israeli colloquial for being meek and obedient—he was, by definition, inferior to the veterans of the Palmach. Ben-Porat internalized these stereotypes. Several times in his book he refers to himself as a "Polish officer"—for example on page 106—and reveals his awareness of Zeira's distinction between natives and "others" (p.107).

For example, compare Ben-Porat's smoldering anger with Zeira's banal smugness. Ben-Porat wrote

> I told you, the reader, the story of my life. . . . I wished to describe the anatomy of a professional intelligence officer, not to impress with [H]olocaust stories. Maybe, one day, when they stop saying [that Jews went to their death] "like lambs to the slaughter" I shall tell my story. Not now." (p.46)

In contrast, Zeira wrote

> I had the great privilege to participate in the establish-
> ment of the State of Israel and to contribute to strength-
> ening her security, so that Jews no longer will go like
> lambs to the slaughter. (p.243)

Neither the years in which Zeira worked closely with Ben-Porat, nor the volumes of literature on the complex meaning of the Holocaust, shook Zeira's attachment to the old cliches.

In the final analysis, it is this dogmatic frame of mind that undermined the military officers. They were all good men, highly intelligent and totally dedicated to the Jewish State. However, they were raised as true believers in a strict orthodox ideology, which held that Galut was bad; that Jewish sovereignty was the supreme value; that the purpose of the Jewish State was to prevent another holocaust; that doing, not thinking, was what really mattered; and that reflection on these time-honored principles was a waste of time. Within this rigid paradigm they were free to be playful and dare, but they were not to question the paradigm itself. So, they, as did their Jewish cousins in Europe, became mired in the status quo. When they themselves reached positions of leadership, they did not know how to question received ideology and doctrine.[9] This is the true meaning of the Mishap of 1973. The Six-Day War made them feel that they had fulfilled their lifelong dream of seeing Israel become a secure and mighty state, immune to another holocaust. At the same time, the victory strengthened their stereotyped view of the Arab enemy as incompetent and weak. President Sadat was the big talker, incessantly making announcements about an impending war. They constantly affirmed their own agency—except now, the doing was easy, and they could enjoy the fruits of their labor. The Yom Kippur War rekindled the old fear. The idea that they, themselves, might have brought about a new holocaust was too overwhelming to behold. Thus, they occupied themselves with building elaborate defenses, the essence of which was that their superiors, not they, should be held responsible for the Mishap.

Twenty years after the Yom Kippur War, the most amazing phenomenon continues to be this escape from responsibility and the lack of accountability among both the politicians and the military. Leadership demands critical reflection. The role of a leader includes both dependence on others, and an ability to exercise independent judgment. A sober understanding of consequences enables leaders to invest historical events with meaning, and to reconstruct them in a broader context. The military officers and their political leaders did not cultivate critical reflection. Even the passage of time—the twenty years that separate us from that war—have not brought about a change in perspective.

A part of the explanation lies within Israeli culture. Israelis are not encouraged to reflect on their actions nor on the meaning of their existence. Eli Wiesel—an outsider—captured this point in his exchange with Mordechai Gur, quoted in the introduction to this review: "Who says you've got to discuss anything? You don't have to," protested Gur. "It's a duty—a privilege—to talk . . . ," responded Wiesel.

Of course, generalization can be deceptive. Not all Israelis shun reflection, and not all Diaspora Jews see it as a duty and a privilege. Still, a sense remains that these books represent a part of Israel—bright, capable, and dedicated people who were raised within a nondiscursive paradigm and were never able to transcend it. These qualities might well have been indispensable qualities in 1948, even in 1967. However, changing circumstances required reflection, the lack of which made the calamity of 1973 inevitable.

Notes

1. Quoted in Amos Elon, *The Israelis, Founders and Sons.* (New York, 1971) 239. Elon's pathbreaking book—a bestseller in its time—was the first critical collective portrait of the Jewish majority in Israel.

2. A. Braun, *Moshe Dayan and the Yom Kippur War.* (Tel-Aviv: 1992) E. Zeira, *The October '73 War: Myth Against Reality.* (Tel-Aviv: 1993); Yoel Ben-Porat, *Ne'ila: Locked-On.* (Tel-Aviv: 1991). All three books are in Hebrew.

3. For example, Zeira was offered a scholarship to study at Cambridge, and then join the Technion's faculty. He refused, and joined the Palmach (Zeira, p. 15).

4. Recall Ben Gurion's famous statement: "Heed not what the Goyim say, heed to what the Jews do." For interesting discussions, see, Shapiro, Yonathan, *Elit Lēlo Mamshichim*, Tel-Aviv, Sifriyat Poalim, 1984; Keren Michael, *Ben-gurion and the Intellectuals: Power, Knowledge, and Charisma*, DeKalb, Ill: Northern Illinois University Press, 1983; Sprinzak, Ehud, *Ish Ha-yashar Be-enav: I-legalizm Ba-hevrah Ya-yisreelit*, Tel-Aviv: Sifriyat poalim, 1986; Slater, Robert, *Warrior Stateman, The Life of Moshe Dayan*, New York: St. Martin's Press, 1991; Z. Shif and E. Haber, *Leksikon Le-vithon Yisrael*, Tel-Aviv: Zemorah, Bitan Modan, 1976.

5. R. Slater, *Warrior Statesman, The Life of Moshe Dayan*. (New York: 1991) 349–360. See, also Z. Schiff and E. Haber, *Israel, Army and Defense, A Dictionary*. (Jerusalem: 1976), 136. The Hebrew equivalent of the "Third Commonwealth" is the "Third Temple."

6. See, Slater, *Warrior Stateman*, 365. According to Braun, Dayan simply deferred to the wish of the daily editors who preferred to develop a strategy of breaking the news to the public by themselves. Braun fails to explain the relationship between his version of the facts and the fact that General Yariv was chosen to address the people.

7. *Sabra* is a colloquial term for a person born or raised in Israel. Literally, it means the fruit of the cactus—sweet inside and rough outside. In Israeli culture, it connotes a liberated personality, or the antithesis of the Jew of Diaspora or Galut.

8. Bartov, Hanokh, *Dado: 48 Shana Ve-od 20 Yom*, Tel-Aviv: Sifriyat Maariv, 1978, vol. 1. Dado returned to Kiryat Chaim. In hindsight, it was an important experience—he left the narrow circle of the Yugoslav group and the Kibbutz, stayed with Sabras and was accepted by them not only as one of them but as their . . . leader. He was no longer a new immigrant. (p. 25)

9. Shapira, *Elit, passim.*

10. *Sifrut HaMa'abarah* (Transit Camp Literature): Literature of Transition

Nancy E. Berg

Eli Amir, *Tarnegol Kaparot* (*Fowl of Atonement*). Sifriyat Ofakim 113. (Tel Aviv: Am Oved, 1983).

Shimon Ballas, *HaMa'abarah* (*The Transit Camp*) (Tel Aviv: Am Oved, 1964).

Sami Michael, *Shavim VeShavim Yoter* (*Equal and More Equal*) (Tel Aviv: Boostan, 1974).

> *Our expectations from the country were great, a mixture of messianic dreams and unrealistic aspirations, but the reality was different: crisis followed crisis—economic, social, religious, and moral. The hardest of all was the search for identity, a search for the personal I and the collective; and on top of all of these came an additional blow—[the crisis] of culture.*
> —Eli Amir[1]

I

$\mathcal{T}$he crises which Eli Amir describes were shared by many upon their arrival to Israel during the period of mass immigration in 1948 to 1951. From their own experiences—and those of their friends, relatives and neighbors—comes the subgenre of immigrant literature—*Sifrut Hama'abarah* (transit camp literature)—a subgenre concerned with the moment of conjunction and confrontation between both the immigrant's personal history and the collective history of Israel. The literature of transition, written predominantly by Israelis of Iraqi origin, is frequently characterized by the sharp contrast between the newcomers' expectations, and the lack of welcome they received, the bleak descriptions of the physical conditions of the transit camps in contrast to life in the country of origin, and the clash between the cultures of the newcomers and the veteran settlers. The plot describes the difficulties encountered by the characters—in particular, the fragmentation of the family unit, and the crisis of identity. These novels, written in the realistic mode, create adolescent protagonists and large casts of secondary characters which often remain underdeveloped. The authors make use of institutions which are central to Israeli society as background, examining them as mechanisms for promoting integration of the characters into Israeli society.

Foremost among these institutions was the *ma'abarah* (transit camp), the precursor of today's *merkaz klitah* (absorption center). New immigrants were settled in the overcrowded *ma'abarot*, often sharing with another family a tin cabin (*pahon*) or a canvas shack (*badon*) that could not withstand the winter rains. The shacks had neither electricity nor comforts. The communal facilities were located as much as a kilometer away or more.[2]

Underlying the situation—and the literature which encodes it—is a certain irony, in that the success of Zionism in establishing a State caused a rupture in the Jewish experience similar to that caused by exile. The Zionist dream of the ingathering of the exiles has, in effect, made exiles of many of the ingathered—if only temporarily. While the movement of the Babylonian Jewish community to Israel was seen as part of the fulfillment of the Zionist dream, literature resulting from this move questions the assumptions of the dream.

II

The realities of Israeli society at the time of each novel's publication have contributed to their respective critical reception and current status. Shimon Ballas's *HaMa'abarah (The Transit Camp)* was published in 1964, the same year as Katzenelson's polemical *HaMahapekhah HaAshkenazit* (The Ashkenazi Revolution). Ballas's book is the first literary work about life in the transit camp by a former resident, but is not without precedent. *Shesh Kenafaim LeEhad (Each One Has Six Wings)*, by Hanoch Bartov,[3] was the winner of the 1955 Keren Kayemet Ussishkin Prize. It was the first work to be recognized as a transit camp novel (*roman hama'abarah*).[4] It takes place in a poor neighborhood outside of Jerusalem, rather than in an actual transit camp, and tells of various immigrants from different countries of origin.

Despite the diversity of the characters' origins, an Ashkenazi perspective dominates, always returning to the experience of the European war, and referring to Mizrachim in stereotyped terms by both its characters and the narrator. A negative view of the mass immigration is expressed by one character. "The Achilles' heel of this aliyah is the lack of selectivity. Backward elements and so forth . . ." (p.246). The criticism is answered by the story's outcome, and even more directly by the protagonist herself, despite her status as Sabra and war hero.

Also included is the story of the young immigrant Menashe who leaves his family to join a kibbutz. In doing so, he realizes the Zionist dream as held by the early settlers. The novel ends happily with the birth of a child to a pair of Holocaust survivors, their own Sabra to be named after the native-born teacher who first helped them adjust to their new life. They choose a name "that isn't a remembrance of anything, so she doesn't carry it on her shoulders" (p.319), less in gratitude than in representation a new start.

Despite the elision of the Mizrachi experience, the book is significant, not only because of the near-centrality of the immigrant experience, but also because it deals—at least marginally—with the issue of communism. "In America they call it—communism, here—Zionism." (p.251).

Ballas's novel is almost a rewriting of *Shesh Kanafaim*. Just as the earlier book describes the development of a neighborhood community, *HaMa'abarah* details the organizing of the transit camp. Both present many characters and their stories in ensemble style. However, it represents an important departure signalled by the opening of the novel. Here, the birth of a baby occurs at the beginning of the narrative, and is hardly a cause for celebration. Rather than a symbol of hope for the future, the baby is born dead. Its stillbirth is a collective tragedy that catalyzes the rest of the plot.

In a significant departure from the earlier model, Ballas privileges the Mizrahi over the Ashkenazi viewpoint. Almost all of the characters are Iraqis. The Ashkenazim serve as the reference group for the protagonists, setting the normative standard. They are called "the Yiddish"[5] by the Iraqis, highlighting the centrality of language. Their presence is evoked by the *ma'abarah* residents to check unruly behavior. "The Yiddish are laughing at us. They say the Iraqis are savages— each at his brother's throat . . . They say we are uncivilized, lazy . . ."[6] Ashkenazim do not play a large role, because it is the transit camp, not the ethnic question, that is under discussion.[7] The main thrust of the novel shows the process of resolving the tensions between the values brought from "back there" and public Zionism in an acceptance of the principles of democracy.

Iraqi readers complained that their past was not well-represented by Ballas's novel,[8] but such representation is clearly not the aim of the work. Life in Iraq remains outside of the narrative, serving as a distant context for life in the camp. Instead, the book emphasizes the present of the *ma'abarah* with only scant references to the glory of the past. Ballas has said, "I wanted to represent a certain reality . . . the reality of life in the transit camp."[9]

The contemporary critics—all Ashkenazim—varied in their judgements of the novel's literary merit. Some even ignored the standard questions of literary criticism, much to the author's dismay.[10] One reviewer dismissed the book as "literary reportage," and commented that it was "not the story of the Second Israel (that is, Jews of Middle Eastern background) which we have long been awaiting."[11] A more favorable review characterized the style as "quasi-documentary," and opined that Hebrew literature was not yet mature enough to include the Tolstoy which such a story required. However, she judged the novel as "readable," "interesting," and "relevant,"[12] and, in a different review, she remarked on the success of the book in being "[a window to a world which] we couldn't find our way to by ourselves."[13]

Another reviewer praised the author's ability to write and to engage the reader from the beginning, as well as his mature perspective. She concluded that "it was good that [HaMa'abarah] was written, and seventy times more so that it was written without bitterness."[14] The writer of the review titled "The genre of 'I accuse' in the transit camp" clearly disagreed with this assessment.[15] It is undoubtedly a very personal reading, as the tone of the novel itself is not bitter.[16] A few of the characters express their dissatisfaction with regret or clever irony.[17] Yet, the bitterness is not directed against anyone, and comes only from the characters, and not the narrator.

More than twenty years after the publication of HaMa'abarah Yahil-Wax described it as "a novel about Israel in which Zionism is not mentioned."[18] The book clearly did not belong to the canon which focused on the collective experience and the promotion of positive values. However, it is not because the book has nothing to do with the discussion on Zionism that it could not fit into the canon, but rather that it asks a different question from those in the canon. Contemporary stories began the quest to define a new Israeli identity for the majority (the Ashkenazi) with recognition of a minority (usually Arab) presence.[19] The canon has had difficulty finding a place for the novel because of its difference.[20] It offers a new perspective on the experience of the ingathered exiles in the promised land of Zion.

III

The decade following the publication of Ballas's book bore witness to the rise of the Black Panthers [*Panterim Sheḥorim*], which came to the attention of the public in 1971. They were a political group which expressed the frustrations and anger of the "Second Israel," and challenged the Ashkenazi hold on political power.[21] The ethnic question, declared politically dead in 1969,[22] was revived as a social issue by the Black Panthers. The protest took most of Israel by surprise. The Panthers achieved modest success before fading into the background.[23] The government continues to be blamed for the *ma'abarot* and the institutionalized discrimination against Middle Eastern Jews.[24] In 1974, Sāmī Michael published his first novel *Shavim VeShavim Yoter,* a book which confronted these issues.

Shavim VeShavim Yoter is the story of David Asher's initiation to a new world, his transition from youth to adulthood, and from exile to absorption. It is set against the backdrop of the Ashkenazi/Mizraḥi conflict.[25] The narrative is told from the point of view of the protagonist, an Iraqi immigrant, and in his own voice. It alternates between David's fighting in the Six-Day War, and his earlier experiences as a youth in the *ma'abarah* with his family where he falls in love with an Ashkenazi girl—to the consternation of her mother. The failure of their marriage contrasts sharply with the conventions of contemporary movies dealing with the Mizraḥim. Here, the marriage of the mixed couple is presented, not as a solution to the ethnic gap, but as a source of greater ethnic conflict.[26]

The two parts of the narrative merge at the end, corresponding to David's integration as a whole person. The integration process is shown to be prolonged and painful. For David, leaving the transit camp does not mean leaving it behind. He achieves both psychological and social integration when he finally accepts Israeli standards, allowing them to complement his original values. By the strength of his inner character, he saves his Ashkenazi army comrade and becomes a wartime hero. While he has not yet won back his Ashkenazi bride, she gives him reason to hope. Yet, his son is the greatest source of optimism. David can now bequeath to him—the result of a mixed marriage—not only his dark skin (Iraqi heritage), but also a hero for a father (Israeli identity).

The Army, which begins as a demoralizing experience, eventually serves to integrate David fully into Israeli society. He enters the war under protest.

> They won't do a job on me ... I go out to war not as a Jew, nor as an Israeli; I go out as a black Sephardi. If I return from this business alive—I'll return to my previous status . . . my skin color and ethnicity marked on my forehead like the sign of Cain.[27]

Previously he refers to various acts of discrimination against Sephardim in the Army, and the high incidence of suicides. "Guys like me had no place in the Army."[28] He emphasizes the ethnic gap when he introduces his unit, which includes "Yoram, the commanding officer—Ashkenazi, of course;" Rafael the Yemenite, and "that Efraim." a Sephardi soldier with special training, who is the exception that proves the rule to Ashkenazi officers and Sephardi privates.[29]

David literally saves his own life through the use of Hebrew, convincing his rescuers that he, too, is an Israeli rather than an enemy Arab soldier. His Palmakh-like heroism during the 1967 War is an act of redemption. This heroism makes him belong. ". . . I am an Israeli citizen. For the first time in my life, I acted as a citizen whose skin color was not an obstacle, not a physical defect."[30] The maturity he gains through his experiences in the Army allows him to go beyond the categories of Ashkenazi/Sephardi, or oldtimer and newcomer, and to become an Israeli.

The critics generally decried the novel's bitter tone and its artlessness. One critic described it as "sewn with a black thread on white fabric."[31] She complained that the writer did not take the situation of the newly established state into account in his protest.[32] Admittedly, while the book shows flaws common to those of a first novel, the oversimplification of issues into binary categories—black and white, good and bad, Sephardi and Ashkenazi—serves to reflect and underline the protagonist's perspective. In questioning the validity of the protagonist's generalizations, the opposing generalizations are called into question as well.

As was the case with the Panthers, the novel was seen as being more radical than it actually is. Such a misreading influenced the critical resistance. While it exposed an issue that is problematic to Israeli society, it did not seek to undermine the structure of society—nor did the Panthers. They did not call for a revolution. Rather, they asked to be allowed to participate in the social institutions of Israel, and—in particular—the Army.[33] In the novel, the Army serves an integrating and democratizing function. *Shavim VeShavim Yoter* validates a primary Israeli social institution, and embraces the mainstream myth of heroism. Of the three novels under discussion in this chapter, it is arguably the most affirming of Zionism and Israel.[34]

IV

The ten years following the publication of Sāmī Michael's novel in 1974 brought many changes to Israel, including a rise in immigration from Eastern Europe and the West. No longer were immigrants automatically associated with Arab and Islamic lands. The Labor party, in power since before the period of mass immigration, was defeated in the elections in 1977. The ethnic question shifted to being constructed as a cultural issue. *Tarnegol Kaparot (Fowl of Atonement)* by Eli Amir reflects this change in emphasis. His novel takes place mostly on the kibbutz, and emphasizes the psychological and cultural crises of the main character, Nūrī.[35]

In *Tarnegol Kaparot,* the kibbutz setting highlights many of the crises of the immigrant, functioning as a microcosm for the Zionist nation. The novel tells the story of a youth caught in the conflict between the Iraqi and the Israeli ways of life. Nūrī is forced to decide between joining the kibbutz—

where he has been placed temporarily—and staying permanently or returning to the *ma'abarah* to help support his family. His dilemma is played out in the cultural context: challenging his musical taste, his accent, his habits, and his religious customs.

His reluctance to abandon familiar customs does not preclude him from entertaining curiosity about the new ways and educating himself. Nūrī's first introduction to Western classical music mystifies him.

> Who was Beethoven? What strange music it was. Everything in it was the same ... And the way they (the Ashkenazim) listened to the music—without interjections, without exclamations of admiration! What point was there to music if it didn't do something to your heart—something that softened your face and your eyes?[36]

It also piques his interest. Nūrī learns about classical music, and, to the surprise of the "locals," participates enthusiastically in the next Western classical music quiz.

His introduction to Israeli or Western culture is less traumatic than is his introduction to Israeli secularism. Along with cultural identity Nūrī is confronted with questions about his religious beliefs and practices. The paradoxical nature of the situation—traditional Judaism as less of a presence in the Jewish State of Israel—is the source of the conflict. The secular nature of the Jewish nation is difficult for Nūrī and his friends to understand. Many of the nation's founders were ardent socialists, intent on creating a society that stood in opposition to the traditional religious enclaves of European Jewry. Nowhere is this secularism more apparent than on the kibbutz, the epitome of Zionist ideology. In order to leave the youth transit camp and get placed on a kibbutz, Nūrī lies about being religious.

In the *ma'abarah,* the move away from religion seems to be an expression of lack of faith, and a further unraveling of society as known in Iraq. On the kibbutz the move toward the secular expresses a specific ideology. Secularization is part of the indoctrination of the prevailing Zionism of the day.

Nūrī and his peers who arrive on kibbutz from their *ma'abarot* are dismayed at the absence of Jewish space and time. Noticing the lack of a synagogue,[37] they wonder where they pray, and what to tell their parents.[38] The Sabbath is not sanctified as the day of rest, nor is there time set aside for religious rituals. Nūrī describes his resentment at this state of affairs in recounting his daily routine.

> . . . occasionally skipping the laying of *tefillin* and feeling a frightening void opening up inside me, simply in order to arrive in time for my stinking, dirty job [in the cowshed].[39]

The great conflict arises when Nūrī brings home a chicken for his family in the *ma'abarah*. His parents don't believe Nūrī when he lies that it was slaughtered according to Jewish ritual. They accuse him of being ruined by the kibbutz. Realizing the enormity of the gap between his life on kibbutz and his life with his family, he is torn by self recrimination.

> How could I have brought a headless chicken home to the *ma'abarah*? Whoever gave a thought about ritual slaughtering on the kibbutz? . . . Ever since the big fight about God in the youth group everyone had stopped thinking about Him. . . . Night after night I was afraid to fall asleep: they had killed God.[40]

This incident gives the novel its title, and serves as a powerful image, all the while recalling the fowl of expiation from the eve of Atonement Day. Caught in the middle of two incompatible communities, the youth must choose what he is to sacrifice from either culture in order not to become a sacrifice himself.

Nūrī's friend Nilly almost becomes just such a sacrifice. Of all the Iraqi teens on the kibbutz, Nilly most wants to be like those who are from the area. However, in abandoning the past, she misreads the moral code and courts disaster with her out-of-wedlock pregnancy. With the help of the counselor, Sonia, and Nūrī she is rescued from a life of shame, and married off to her Sabra boyfriend. Her parents reconcile with her when she names the child after her grandfather.[41] In this book—written a generation later—the choice of name serves as a counterpoint to the baby-naming scene in *Shesh Kanafaim*. Here, tradition and remembering take precedence over revolution and fresh starts.

Nūrī's desire to adapt to Israel is constrained by his loyalty to the family.[42] Even without family considerations, Nūrī is hesitant to accept the immediate transformation which the new place seems to expect. He explains:

> They tried to provide us with ready-made identities, which we were supposed to put on like a new suit of clothes in order to be like them. We had, indeed, shed our old clothes, but the new ones were too new, as uncomfortable as brand new shoes. [43]

The renaming of the immigrants symbolizes this process, this imposition of instant Israeli-hood. Nūrī balks at becoming Nimrod, the Biblical hunter (Genesis 10:8–10), and retains his Iraqi name.[44] He carefully walks the thin line between adaptation and absorption.

Like Menashe in the opening scene of *Shesh Kanafaim*, Nūrī returns to his humble neighborhood to recruit on behalf of the kibbutz. Despite Nūrī's pride at wearing the kibbutz clothes, and in representing the kibbutz to the people of the *ma'abarah*, he does not choose to join. He rejects the ready-made identity and the call to rebellion. The rebellion urged by the counselors is, in effect, based on conformity to a Eurocentric ideal and life experience. It is also a limited rebellion, to be directed only against the families and values imported to the *ma'abarah*, and not against the counselors and the kibbutz. However, when he returns to the transit camp, he is fluent in Hebrew, Beethoven, and the ideals of the kibbutz—the combination of which, of course, attests to the identity conflicts of the Ashkenazi Sabra.

Although still critical of the establishment and the Ashkenazi domination over Israeli culture, the *Shesh Kanafaim* is much less overt in its criticism than is Michael's *Shavin VeShavim Yoter*. Even the familiar scene in which the elegantly clad arrivals are sprayed with DDT at the airport—described as humiliating in *Shavim*—is presented with humor by the narrator-protagonist in *Shesh Kanafaim.* Nūrī remembers his father leading the entire hall with infectious laughter at the sight of his younger son's evident bewilderment. (p. 32–33)

Tarnegol Kaparot presents a further elaboration of the us/them categorization scheme in *Shavim VeShavim Yoter.* In this novel, "they" are divided into the red-headed Ashkenazim and the blond Sabras. The Sabras, or locals, are models for integration, and greatly admired by the Iraqi youth, while the Ashkenazim are generally negative characters.[45] "Why did every place have to have its own redhead?" the narrator asks in dismay.[46] Yet, the Ashkenazim cannot be easily dismissed because of their dominance over early Israeli society. The novel calls for mutual recognition of the Other, and cultural coexistence.

The novel has enjoyed a warm reception by critics and the Israeli establishment alike.[47] It received the Youth Aliyah Prize for Literature, and was adopted by the Department of Education for inclusion in the high-school curriculum. One journalist proclaimed it "a revelation for understanding the social and political upheavals of the seventies."[48]

Despite the critical acclaim, in actuality, *Tarnegol Kaparot* is more revolutionary than the books preceding it. It is critical of the kibbutz—"the experiment that did not fail,"—that bastion of Zionist principles, equality, and communism. In this story, the kibbutz does fail. It fails to offer true hospitality to the Iraqis. It also fails to integrate them into the values of Israeli society, and, most importantly, it fails to convince them to join the kibbutz. This book also presents a surprising transformation in which the value of self-realization becomes a reason for joining the kibbutz rather than for leaving it.[49] The positive reception of this book reflects a shift in societal attitudes. In the wake of the Yom Kippur War, the political upheaval of 1977, and the unpopular 1982 invasion into Lebanon, previously accepted assumptions and values were being questioned by the larger society as well.

V

The books and the reactions to them are reflective of their times. In *HaMa'abarah*, the emphasis is more on the contrast between present and former status, rather than settler versus immigrant, Ashkenazi versus Mizrahi, and native versus foreign-born. As previously mentioned, the presence of the "Other"—the settler, the European, and the native born—is scarcely felt and hardly as central as in the later books. *Shavim VeShavim Yoter* highlights and polarizes these oppositions. *HaMa'abarah*'s lack of emphasis on the Ashkenazim is in stark contrast to *Shavim VeShavim Yoter*, where the conflict is all-encompassing. The title itself expresses the notion of inequality and otherness. The basic conflict in the book is the perceived inequality between the Mizrahim and the Ashkenazim—or the "other." The act by which the protagonist achieves his position is necessarily one of epic proportions. It takes a dramatic event to actuate a change so extreme according to the book's ruling paradigms. Although the oppositions at the core of Michael's novel are present, in *Tarnegol Kaparot*, they play a less central role. Nūrī's heroic actions are less dramatic, and they display a grasp of the more subtle criteria of status and prestige.

The arrival scene is absent in Ballas's work because the scope of the novel is almost entirely confined to the transit camp, its characters, and the events within it. The story begins and ends in the coffeehouse that serves as the focal center for both the *ma'abarah* and the novel. In *Shavim VeShavim Yoter*, the humiliation of the experience is presented as justification for the narrator's anger and antiestablishment stance. It belongs to the era of the Black Panther protests. This contrasts with the humorous portrayal in Amir's novel, which has been made possible, perhaps, by the further passage of time, and the changes taking place in Israeli society.

Common to all three of the stories are the adolescents' struggle for identity, and their refusal to accept the identity imposed on them by their new home. Their struggle is part of the maturing process as well as that of integration. They must resocialize if they are to be successful in leaving exile behind. As adolescents, they must be free to define themselves as individuals. The conflict between the needs for resocialization and individuation is the source of the tension in these novels, and in the metaphor of adolescence.

VI

Until recently, this literature has assumed a marginal position despite the centrality of the concerns addressed within these books to a country of immigrants. *Ma'abarah* novels began to appear while Israeli literature was undergoing a transition from social realism to existentialism and experimentation with modernism. Written in the style which mainstream Israeli writers considered to be passé the *ma'abarah* literature did not appeal to the literary taste of the period, and, as a result, was either judged unfavorably or ignored.

The *ma'abarah* novels continued in the social realism trend of the literature of the 1940s and 1950s. An assumption of shared values common to the author, narrator, characters, and audience serves the literature of the War of Independence.[50] Identification with these values has created the "novel of the collective."[51]

> Literature of the War of Independence was born, due to the circumstances which shaped it, with the sign "we" . . . and asked . . . what right of existence does the "I" have without any connection to social realism.[52]

The implied author, narrative voice, and characters generally share similar perspectives, leaving little room for ironic discourse. Characters tend toward types. Plots follow an establish course.[53] The language used is, generally, highly stylized and formal—whether, as Shaked suggests, to express the noble greatness of the values expressed,[54] or due to the lack of a modern literary idiom.[55] Nurit Gertz emphasizes the core of shared values in creating the genre.

> The possibility of using different aspects of the work (especially plot and external characterization) in order to shape and direct the moralistic norms comes from complete confidence in these norms.[56]

This confidence waned in the so-called "New Wave" literature of the next generation.[57] The belief in shared values that is central to the realization of Zionist collectivism and pioneerism is also questioned when reality falls short of the high moral ideal.[58] The disillusioned and alienated individual wanders through these works as an anti-hero. The confusion in values and goals is expressed through irony, unreliable narration, and the absence of any clear authority. The narrator or protagonist's point of view is differentiated from—and undermined by—that of the implied author.[59] The almost classical style of the earlier works gives way to a more colloquial, nonnormative language, and is considered to be more sophisticated than is Palmah literature. The notion of exile was transformed from a national concern, resolved by the establishment of the State of Israel, to a metaphor for modern life.

Written during the period of New Wave literature, but in a style closer to that of the Palmah novels, *sifrut hama'abarah* belongs to neither of the two literary generations. These are novels of collective alienation, exploring the shared, rather than the individual, experience of not belonging written in response to the exclusion from the collective or Ashkenazi identity. They question the values lauded in the writing of the 1940s, and challenged in the 1960s from the position of the outsider wanting to come inside. Instead of the Sabra protagonists of both the Palmah and the New Wave novels, the characters central to the stories of the *ma'abarah* are marginal to Israeli society. In this respect, the literature of the *ma'abarah* preceded mainstream Israeli literature, which incorporated marginal characters in the 1980s.[60]

The *ma'abarah* literature works within the conventional schema of the canon, in form, if not in content. The language and rhetorical style follow the development of the literary idiom in mainstream Israeli literature. The Hebrew of *HaMa'abarah* echoes the earlier classical style, while Arabic is used to demonstrate the characters' distance from their surroundings. In *Shavim VeShavim Yoter,* the language is more informal and less stylized, as Arabic words and phrases signal dialogue between fellow outsiders. *Tarnegol Kaparot* is written in a language closest to the daily idiom. The use of Arabic and nonstandard items seems to be the least self-conscious, and nearest to the spirit of contemporary works.

VII

When Bartov's *Shesh Kenafaim LeEhad* was published,[61] the critic Azriel Ukhmani recalled an earlier remark from Palmah writer Moshe Shamir. In his response, Ukhmani refers to Bartov's character who integrates into Israeli society so successfully that he returns to the neighborhood of immigrants as a representative of the kibbutz.

> A year or so ago someone declared that the child who grows up in a transit camp will write the first *ma'abarah* novel. Apparently it was not Menashe who wrote the first story about the neighborhood of immigrants.[62]

These, then, are the stories by the Menashes of the transit camps.

The literature of the *ma'abarah* serves as a window to the transit camps for those who were fortunate enough not to experience them, as well as gives a sense of perspective to those who were less fortunate. These works also explore the meaning and condition of exile in a larger sense, centering on the metaphor of adolescence. They consider the experiences of Iraqi characters uprooted to Israel during the early 1950s. While these novels deal with the specifics of the fictional characters and their situations, many of the issues presented are common to all new immigrants in Israel—and, indeed, anyone who is not at home. At the same time, the novels are, at the very least, as revealing about Israeli society as the hero novels of the Palmah generation, or the New

Wave novels of alienation. They enlighten—or remind—the reader about the experiences of the exile and the immigrant, as well as the reception given them by a country of immigrants. Although underexamined, *sifrut hama'abarah* represents a significant contribution to Israeli literature. It examines issues crucial to Israeli society that offer consistent exposure of implicit tensions which are otherwise left untended.

For each of the writers discussed here—Amir, Ballas, and Michael—the *ma'abarah* novel is the first stage in their respective Hebrew literary careers. Each of the authors has made use of institutions fundamental to Israeli society—the *ma'abarah* now replaced by absorption centers; the Army; and the kibbutz—in order to present the experience of the immigrant and the Mizrahi to the mainstream Israeli audience. By depicting an alternative view of the ingathering of the exiles, they question the integrity of the values which are basic to Israeli society, as well as the success of Zionism. The novels illustrate the society's efforts to absorb the immigrants, and the adverse effects of having created such a powerful culture—that is, the failure of success. "The one who has lived the reality of the *ma'abarah* is obligated to write about it."[63]

Notes

1. Eli Amir, "HaMahapekha BeHayai," *'Al HaMishmar.* 10 January 1986.

2. Heskel Haddad, *Flight from Babylon* (New York: McGraw Hill Book Co., 1986) chapter 36.

3. 3. Hanoch Bartov, *Shesh Kenafaim LeEhad* (Tel Aviv: Sifriyat Po'alim, 1954). Bartov was born in Petah. Tikvah.

4. 4. Azriel Ukhmani, *"Gidulo Shel Mesaper,"* *'Al HaMishmar.* 18 February 1955.

5. Ballas, *HaMa'abarah.* 128 and elsewhere.

6. Ballas, *HaMa'abarah.* 128, 148.

7. The only exceptions to the absence of Ashkenazi characters are the government official in charge of the *ma'abarah,* and the blond Sabra, or native Israeli, named Zvi who shares a cell with some of the *ma'abaranikim* or transit camp residents in prison. This character stands in ironic opposition to the heroes of novels which were popular in the previous generation. Those blond Sabras represented the ideal "new Israeli," and often died fighting for their

country. [See, Gershon Shaked, "Literature and Its Audience: On the Reception of Israeli Fiction in the Forties and the Fifties," *Prooftexts* 7 (1987) 207–223.] In explaining why he is in jail Zvi states, "I was simply sick and tired of staying in the army. There are all sorts of characters and each one gives an order. I can't stand orders." (p.164)

The contrast of the character to the accepted ideal can be seen as criticism of the earlier literature which excluded anyone other than the blond Sabra heroes, or as a redefinition of the hero according to criteria of individualism over group cohesion. By placing Zvi in prison, the novel also equalizes the Sabra and the newcomer, and thereby calls the established hierarchy into question.

8. P. Azai, "Shimon Ballas, Meḥaber *HaMa'abarah*," *HaAretz*, 19 April 1964.

9. Interview with Shimon Ballas in Tel Aviv, 9 May 1989.

10. Ibid.

11. Mordekhai Avishai, *"Yisrael HaSheniyah BeRoman Ḥiver"* Bet HaSofer Tchernichovsky Archives. Tel Aviv. 28 August 1964.

12. Aliza Levenberg, *"Ḥayei HaMa'abarah MiBifnim."* Bet HaSofer Tchernichovsky Archives. Tel Aviv. 25 July 1964.

13. Aliza Levenberg, *"Eshnav HaMa'abarah,"* *Ma'ariv*, 30 April 1964.

14. Ruth Cohen, "HaMa'abarah l'Shimon Ballas." Bet HaSofer Tchernichovsky Archives. Tel Aviv. 29 May 1964.

15. T. Golovsky, *"Tivo Shel Ha'ani Ma'ashim' BaMa'abarah,"* *Tarbut, Sifrut VeOmanut.* 6 May 1964.

16. Other critics support my assessment. See, for example, Lev Hakkak, *"Terumatam Shel Yoẓei Irak LaSifrut HaIvrit Ba'arez,"* *Iton* 77:5–6 (November/December 1977) 22–23. Hakkak characterizes the tone as muted.

17. One immigrant in *HaMa'abarah* coins the phrase "the Second Babylonian Exile," inverting the idea of the original exile of the Jews from the land of Israel to Babylon to signify the return of the Babylonian Jews to the land of Israel. (p. 76) His neighbor composes a poem in the form of longing for Zion to lament their fate. *"Hoy yonah homeiha bekirvati/hoy Shekhinah, lu yada'at tsorati."* (p. 76) ["O dove cooing close by me; O Shekhinah (Divine Presence), if You only knew of my sorrow"]

18. Miriam Yaḥil-Wax, *"HaEmdah HaShlishit,"* *Iton* 77:91–92 (August/September 1987) 18–21.

19. See, for example, Hannan Hever, "Israeli Fiction of Early Sixties," *Prooftexts* 10 (1990) 129–147.

20. Yaḥil-Wax notes that "the attempt to integrate it in the canon as an ethnic novel were forced and failed anyway." Yaḥil-Wax, *"HaEmdah,"* 19.

21. See, Erik Cohen, "The Black Panthers and Israeli Society," in Ernest Krausz, ed., *Studies of Israeli Society* (New Brunswick, New Jersey: Transaction, Inc., 1980), 147–164.

22. Shlomo Deshen, "Political Ethnicity and Cultural Ethnicity in Israel During the 1960s," in Ernest Krausz, ed., *Studies of Israeli Society* (New Brunswick, New Jersey: Transaction, Inc., 1980), 126.

23. Hypotheses for the dissolution of the Israeli Panthers vary. While lack of organizational strengths contributed to its demise, Erik Cohen, in "The Black Panthers," suggests that the most profound reason was their inability to

> create a new "social myth" . . . [they] were still too much attached to the fundamental assumption of the "unity of the Jewish nation" and had too strong a stake in the survival of Israel as a "Jewish state," to create a radically separatist Oriental ideology. [160]

24. See, for example, Ernest Krausz, *Studies of Israeli Society* (New Brunswick, N.J. 1980); and Charles Liebman and Eliezer Don-Yehiya, *Religion and Politics in Israel* (Bloomington: Indiana University Press, 1984), 117.

25. In the story, "Sephardi" is used instead of *"Mizrahi."*

26. "In most 'bourekas' films, the ethnic/class tensions and conflicts are solved by a happy ending in which equality and unity are achieved by means of unification of the mixed couple." Ella Shohat, *Israeli Cinema: East/West and the Politics of Representation* (Austin, Tex.: University of Texas, 1989) 134. See, also, Shohat, 115–178.

27. Michael, *Shavim VeShavim Yoter*, 54.

28. Ibid., 142.

29. Ibid., 9.

30. Ibid., 254.

31. Iza Perliss, *"Aflayah Adatit BaRoman," Davar.* 23 August 1974.

32. Ibid.

33. One of their demands was to increase their eligibility for Army service. See, for example Cohen, "The Black Panthers," 148–149.

34. Michael's *ma'abarah* novel for younger readers, *Pahonim VeHalomot [Shacks and Dreams]* (Tel Aviv: Am Oved, 1979) deals with many of the same issues, in a gentler fashion, and end on a note of joy, delight, and hope.

35. Although most of the story is set in a kibbutz, I include this novel in our discussion of *ma'abarah* literature because the protagonist, and many of the other characters, are products of the camps. It also covers the same period as the other books, and many of the same issues.

36. Amir, *Tarnegol Kaparot*, p.118.

37. " 'What? Jews without a synagogue?' growled 'Abd al-'Azīz, the son of the rabbi of the Kfar Ono *ma'abarah* [upon his arrival to the kibbutz]." Amir, *Tarnegol Kaparot*, 41.

38. Ibid.

39. Ibid., 65.

40. Ibid., 200.

41. Ibid., 145.

42. "When we arrived here, I swore that I would root myself in Kiryat Oranim, that I would become a part of it." Amir, *Tarnegol Kaparot*, p.118.

43. Ibid., 186.

44. Ibid., 42. In the novel *Tehom Shemesh*, David Rabeeya goes one step further. The immigrants are assigned Yiddish rather than Hebrew names by veteran Israelis, ". . . telling Salman that his new name would be Zelig, and his parents would be called Zalman and Zelda." (Rabeeya, *Tehom Shemesh*, Tel Aviv: Alef, 1983: 47).

Also, "Ya'akov became Yankele, Yitshak became Yitshakele . . ." Ibid., 50.

This establishes an ironic connection between the Mizraḥi immigrants, and the *shtetl* Jews left behind by the Ashkenazi Israelis. At the same time it points to the cultural coercion implicit in these ready-made identities. Salman's attempts to be like "the Baltic," as he even recites the kaddish for his father in a Baltic accent, virtually denying his identity as Iraqi-born. (Ibid., 77) which begins with his acceptance of his new and name ends in a loss of identity and insanity, "What is my name?" (Ibid., 107)

45. There are several exceptions. The nice Ashkenazim who fall outside this scheme do not have red hair. The counselor, Sonia, has "silver threads interwoven in her black hair" (Amir, *Tarnegol Kaparot*, 34), while Dolek's hair color is never described. In any event Dolek has been purified by the Holocaust (chapter 14), as has the grey-haired Aunt Olga (chapter 2). (See, Amir *Tarnegol Kaparot* 168–169.)

46. Amir, *Tarnegol Kaparot*, 48. Here, too, as in *Shavim VeShavim Yoter*, the Holocaust survivors are omitted from the negative characterization of the Ashkenazim.

47. See, for example, Ruti Tradler, *"HaDekel Lo Meḥubar Tov LaAdamah, Kamoni," Moznayim* 57:5–6 (October–November 1983) 88; Ya'akov Rabi, *"HaSipur VeHaTe'udah," 'Al HaMishmar*, 16 March 1984; Yaron Elikayam, "Ma'aseh Ḥinukhi," *Ma'ariv*, 6 December 1988.

48. Philip Gillon, "Robbed of Dignity," *Jerusalem Post Magazine*, 11 March 1988.

49. As in S. Yizhar, *"Efrayim Hozer LaAspeset"* (Ephraim Returns to the Alfalfa) (1938), or many of Amos Oz's kibbutz stories.

50. Terms used to label the writers of this literature include the generation of 1948; *dor hapalmah* (the Palmach generation), *dor ha'aretz* (first generation of native Israelis), native writers, and others.

51. Gershon Shaked credits Dan Miron with formulating the term. Shaked has, himself, written about these works under the title "First Person Plural." Gershon Shaked, *The Shadows Within* (Philadelphia: Jewish Publication Society, 1987) 145–163.

52. Shaked, *Gal Hadash BaSiporet HaIvrit* (Tel Aviv: Sifriyat Poalim, 1970) 11–12.

53. Shaked, "Literature and Its Audience: On the Reception of Israeli Literature in the Forties and Fifties," *Prooftexts*, 7:3 (September 1987) 207–208.

54. Shaked, "Hebrew Prose Fiction After the War of Liberation," *Modern Hebrew Literature*, 1979. 21–34.

55. Ibid., 23–24.

56. Nurit Gertz, "Temurot BaSifrut HaIvrit," *HaSifrut*, 29 (December 1969) 71.

57. *HaGal HaHadash*: Gershon Shaked's term has been widely adopted by scholars of Israeli literature.

58. See, for example, Shimon Sandbank, "Contemporary Israeli Literature: The Withdrawal from Certainty," *Triquarterly* 39 (1977) 3–18. Also Arnold J. Band, "The Evanescence of Nationalist Themes in Israeli Literature," in Michael C. Hillman, ed. *Literature East and West: Essays on Nationalism and Asian Literatures* 23, (1987) 111–116.

59. For a more detailed discussion, see, Gertz, "Temurot," 69–75.

60. Note, for example, the title character of A. B. Yehoshua's *Molkho* (Tel Aviv: HaSifriyah, 1987), and the popularity of Dan Benaya Seri's writing: *'Ugiyot HaMelah Shel Savta Sultanah* (Jerusalem: Keter, 1988); and *Ziporei Zāl* (Jerusalem: Keter, 1988); and of course, Lizzie Badih.i in Shulamit Lapid, *Mikomon* (Jerusalem: Keter, 1989).

61. Bartov, *Shesh Kenafaim LeEhad*. Tel Aviv: Sifriyat Po'alim, 1954.

62. Cited in Dan Laor, "Ha'Aliyah HaHamonit Ke'Tokhen VeNose' BaSifrut Ha'Ivrit BiSh'not HaMedinah HaRishonah," *HaZiyonut*, 14 (1989), 161–175.

63. Shimon Ballas in an interview with P. Azai, 19 April 1964.

11. Historical Memory: Israeli Cinema and Literature in the 1980s and 1990s

Nurith Gertz

Films

Uri Barabash, *The Dreamers*, 1987

Uri Barabash, *One of Us*, 1989

Eli Cohen, *Avia's Summer*, 1988

Baruch Dinar, *They Were Ten*, 1960

Eitan Green, *Till the End of the Night*, 1985

Menachem Golan, *Eight Trail One*, 1964

Yosef Milo, *He Walked in the Fields*, 1967

Ilan Moseheson, *Wooden Gun*, 1979

G'ad Ne'eman, *Paratroopers*, 1977

Akiva Tevet, *Atalia*, 1984

Dan Volman, *Soldier of the Night*, 1984

Dan Volman, *Hide and Seek*, 1980

Yoel Zilberg, *HaSamba*, 1971

Book

A. B. Yehoshua, *Mr. Mani* (Tel Aviv: Hakibbutz Hameuchad and
Siman Keriaa, 1990).

I. Introduction

uring the 1970s and 1980s, the political Right gained
the upper hand in Israel. As the Right ascended, so
did the views that the country's isolation in the world was
permanent, and that Israeli society must rely on armed force
and resign itself to a permanent state of war. Although Leftist circles opposed these conceptions, they failed to provide
an ideological alternative. The absence of such an alternative
is amply reflected in Israeli cinema as well as literature and
other texts. During the 1980s and the 1990s leading figures
in these two arts—literature and cinema—were allied with
left-wing circles, and expressed the critical reactions of the
left toward the prevalent right-wing dominant ideology. In
this, they followed a long tradition of close affiliation between
the intellectual strata in Israel and the Left. The central
cinema of the time expressed these tendencies in the most
blatant manner.

The protagonists in films made in the 1970s and 1980s
find themselves worn down by a militaristic, violent society
in which they cannot exist, and from which they cannot flee.
The films expose this alienation by reference to older texts.
They revert to the nationalist cinema and the literature of
the pre-independence and early independence period of 1950
to 1960, using the national models of those years as tools in
their dispute with the dominant ideology of the present. The
themes of action and valor, and the spirit of voluntarism and
camaraderie of the fighters, both of which were cornerstones
in the nationalist cinema and literature of the past, are represented in the so-called "left wing" cinema of the 1980s as
meaningless forms. National values of the past, as reflected
in the War of Independence culture, are presented as empty

cliches. These cliches—so abundant in the national cinema—
are exposed and parodied now.

Although the dispute is, indeed, with the past, it addresses itself to goals that became very dominant in Israeli
society after the 1967 war—such as the ideological narrative
that places heroism and battle, as well as nationalism and
militarism at its center. In the process, history is kaleido-
scoped, and the past is perceived as a mirror-image prefigur-
ment of a dreary present.[1] This explains the tone of despair
that dominates the films. Their depictions of reality in the
past and future suggest nothing different from their portray-
als of the present.

In the late 1980s and early 1990s, two seemingly unre-
lated changes occurred in Israeli culture—namely, the weakening of the Right, coupled with a growing tendency among
many Israelis to seek possibilities of dialogue with the Palestinians; and the appearance of Western postmodern models
in Israeli literature and art. These two processes come together in some literary and cinematic works of the 1990s. In
the spirit of postmodernism, these works reject the possibility of creating continuity or order in a fragmented history.
They rule out the very ability to grasp the past beyond its
inherent images. The very awareness, painful as it is, that no
truth lurks behind the words and images[2] allows these works
to set texts, images, and quotations against each other, thus
presenting history as a stage of unrealized possibilities in
both past and present. In the style of Western postmodern
writing, they reject a clear linear story line. They form a
collage built of quotations and information, and they juxta-
pose different perspectives with one another, never letting
one of them overpower the other. Thus, they surrender their
pretentions of representing the past, and suffice with a substitute, such as portraying our own stereotypes and images
of this past. In this, on the one hand, they show the impossi-
bility of penetrating reality beyond its fragmented imagery.[3]
On the other hand, they confront the static perception of
time that had dominated Israeli cinema and literature in

previous years—that is, viewing the past as a mirror image of the present. In its stead, they present a multitude of interpretations, debates, and fantasies of historical possibilities that were, or were not, in existence, or that would, or would not, come true. Thus, the literature and cinema of the early 1990s invoke postmodern models to grope for new historical interpretations that seemed altogether inaccessible in the cinema and literature of the 1980s.

Because the dispute with earlier works is especially highlighted in films of the 1980s, these will be analyzed in the second part of this chapter. The postmodern deconstruction of history, however, is best characterized by some literary works of the 1990s, among which is A. B. Yehoshua's influential novel *Mr. Mani*. Hence, the third part of the chapter will be dedicated to this novel.

II. Israeli Cinema in the 1980s

The last words of Josef Trumpeldor (who fell defending the settlement of Tel Hai in 1920)—"It is good to die for our country,"—are truncated by the protagonists in the films of the 1980s into "It is good to die" or "It is not good to die" (*Summer Blues*, *Atalia*). A famous poem by the poetess Rahel, written in the 1920s, is altered beyond recognition. The original poem contains the following verses:

> I did not sing to you my Land
> nor glorify your name
> With acts of heroism, with the spoils of war
> Only a tree my hands did plant
> On the still Jordan shores
> Only a path my feet did trace
> through the fields.

In the film *Repeat Dive* (1981 directed by Shimeon Dotan) it became: "I did not sing to you, my Land/Because there was no reason to."

In the texts of the past, the Zionist goals—establishing a just Jewish Israeli society that cultivates and lives on its land—gave military action its justification. In the films of the

1980s, the Zionist goals vanish, leaving only the military operations. In the national cinema of the past, individuals found their purpose in life in the actions of the national collective. The political cinema of the 1980s contrasts Army life with the private, individual world that might have provided a refuge from the collective, had individuality not been smothered and suppressed by it. In fact anything beyond the fighting military collective—including the protagonists' private lives—is devoid of value.

This fissuring of the national and personal basis in Israeli society is explored in the cinema of the 1980s, especially through the persona of the "other," whom society bans. The reversion to past models, in this case, permits this cinema to examine the extent to which society has lost its identity by outlawing the others within it. The others, in this case, are those who are unable or unwilling to accept the national norms. Protagonists who are too weak—physically or psychologically—to tolerate the Army life that is thrust upon them (*Paratroopers, Soldier of the Night, Atalia*); heroes on the fringes of society (the widows in *Atalia* and *Repeat Dive*; the Christian clergyman in *Till the End of the Night*; the Holocaust survivors in *Wooden Gun* and *Avia's Summer*); or heroes whose ideological views or aberrant behavior cast them out of society (the pacifist in *Summer Blues*, the homosexual teacher in *Hide and Seek*, the rebellious soldier in *One of Us*)—all of them are either crushed by society or assimilated against their will.

Alternatively, they seek an impossible way out, attempting to abandon their Israeli identity and its history. Most of these attempts end in failure. Despite being portrayed as decadent and stagnant, the collective still imposes its authority on the would-be deviant. The films, and their protagonists, find no meaning outside the social-collective order that they reject. Neither does the banished outsider offer any alternative. His world, too, is subordinate to the world against which he rebels. Thus, the films drain the national models of their original content, but also attest to the fact that, for the moment, there is no alternative in the present to these empty frameworks.

This subject was first raised by one of Israel's most influential film directors, Jad Ne'eman. His film, *Paratroopers* (1977),
was the first to criticize Army life as a metaphor of Israeli
culture, and to fully capture the despair of those who could not
decipher its ethical equivalent. Other directors followed suit.

The protagonist of *Paratroopers* dies when he trips over
a grenade he himself has thrown. This death is a replay of
another death—that of Uri, the hero of the novel *He Walked
in the Fields*, written in 1947 and considered for years to be
the great epos of the period of the struggle for independence,
culminating in the war of 1948. The differences between the
two versions is a clear measure of the changes that have
taken place in the intervening years. In the novel, *He Walked
in the Fields*, as in the film *Paratroopers*, the tough guy
forces the faint-hearted soldier to hurl a live grenade. In both
cases, the protagonist uses similar arguments. He tries to
help the soldier overcome his fear, and convince him that he
is capable of doing something that he imagines that he cannot do. In both cases, similar words are also used. In *He
Walked in the Fields*, Uri says, "Let him be a man for once!
. . . Stop being so afraid. Stop being such a coward! Get on
with it, Simon. Show us what you know." In *Paratroopers*,
the tough officer says, "Stop being such a coward, Weissman.
You don't know what you can and can't do.") Here, however,
the similarity ends. In *Paratroopers*, the main hero is not the
tough soldier but rather the coward, who was a marginal
and unimportant character in *He Walked in the Fields*. This
soldier achieves nothing by his death, as he has nothing to
achieve. *Paratroopers* returns to the novel, *He Walked in the
Fields*, in order to retell a familiar story about a group of
fighters who force the misfits to become part of the collective
framework. In this case, however, there is a difference—the
national objective to this deed is missing.

In his final act, Uri, the hero of the novel, *He Walked in
the Fields*, succeeds in merging his private set of values into
the collective or national one. Although he has tried to achieve
this throughout his life, he especially manages to achieve it
in death. By throwing himself on a grenade that has been

hurled by his subordinate, he saves his soldiers' lives and displays his human sensitivity. By sacrificing himself for the collective, he displays national valor.

Paratroopers exposes the fallacy on which this ostensibly harmonious fusion of values is based. The vulnerable, frightened soldier unquestioningly accepts a military goal to which he is not suited, thus falling victim to a well-oiled machine in which there is no place for him. His death removes him from the stage, and the machine grinds on without him.

For lack of an alternative, the film presents the military framework as the ultimate goal for past and present heroes alike. This duality is reflected in its structure—which is torn in half, each part with its own protagonist and plot. The protagonist of the first part is Weissman, an outsider unable to adjust to military life. He is abused by soldiers and officers alike until, unable to bear the tension, he commits suicide. The outsider's agonies and ordeals are used in this section of the plot to examine the norms of the fighting collective, which has turned toughness into a paramount value by trampling on any human or personal manifestation that does not conform with it.

In the second part of the film, the dead soldier's officer becomes the hero. As the plot accompanies him and examines his moral barometer, we discover in him the very qualities that he despised in his subordinate—sensitivity, fear, weakness, and doubts. The first part of the film shows that even the protagonist who does not fit into the male military order is totally dependent upon it. He has no alternative to offer, either in life or in death. In fact, his credo is the same as the officer's, and his true ambition is to complete his training successfully and become a paratrooper. Thus, the values of the past had been reduced to degenerate militarism, for which a proper substitute is no longer available. This judgment becomes most apparent in the second part of the film. The officer's dictate, which is composed of two very simple rules—be like everyone, and, like everyone, be courageous and tough—appears to be inhuman in the first part of the film, as witnessed in scenes of abuse inflicted on the weak soldier. However, in the second section of the film, when the officer conducts his own soul-searching, this credo is seen as a refuge from total emptiness. "We tried to make a soldier out of him," says the officer, when drunk, and as he admits that the attempt failed. "And now he's dead. Just dead." Yet, he knows no other way.

The film poignantly expresses this entrapment through cinematic techniques. Throughout the first part, the camera never closes in on the protagonist, Weissman—therefore avoiding subjecting his agony to close scrutiny. Moreover, most of the first part of the film—even in its most intimate moments—is composed of long shots, at a distance, in which even the individuals are perceived as a part of a group. While the plot attempts to reveal the individual's anxiety, the cinematography shows the futility of these attempts. The second half of the movie is typified by more close-ups. Yet, these mainly expose the commander's embarrassment—rather than the the world of the outsider—thus emphasizing the notion of impasse that arises from the plot. This notion is further shaped by the structure of the film.

On the face of it, it is constructed in two separate parts, and featuring two separate protagonists. In fact, however, the two parts are intertwined, right down to the minutest details, and as each detail of the first part finds its correspondence in the second. In this way, we discover that the sensitive, weak soldier, and the tough commander, are but two sons of the same society, and two faces of the same identity. All that the commander has managed to crush in his soldier—fear, weakness, and doubts—he has actually crushed in his own soul.

Paratroopers dismantles the national literary model of the past. It contemplates the novel, *He Walked in the Fields,* and sees in it, neither harmony between the individual and the collective, nor a fusion of national and personal goals. In this way, it uses the text of the past in order to present a total collapse of values in the present.

Another way in which the cinema of the 1980s explores these collapses of values is by dismantling the family relationships that characterize the works of the past. Such family ties were more than mere blood relations. They brought together protagonists with rival ideologies, proving the existence of allegiances that transcend rivalries and irreconcilable views, and proving that there is a deeper love—such as that between brothers or between parents and children—that is immune to ideological differences. The cinema of the 1980s dismantles family relationships such as these, drawing ideological boundaries between brothers, and between fathers and sons.

The novel, *He Walked in the Fields*, focuses on two generations that vacillate, each in its own way, between collective and private goals. The film resolves these conflicts in harmony. The son sacrifices himself for the collective and, thereby, displays his sensitivity as an individual. The father, who has devoted all his life to the collective, rediscovers his place in the family and raises his grandson. Therefore, together they reconstruct the harmony between the individual and collective life.

As in *He Walked in the Fields*, similar father-and-son pair resurfaces several years later in Eitan Green's film, *Till the End of the Night*. They have similar characteristics, and are played by the same actors with Asi Dayan as the son, and Yosef Milo as the father. Now, however, it is clear that the conflict between them cannot be solved within the family, nor within the same set of beliefs. Whereas the son is now immersed in an empty bourgeois existence cloaked in a military halo, the father—a Christian by belief—lives outside society, and outside both the military and the bourgeois milieus, outside Israeli history. The contrast between them is evident at all levels in the film—above all, in the way in which the film is shot, and in the background settings. The son is usually pictured in his bar, from afar and through a clutter of people and objects, with dim lighting and lots of noise. The father appears in several major scenes illuminated from the side, and surrounded by an aura in an empty, silent room, and to the occasional accompaniment of a Bach sonata or clarinet music. The contrast between the lifestyles of father and son is further reflected in the contrast between the density, noise, and grey light of Tel Aviv, where the son lives, and the Jaffa church that the father frequents. The shafts of light penetrating the windows and doors of the church, and the background of vaults and palms, seem to belong to another, more tranquil and serene existence, which stands in stark contrast to the commotion of Tel Aviv.

In the book, *He Walked in the Fields*, Uri sacrifices himself on the altar of his beliefs, and his death leads to a resurrection. The film adaptation of this book emphasizes this point. The film ends with a shot of the son against a backdrop of a tall tree, a symbol of growth and continuity. In *Till the End of the Night*, the father is sacrificed on the altar of his son's pointless life, when the local underworld mistakenly kills him instead of his son. Moreover, his death does not augur a resurrection. It is a sterile death, brought about as a sacrifice to a sterile life—namely, that of his son. Thus, the destruction of the family in *Till the End of the Night* is projected onto that of the families that preceded it—that of 1947 (when the novel *He Walked in the Fields* appeared) and that of 1967 (when the film based on this novel reached the theaters). These other families are presented as one—a single family always living in false harmony and fraternity. The family relationship that had transcended divergent attitudes and ideologies has now been ruptured. The schism of those still within society and those cast out—such as the Christian father—is now portrayed within the family itself.

In settling accounts with the models of the past, several films of the 1980s turn to the pre-independence or the early-independence period. In these cases, the cinematic and literary models of the past are not merely mediators in the polemic with the present. They also serve as tools for a re-creation of one period in the image of the other.

The film *Wooden Gun* (1979) is set in the early 1950s. Here, already into the so-called "heroic" period, it marks the disintegration of national values. The film is built along the model of adventure books and films—such as *Eight Trail One* and *HaSamba*—produced after the War of Independence and subsequent wars. Here, however, this model is held up to parody. In the postwar books and films, a group of children joins the war effort, exposes enemies and hidden spies, and helps the adults win. In *Wooden Gun*, a group of children invents a make-believe war, but victory in this war results in catastrophe.

The film portrays the group of children at study and play. The two worlds—study and play—are closely intertwined. Their national-Zionist education is saturated with the slogans and cliches about the old valorous struggles of the few against the many, and the children act out these cliches as they play. A child dons a fake beard and delivers a speech by Herzl on the rebirth of the nation in its ancient homeland. A teacher takes his pupils to the top of an unforested mountain, where he orates on the nation's yearning for Jerusalem, its capital. The principal lectures the bored pupils on Israeli youth—to which the eyes of the entire nation turn, and so on. This ideology, communicated from the very outset as a collection of cliches and slogans, is totally distorted when it infuses into the children's war games. In these games, all dreams, all ideas, and all opinions condense into a vision of war in which courage must be shown in order to vanquish the tyrant. Once again, war has become an end unto itself. In this case, the "tyrant" is an orphan whose parents perished in the Holocaust. After the Independence Day school play—in which he portrays Herzl—his friend wounds him by gunfire before he has time to even remove his makeup.

As in other films of the time, this one analyzes what had only been latent in the national cinema—that is, the contraction of the entire Zionist dream into one of war. This dream of war is shown for what it is, not only through the use of parody (a preposterous child's game) but also by means of the so-called "other," the misfit, or crazy Palestina, who lost her entire family in Europe and has become a target for the warrior-children's abuse. Palestina endows the film with a different landscape—the sea, as opposed to the shanties and huts of the city. (Apart from these scenes, the entire film is shot in tiny apartments, basements, and yards, as is customary with other films as well.) Palestina also provides a different psychological world—an insane, lyrical, and poetic one—that the children rebuff. However, it transpires that Palestina is not the only Holocaust survivor in the film. In fact, the Holocaust encompasses all the children, filtering through to them from their parents and relatives. By assuming the identity of rugged combatant, and the legacy of the War of Independence, they disown not only Palestina's sensitive, and lyrical world of fears, but also their parents' past—which is also their own.

In many cases, the "other" through whom the collapse of the Zionist dream is viewed is a Palestinian Arab. These films discover that, to disregard his existence is to disregard substantial facets of Zionist-Israeli existence. Once again, the films expose these facets by using texts of the past. Uri Barabash's film *The Dreamers* (1987) illustrates this point. Describing the early Jewish settlements in Palestine, he uses a film made in 1960 on the subject, but modifies its structure and contents, describing the beginnings of the settlement drive as if they were its end.

They Were Ten (1960) describes the establishment, in the beginning of the century, of a settlement by a group of Jewish pioneers on the slopes of a barren hill. This is no easy matter, and many serious problems arise. First, nature, in the form of biting cold and drought, is against them. Then, the Arabs gang up against the Jewish farmers at ploughing time, refusing to share their water. Finally, the protagonists fail in their attempts to merge their personal needs into the collective goals. In the final analysis, all these problems boil down to a single, overriding one—the difficulty of exchanging the diaspora identity for that of the tough, hard-bitten peasant, who are new people in a new society. This difficulty is overcome only when the protagonists refuse to submit to the Arabs. They stand up for their rights, and achieve victory.

In *The Dreamers*, a similar group of pioneers settles on a similar hill. They share the same purpose, and they face the same difficulties. Here, however, the similarity ends. The heroes of *The Dreamers* have no way to surmount their difficulties.

The protagonists who stand up for their rights and fight the Arabs in *They Were Ten* prove, by means of their struggle, that they are no longer mere mortal Jews. They fight for a just cause, and their struggle endows the concept of justice with a universal dimension, which even gentiles must acknowledge. In *The Dreamers*, the Jews who stand up for their rights negate the Arabs' rights. There is no middle road between the two types of rights, or the two types of justice. The concept of justice as a universal force expires irreversibly.

The pioneers of *They Were Ten* ultimately find a personal refuge within the collective, as demonstrated when a pair of lovers, helped by their friends, start building a home for themselves. In *The Dreamers*, as in other films, the possibility of building a private refuge of this type is nonexistent. The collective would not tolerate it, because it demands that the individual sacrifice everything—personal effects, books, clothes, and even love—for the common good. Not content with its dispute with these abstract themes, the film also delves into the nuances of cinematic poetics. *They Were Ten* opens by setting forth the tension between the dynamism of the Arabs—who either move across the landscape on horseback or drive their flocks—and the passivity of the Jewish settlers, who confine themselves to their shacks and fields. This tension is vitiated as the plot progresses. The Jews learn to ride horses, venture across the stretch of land between their settlement and the Arab village, and learn how to till the land. Now they, too, are able to gallop across the landscapes. In this film, as in others of its kind, dynamism in space is linked with dynamism in time. As soon as the protagonists of *They Were Ten* acquire the ability to move around freely, they are also able to get the plot moving—to dictate the nature of their struggle with the Arabs, as well as its rhythm, duration, and their success in it. In this struggle, they consolidate their beliefs, construct an Israeli identity, justify it on universal grounds, and change the way in which the world relates to them.

The protagonists of *The Dreamers*, by contrast, remain static throughout the film. They cannot even drive the plot. The Arabs are the agents who control the action, while the Jews are reactive and pulled in their wake. This stasis is construed at the beginning of the film by means of documentary scenes that shift from shots of armies stampeding across continents to photos of dead Jews. The decision to emigrate to Palestine to build a new identity and society was supposed to have changed all this. It has not succeeded. Throughout the plot, the Jews are usually enclosed in their courtyard while the Arabs roam around freely. The open landscape of the film is one of foothills or mountains and cliffs. This landscape is filmed with exceedingly slow pans and zooms running along its length, breadth, and depth. The camera caresses it, as it were, from its lowest valleys to its highest peaks in an up-down tilt. However, it is not a Jewish landscape. As in many other Israeli political films, the landscape of *The Dreamers* is an Arab one.

The cracks in the harmony of the past are exposed in the widening gap between the heroes' words and actions, as well as their intentions and deeds. The soundtrack is a voice-over reciting from the pioneers' diaries. The words express dreams of nascent freedom and justice, dreams of a people without a land returning to a land without a people. However, instead of supporting the soundtrack, the camera contradicts it directly with a shot of the Arab community—another people residing in this same land. From its point of departure—a dialogue with the patterns of time, space, plot, and soundtrack that appear in *They Were Ten*—*The Dreamers* penetrates a level which is even more concrete—that is, a dispute with specific scenes.

In *They Were Ten*, the conflict between Jews and Arabs comes to a head one dark evening when the pioneers are busy celebrating, and one of the Arabs sneaks into their compound and steals their horse. This is the point at which the conflict develops, until the Jews show that they are able to fight for justice—as in recovery of the horse—and earn the Arabs' respect. *The Dreamers* replays this scene, but turns it inside out. It is now the Jew, Amnon, who sneaks into the Arab stables one dark night, as the Arabs are busy celebrating, in order to retrieve the horse that they have stolen. He is caught by his friend, the sheikh's son, and their subsequent conversation is in fact a reply, years delayed, to the heroes of *They Were Ten*. Victory cannot be found through struggle, they agree. Any struggle simply leads to further struggle. This covenant between Jew and Arab, occurring at exactly the same point where the conflict erupted years earlier, indicates that a solution is possible. However, this solution is not adopted because neither society is ready for it.

This brings us to the final difference between the otherwise identical endings of the two films. The woman—the central persona of the group in *They Were Ten*—dies of an illness. The film, however, does not end here. It ends with a long-awaited rainstorm spattering on her grave, heralding the end of the drought, and a shot of a tree in sprouting shoots and blossoms. Such endings are very common in the national films, in which they symbolize the prosperous future that awaits the heroes even after death.

In *The Dreamers*, however, this promise of the future— the same tree and the same plentiful rain—is delivered after the heroes' hopes and dreams have shattered. It is meant to prove that the possibilities suggested by the national films are, in fact, impossible. Here, the blossoming tree is accompanied by a voice-over of the heroine, narrating from the group's diary. "At the price of suffering, we learned to forgive ourselves. We compromised with the dream." Behind this optimistic remark, as with the blossoming tree, there is no substance. The sensitive, compromising, forgiving heroes either died or returned to Europe. In fact, there is no one left with whom to compromise, and no one to forgive. Thus, the blossoming tree symbolizes a rebirth that will never occur. It is a metaphorical blossoming that has no basis in reality.

III. Israeli Literature in the Early 1990s

Israeli cinema of the 1980s examined the past from the painful perspective of the present. It tried to decompose the dichotomies of which the past national narratives had been composed, and disrupt the appearance of harmony that these narratives had created between the individual and society, between the Israeli and the world, between nationalism and humanism, and between symbols and deeds. In this way, it fought a battle against the national and military values of contemporary Israel society, and exposed the rifts that fissure the national models of the past and present together. However, these films did not propose an escape route, nor an alternative value system to replace the collapsing existing systems. Their preoccupation with the past expresses a sense of an ideological dead end that characterizes, in the 1980s, cinema, literature, and Israeli culture in general.

In the late 1980s, when the Intifada gathered momentum and the Israeli public became increasingly exausted by the policies of the Right, new options began to surface in Israeli politics and culture. Literature might have been the first medium to examine them in the course of its reexamination of both the past and the present. Israeli cinema followed suit. To do so, some literary works used Western postmodern models. By these means, they portrayed Zionist history as a collection of images, quotations, posturings, and possibilities—some fulfilled, and others not. Thus, they deconstructed this history and presented other, imaginary histories. Thus, too, they resurrected discarded postulates as new options for the present, and elicited new directions in the past and the present together. The option of Arab-Jewish binationalism—a partitioning of the land between Jews and Arabs, a cosmopolitan co-existence based on cooperation, an indigenous movement that wishes to detach itself from the Jewish heritage and integrate into the Middle East, and more—

they attempted to present, albeit as a fantasy or dream, a reality as-yet unrealized either in the present or past.

A. B. Yehoshua's novel, *Mr. Mani*, might serve as an example of this type of writing, as it is composed of five dialogues revolving around the Mani family. The first of these dialogues is set in the late 1980s, at the start of the Intifada. Each of the subsequent dialogues takes place in a generation previous to that described before. The fifth and final dialogue is set in the middle of the eighteenth century. Here, as the text reaches its end, the origin of the Mani dynasty is revealed. In this fashion, the end and the beginning come together. Past and present collide.

The temporal confusion in the book corresponds to an utter confusion of places and identities. The son of the narrator in the fifth chapter moves to Jerusalem, and becomes the prisoner of a fixed idea that the Muslim residents of the country are, in fact, Jews who have forgotten their identity—"who still don't know that they're Jews"—and that it is his duty to show them what they've forgotten. To this end, he leaves his home and his wife, steps through the boundaries of the Jewish community, and spends most of his time in the Christian and Muslim quarters of the city. In his wanderings, he is supported by the British Consul in Jerusalem, who believes that the Jews are Christians who are destined to return to Christianity. Therefore, he regards them, not as flesh-and-blood people, but as "literary heroes, who stepped out of the Old Testament and are fated to enter the New Testament in the End of Days; all we must do in the meantime is make sure they don't enter another book by mistake" (p. 309).

In the end, the direction in which the son of the narrator is heading is not altogether clear. Is he indeed attempting to remind the Muslims that they are, in fact, Jews? Or is it the other way around? Is he trying to forget that he himself is a Jew? "Instead of discovering Jews who forgot they are Jews, he will himself become something like that in the meantime, a master copy of sorts" (p. 340). The two processes actually express a single desire—one "that knows no satisfaction, that always seeks to mix with people and fight what it regards as insularity or self-segregation" (p. 325). Eventually, when the hero approaches the "others" to remind them of their Jewishness, he assimilates into their community and remains with them until his death. Thus, the novel leads to the collapse of all national identities—Jews are not Jews, Christians are not Christians, and Muslims are not Muslims. All come together in one great universe. This universe, however, is but a dream and a fantasy, and the son who dreams and fantasizes it is, ultimately, sacrificed on its altar.

Nevertheless, the literature and cinema of the late 1980s and the 1990s are replete with such dreams. It is the postmodern writing that helped them reopen closed issues, again ask questions that had already been answered, untie the common denominator that unites the Zionist ideologies, undermine the old narratives, and, in so doing, dredge up a wealth of new historical options that had seemed inaccessible in the cinema of the 1980s and have resurfaced in the 1990s. Thus, in Israel, in the 1990s, the postmodern writings march hand-in-hand with the ideological quest for a different history—a different past that will serve as a base for a different future.

Notes

1. In Benjamin's words, the cinema—as does other texts in Israeli culture in this specific stage, did not discover "the revolutionary possibilities of time." See, Walter Benjamin, *Poesie et Revolution* (Paris: Denoel, 1971); and Rainer Nagele, ed., *Benjamin's Ground* (Detroit: Wayne State University Press, 1988).

2. Jean-François Lyotard, *The Postmodern Condition: A Report of Knowledge* (Minneapolis: University of Minnesota Press, 1984).

3. See Umberto Eco, "Postmodernism, Irony, the Enjoyable," postscript to Umberto Eco, *The Name of the Rose* (New York: Harcourt, Brace, Jovanovich, 1984)p; and Frederic Jameson, *Postmodernism* (Durham: Duke University Press, 1991). For a postmodern view of history, see, Amos Funkenstein, "History, Counterhistory, and Narrative," in Saul Friedlander, ed., *Probing the Limits of Representation* (Cambridge, Ma.: Harvard University Press, 1992); Robert A. Rosenstone, "History in Image/History in Words: Reflecting on the Possibility of Really Putting History Onto Film," *American Historical Review* 93:5 (October 1988); Hayden White, *Tropics of Discourse* (Baltimore and London: Johns Hopkins University

Press, 1978); Hayden White, "Historical Emplotment: Two Kinds of Ruin," in Saul Friedlander, ed., *Probing the Limits of Representation* (Cambridge, Ma.: Harvard University Press, 1992); Anton Kaes, "Holocaust and the End of History: Postmodern Historiography in Cinema," in Saul Friedlander, ed., *Probing the Limits of Representation* (Cambridge: Ma.: Harvard University Press, 1992); and Anton Kaes, *From Hitler to Heimat* (Cambridge, Ma.: Harvard University Press, 1989).

4. Moshe Shamir, *He Walked in the Fields* (Merhvia: Sifriyat Poalim, 1947).

NOTES ON CONTRIBUTORS

Mohammed Abu-Nimer received his doctoral degree in Conflict Analysis and Resolution at George Mason University in Fairfax, Virginia while conducting research on Israeli-Palestinian dialogue groups. He has worked with Israelis and Palestinians for more than a decade, facilitating dialogue groups and in other educational projects. Currently, he is associate professor of Sociology at Guilford College in Greensboro, North Carolina.

Kevin Avruch is professor and coordinator of Anthropology at George Mason University in Fairfax, Virginia. His specialties include conflict resolution, politics and culture, and the anthropological study of Israel. He is the author of *American Immigrants in Israel: Social Identities and Change* (Chicago: University of Chicago Press, 1981); and co-editor of *Conflict Resolution: Cross-Cultural Perspectives* (Greenwood, 1991).

Efraim Ben-Zadok is professor of Public Administration in the College of Urban and Public Affairs at Florida Atlantic University. He was a faculty member at the State University of New York and Tel-Aviv University. His fields of interest include public policy analysis and urban politics. His recent book is *Local Communities and the Israeli Polity* (Albany: State University of New York Press, 1993).

Nancy E. Berg received her doctoral degree from the University of Pennsylvania in Modern Hebrew and Arabic literature. She is an assistant professor of Hebrew and Comparative Literature at Washington University in St. Louis. The author of *Exile from Exile: Israeli Writers from Iraq* (Albany: State

227

University of New York Press, 1996), she is currently writing about the politics of literary reception in Israel.

Nurith Gertz is associate professor at the Open University of Israel. Her recent books include *Motion Fiction: Israeli Fiction in Film* (Tel Aviv: The Open University); and *Captive of a Dream: National Myths in Israeli Culture* (Tel Aviv: Am Oved, Ofakim).

Jeff Halper is an Israeli-American urban anthropologist who has worked in Jerusalem for the past twenty-five years. He directs the Middle East Center of the Friends World College, an international program of Long Island University, where he also serves as professor. He is the author of *Between Redemption and Revival: The Jewish Yishuv of Jerusalem in the Nineteenth Century* (Westview, 1991).

Samuel Krislov has taught at the University of Minnesota since 1964. A former president of the Law and Society Association, he has been a recipient of Guggenheim, Ford, Rockefeller, and Russell Sage fellowships. He has taught at universities in Poland, Israel, and Turkey, and is the author of numerous books, and a frequent contributor to legal and social-science journals.

Pnina Lahav teaches constitutional law and comparative law at Boston University. Her book, *Judgement in Jerusalem: Chief Justice Simon Agranat and the Zionist Century*, was published by the University of California Press in 1996.

Ofira Seliktar is the Ann and Bernard Cohen professor of Israel Studies at Gratz College, and a fellow at the Associates for Middle East Research in Philadelphia. She is a collaborator on a large project on water resources in the Middle East based at the University of Pennsylvania. She is also the author of numerous articles and books on the Middle East.

Walter P. Zenner is professor of Anthropology at the State University of New York at Albany. His works include *Persistence and Flexibility: Anthropological Perspectives on the American Jewish Experience*, and *Minorities in the Middle: A Cross-*

Cultural Analysis, both published by State University of New York Press. He was co-editor of *Critical Essays on Israeli Social Issues and Scholarship (Books on Israel, III)*, and is editor of the SUNY Press series in anthropology and Judaic studies.

Zvi Zohar directs the Shalom Hartman Institute's Center for Halakha in Jerusalem and teaches the history and culture of Jews in Muslim lands in modern times at the Hebrew University's Institute of Contemporary Jewry.